D1319805

MEXICAN CULINARY TREASURES

RECIPES FROM MARIA ELENA'S KITCHEN

THE HIPPOCRENE COOKBOOK LIBRARY

Afghan Food & Cookery
African Cooking, Best of Regional
Albanian Cooking, Best of
Alps, Cuisines of The
Aprovecho: A Mexican-American Border Cookbook
Argentina Cooks!, Exp. Ed.
Austrian Cuisine, Best of, Exp. Ed.
Belgian Cookbook, A
Bolivian Kitchen, My Mother's
Brazilian Cookery, The Art of
Bulgarian Cooking, Traditional
Burma, Flavors of
Cajun Women, Cooking with
Calabria, Cucina di
Caucasus Mountains, Cuisines of the
Chile, Tasting
Colombian, Secrets of Cooking
Croatian Cooking, Best of, Exp. Ed.
Czech Cooking, Best of, Exp. Ed.
Danube, All Along The, Exp. Ed.
Dutch Cooking, Art of, Exp. Ed.
Egyptian Cooking
Eritrea, Taste of
Filipino Food, Fine
Finnish Cooking, Best of
French Caribbean Cuisine
French Fashion, Cooking in the (Bilingual)
Germany, Spoonfuls of
Greek Cuisine, The Best of, Exp. Ed.
Gypsy Feast
Haiti, Taste of
Havana Cookbook, Old (Bilingual)
Hungarian Cookbook
Hungarian Cooking, Art of, Rev. Ed.
Icelandic Food & Cookery
India, Flavorful
Indian Spice Kitchen
International Dictionary of Gastronomy
Irish-Style, Feasting Galore
Italian Cuisine, Treasury of (Bilingual)
Japanese Home Cooking
Korean Cuisine, Best of
Laotian Cooking, Simple

Latvia, Taste of
Lithuanian Cooking, Art of
Macau, Taste of
Mayan Cooking
Middle Eastern Kitchen, The
Mongolian Cooking, Imperial
New Hampshire: From Farm to Kitchen
Norway, Tastes and Tales of
Persian Cooking, Art of
Poland's Gourmet Cuisine
Polish Cooking, Best of, Exp. Ed.
Polish Country Kitchen Cookbook
Polish Cuisine, Treasury of (Bilingual)
Polish Heritage Cookery, Ill. Ed.
Polish Traditions, Old
Portuguese Encounters, Cuisines of
Pyrenees, Tastes of
Quebec, Taste of
Rhine, All Along The
Romania, Taste of, Exp. Ed.
Russian Cooking, Best of, Exp. Ed.
Scandinavian Cooking, Best of
Scotland, Traditional Food From
Scottish-Irish Pub and Hearth Cookbook
Sephardic Israeli Cuisine
Sicilian Feasts
Slovak Cooking, Best of
Smorgasbord Cooking, Best of
South African Cookery, Traditional
South American Cookery, Art of
South Indian Cooking, Healthy
Spanish Family Cookbook, Rev. Ed.
Sri Lanka, Exotic Tastes of
Swedish, Kitchen
Swiss Cookbook, The
Syria, Taste of
Taiwanese Cuisine, Best of
Thai Cuisine, Best of, Regional
Turkish Cuisine, Taste of
Ukrainian Cuisine, Best of, Exp. Ed.
Uzbek Cooking, Art of
Warsaw Cookbook, Old

MEXICAN CULINARY TREASURES

RECIPES FROM MARIA ELENA'S KITCHEN

Maria Elena Cuervo-Lorens

HIPPOCRENE BOOKS
NEW YORK

To my children,
and my grandchildren,
a blessing in my life
and a source of continued joy

With all my love

The author gratefully acknowledges permission to reprint an excerpt from the following material:

From *La cocina mexicana através de los siglos. El pan de cada día.* p. 23. Mexico: Clío, Fundación Herdez, 1996. Used by permission of Clío, Fundación Herdez.

Book and jacket design by Acme Klong Design, Inc.
Food photography: Madeline Polss.

For more information, address:
HIPPOCRENE BOOKS, INC.
171 Madison Avenue
New York, NY 10016

ISBN 0-7818-1061-2
Cataloging-in-Publication Data available from the Library of Congress.
Printed in the United States of America.

The culinary art is not a mechanical task, it is something that has to be done with your soul, with sentiment and style, like any other form of art.

El arte culinario no es una tarea mecánica, es algo que hay que hacer con alma, poniendo sentimiento y estilo, como en todo arte.

— La Cocina Mexicana Através de los Siglos
Fundación Herdez

TABLE OF CONTENTS

Acknowledgments 3

Foreword by Marilyn Tausend 5

Introduction 7

The Privilege of Taste 9

Map of Mexico 11

Hints from the Author 13

Appetizers 15

Soups 27

Rice and Pasta 43

Chicken 55

Beef and Pork 73

Seafood 87

Tamales and Stuffed Chiles 99

Antojitos 119

Salsas 145

Beans 161

Salads, Crepes, and Vegetarian Casseroles 171

Beverages 191

Breads and Desserts 215

Glossary 233

Bibliography 239

Index 241

ACKNOWLEDGMENTS

I WISH TO EXPRESS MY THANKS AND GRATITUDE to the countless persons that are usually part of a book. First and foremost, Roger Ruth, my friend and student, who "only offered another set of eyes" but proved to be the most patient, thorough, and reliable "set of eyes." She was always willing and always available.

Thanks also to Roberto Márquez who, expecting nothing in return, was kind enough to provide me with interesting notes to add to this book.

Thanks to my husband, who was always there for the testing of new recipes, unfailingly providing his knowledgeable opinion on the end result.

Special thanks to my good friend Marilyn Tausend from the International Association of Culinary Professionals, who most graciously found the time to help in the editing of the recipes while at the same time using her expertise to contribute innumerable suggestions and insights.

Last but not least, thanks to my daughter-in-law Carla, who made time in her busy schedule as a lawyer and mother of my two precious grandchildren, to help in the editing of some of the texts.

FOREWORD

by Marilyn Tausend

It is a long time between a polite thanks and the words that I now write.

Twenty years have passed since my family and I joined a crowd of hundreds one summer evening trying to find a place where we could watch the fireworks display in the famed Butchart Gardens on Vancouver Island. This was our first time, and we hadn't come prepared with folding chairs or anything to sit on, and just as we were about to give up, a couple on a large blanket offered to share their space with us. After they introduced themselves and we started talking, I professed my passion for Mexican cooking and that I was leading culinary tours with Diana Kennedy to various regions in Mexico, and had just written my first cookbook, *Mexico the Beautiful*. They then told me about a friend of theirs, Maria Elena Lorens from Mexico City who was teaching Mexican cooking and who had just published a small cookbook with her recipes.

Maria Elena and I began to correspond and soon my husband, Fredric, and I were asked to visit her home in Victoria where we joined her husband and her in a meal featuring an elegantly balanced mole that she had prepared for us. When parting, I thanked her and said that I hoped that our paths would cross again. And they have, many times since then, as our friendship grew.

Later, when interviewing Mexican immigrants for my next book, *Cocina de la Familia*, Maria Elena very generously shared recipes with me, and, without exception, the instructions were easy to follow and each dish came out as a piece of edible art. Such were her elegant crepes flecked with cilantro, encasing a chile-tinged wild mushroom filling—so typical of the Mexico City cuisine that she ate while growing up. In fact, she loved crepes so much that her mother made them for her at least once a week.

With this in mind, when Maria Elena came to me and asked my advice on a new book she wanted to write, I urged her to focus on the foods of Mexico that she knew the best—those of Mexico City and the central region of the country where she grew up, and to share her stories, just as she had told them to me. From the time the Aztecs built their magnificent capital of Tenochtitlán (now Mexico City), it was the hub into which all roads led, bringing goods and different types of food to trade and sell from distant parts of their empire. It is still today, the culinary center of Mexico, and growing up here provided Maria Elena a wide spectrum of ingredients and dishes from which to sample. The book that evolved is about Mexico City—its style of life and its foods.

Maria Elena's recipes include the earthy flavors of the beef and cheese tacos sold by vendors on the busy street corners, the celebratory tamales traditionally made for her father's birthday, as well as more sophisticated dishes such as tender pieces of chicken simmered in a sauce of red wine and prunes. Her book truly evokes the tastes and textures, and even the smells of Mexican cooking and everyone who loves the cuisine of Mexico like I do, should find *Mexican Culinary Treasures* a very valuable resource.

INTRODUCTION

I WAS BORN IN MEXICO CITY and lived there for thirty-six years until 1976, when I moved with my husband and young children to Victoria, British Columbia.

I have many fond memories of my childhood in Mexico. I cherish the countless occasions I spent with my mother in her kitchen, "helping" her prepare meals for the family. My mother, like her mother before her, was an accomplished and enthusiastic cook. She instilled in me her sense of culinary adventure. From a very young age, I welcomed the opportunity to

try new foods, including the exotic, such as *cuitlacoche*, a corn fungus, despite its black appearance and damp smell. After being completely forgotten by the upper classes, this vegetable was resurrected years later for distinguished guests, like the shah and empress of Iran, for whom crepes with *cuitlacoche* seasoned with serrano chiles, onion, and the aromatic herb epazote were the highlight of the Iranian state dinner.

My mother was born in the central state of Querétaro. In her cooking, she favored the use of chiles, cactus pads, and different moles. One of her favorite soups was *Mole de Olla*, which is not exactly a mole as it is commonly known, but a hearty soup made of chicken broth, pork ribs, corn, and zucchini in a base of tomatoes blended with guajillo chile, and served with lime juice and warm tortillas.

My father was born in Zacatecas, a northern state highly influenced by the French occupation of 1862–67. Consequently, my paternal grandmother favored dishes with a marked French influence. One of her trademarks was Zacatecas-Style Roast Hen, a hen or chicken marinated in dry sherry with onion, bay leaves, peppercorns, and ground cumin, with a savory stuffing that included tomatoes, apples, raisins, almonds, olives, and ground pork, marvelously seasoned with cumin, cinnamon, and pepper (page 70).

After her marriage, my mother also cooked in the style of her mother-in-law, and so French-Mexican food was frequently served in our house. Mexico City, being quite cosmopolitan, my mother enjoyed experimenting in the kitchen and trying dishes indigenous to other parts of the country. I naturally reaped the benefits of this and inherited this blend of cuisines.

As an adult, I lived in Puebla, whose cuisine is known for wonderful spicy and aromatic flavors. My cooking was greatly influenced by *la cocina poblana*, as you will see from my extensive use of chipotle chile, my favorite dry chile.

I have been collecting recipes since my teenage years. Most of the recipes are family recipes; others, from Mexico City restaurants. For this book, I have selected only those dishes that are quick to prepare and whose ingredients are either not difficult to obtain or where substitutions will not result in culinary catastrophes.

In recent years, interest in Mexican cuisine has been nothing short of explosive. This has brought about increased availability of an unbelievable assortment of authentic ingredients, especially produce, at major groceries. In the United States, Mexican salsa is the new condiment-sales leader, and you would be hard pressed to find a grocery store that does not sell some version or another of the delicious Mexican tortilla.

This is a book for a knowledgeable and enthusiastic "aficionado," which does not necessarily mean that it is beyond the reach of the novice or casual cook. It does mean, however, that the serious and more adventurous cook will not be disappointed.

Having made these dishes myself on countless occasions, I can confidently say that the recipes are indeed worth trying.

THE PRIVILEGE OF TASTE

MEXICAN POET OCTAVIO PAZ won the Nobel prize in 1986, in part for *Los Privilegios de la Vista*, a book not of poetry but art. The title was taken from Luis de Góngora, the great classicist of the Spanish Golden Age. The original stanza by Góngora reads as follows:

> *Ejecutoriando en la revista …*
> *todos los privilegios de la vista.*

Translated very freely and inevitably losing much of Góngora's charm and elegance, this reads:

> Executing in the review …
> all the privileges of the eye.

Góngora and Paz both refer to the beholding of great art during which "all the privileges" of the eye are rewarded.

Somehow, I have always related this "executing … all the privileges" with the wonderful world of the true epicure. In one way or another, all cultures, even the most isolated ones, have their own typical and characteristic dishes. Many consider that the vast majority of these are based on a narrow range of tastes, like a painting done in only two or three basic colors. It takes a certain set of historical contingencies to bring about the great culinary schools. These, of which there are only a few in the world, are great precisely because they allow the execution of not just a narrow range, but the full spectrum of the privilege of taste.

If anything is characteristic of Mexico's great culinary tradition, it is the fact that it offers in its own richly colorful idiom, a full range of the privileges of the palate, from exquisitely subtle delicacies to the most robust sensations. The collection of recipes in this book were selected precisely because they exhibit the full spectrum of taste.

I guarantee that after having tried some of the recipes, you will have embarked on a real culinary and cultural adventure. More importantly, you will have experienced exciting new flavors and tastes, thereby awakening a whole new palette of taste sensations

R. C. L.

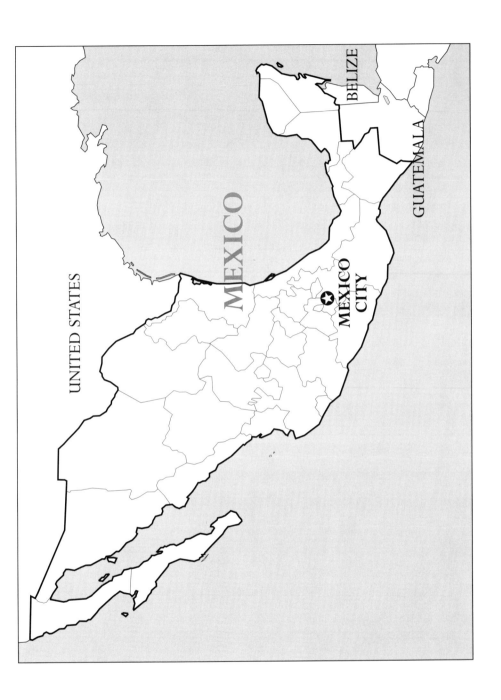

HINTS FROM
THE AUTHOR

WHEN I AM TEACHING A COOKING CLASS, I always make people aware of things that might change the result of a dish. The cooking time, the amount of oil used, the weight of packaged foods that varies by country, the size or the ripeness of fruits and vegetables, the spiciness of the chiles, the inconstant flavor of the tomatoes, and so on.

Success in cooking lies not so much on the accuracy of the ingredients but more on an awareness of the condition of the ingredients, the ability to juggle these when necessary, and to use your senses to discover, before it is too late, that something needs to be altered. I do hope these hints are helpful in being able to cook a successful dish.

- OIL FOR FRYING: Use oil as needed. We do not want to use more oil than is absolutely necessary, so add oil, little by little.
- COOKING TIME: I live at sea level, so cooking times may vary if you live at a higher altitude.
- CANNED GOODS: Keep in mind that sizes and weights vary from country to country. Sometimes it is better to use kitchen measures to ensure accuracy.
- CORN TORTILLAS: The recipes in this book use the standard size, which are generally 6-inches in diameter.
- FLOUR TORTILLAS: The recipes in this book use the standard size, generally about $7^1/_2$-inches in diameter.
- METRIC MEASUREMENTS have been rounded for simplicity and ease of understanding.
- CHICKEN/BEEF BROTH: In Mexican cuisine a homemade broth is the base of a good soup, mole, or sauce. You will find in this book, many recipes where chicken or beef is poached. The cooking liquid makes a good broth and can be frozen and used at a later date. Remember, it does make a difference in the flavor!

APPETIZERS

BOTANAS (APPETIZERS) ARE EXTREMELY POPULAR and ingrained in Mexican culture. It is believed that they were first offered in the port of Veracruz, where all the ships from Spain and France arrived, loaded with European cheese, olive oil, capers, and olives from Seville.

At the beginning, *botanas* were very similar to the Spanish tapas, which consisted of small pieces of cold *tortilla a la española* (Spanish omelet), *butifarras* (small pork sausages), tiny pieces of dry fish, possibly sardines, capers and olives, and it was not until the 1920s when pubs, encouraged by the beer companies, started serving Mexican antojitos (snacks) as *botanas* to accompany beer.

Botanear, the word *botana* converted into a verb, aptly describes Sunday extended family gatherings. Despite different work schedules of all the family members, daily conviviality around the table is still maintained, and Sundays continue to be a family day par excellence, a day for a *comida dominguera* (Sunday meal), signifying a special time and usually more elaborate dishes than everyday life permits.

These *comidas* unfailingly start with *botanas* and a drink; and, depending on each family's budget, may be composed of a variety of cheeses, crackers, sardines, olives, smoked oysters, spicy dips, *quesadillitas*, crispy *taquitos*, pork rind with guacamole, and so on. The list is endless.

AVOCADO MOUSSE

Botana de Aguacate   *8 to 10 servings*

THE WORD AGUACATE IS OF NÁHUATL ORIGIN and is derived from ahuácatl, *meaning "testicle tree" because the fruit was thought to resemble that body part. The word* guacamole *combines* aguacate *with* mole, *meaning sauce. Avocados were first cultivated hundreds of years ago, in Perú and eventually throughout Latin America. When Hernán Cortés brought avocados back to Spain,* ahuácatl *became* aguacate, *which in turn changed to* avocado *in the English countries, and* avocat *in French.*

Avocados, despite being high in fat, are low in calories and high in protein, both contained in the avocado's oil. Another well-known fact about this delectable fruit is that its oily nature and high content of vitamins E and A are wonderful for maintaining healthy skin. Avocado and olive oil facials are among the best remedies for dry complexions. Whether eaten for their savory flavor or used for a facial, avocados are definitely a worthwhile addition to your shopping list.

In countries where the trees flourish, avocados are also used as aphrodisiacs: The pits are grated and brewed as a tea to stimulate passion and stamina. There are many varieties of the original avocado that was taken from Atlixco, Puebla, to the United States, Europe, and Asia such as Haas, criollo, and mantequilla to name a few.

Avocados are at their best when they feel firm and only slightly soft to the touch. If you do not intend to use an entire avocado, do not peel it, but cut away only the wedge you wish to eat, leaving the rest intact. Sprinkle a few drops of lime juice on the exposed areas of the avocado and refrigerate it, covered, until you are ready to use it again.

▼▼▼▼▼▼▼▼▼▼▼▼▼▼▼▼▼▼▼▼▼▼▼▼▼▼▼

3 ENVELOPES (1 TABLESPOON EACH) UNFLAVORED GELATIN

1/2 CUP BOILING WATER

1/2 CUP CHICKEN BROTH

1 PACKAGE (8 OZ / 250 G) CREAM CHEESE

2 LARGE RIPE AVOCADOS, PEELED AND PITTED

JUICE OF 1 SMALL LIME

5 TABLESPOONS HOMEMADE MAYONNAISE (PAGE 147)

2 TABLESPOONS CHOPPED FRESH CILANTRO, PLUS EXTRA WHOLE LEAVES FOR GARNISH

1 TABLESPOON CHOPPED ONION

2 CHOPPED SERRANO CHILES

SALT

In a small bowl, dissolve the gelatin in the boiling water. Transfer the dissolved gelatin to a blender or food processor; add the chicken broth, cream cheese, avocados, lime juice, mayonnaise, cilantro, onion, and chiles and blend the mixture in short bursts until puréed. Season with salt and, if you desire more piquancy, add another chile. Pour the mixture into a mold and refrigerate at least 2 hours, or until set.

Just before serving, dip the gelatin mold in warm water for one minute and quickly invert onto a serving platter. Garnish with cilantro leaves and serve with crackers arranged around the mousse.

GARLIC AND AVOCADO DIP

Dip de Ajo y Aguacate   *Yields about ³/₄ cup*

PUNTA ARENA, *A RELATIVELY NEW RESTAURANT in Lomas de Chapultepec, an affluent area in Mexico City, serves this smooth, tasty dip with all their fish appetizers, such as sliced octopus, scallops, and fish croquettes. It may also be served with corn chips or with* chicharrón, *that delectable fried pork rind all Mexicans love to eat as a snack with lime juice and different salsas or guacamole. Outside of Mexico, pork rind may be found in major supermarkets with the potato and corn chips. These vary in size and name, but Porky's seems to be the most popular brand.*

Choose the hottest serrano chiles you can find—usually the smallest are the hottest—and if you enjoy spicy food, you will agree that this delicious dip goes incredibly well with all of the above.

2 TO 3 SERRANO CHILES, STEMMED
AND SEEDED

2 MEDIUM CLOVES GARLIC

1 LARGE RIPE AVOCADO, PEELED
AND PITTED

JUICE OF ¹/₂ LIME

SALT

In a *molcajete* or mortar and pestle, mash the chiles and garlic to a paste; add the avocado in small chunks, and mash until puréed. Stir in the lime juice and salt to taste. Blend all the ingredients to a smooth paste.

Serve at once in a small *molcajete* or a nice serving bowl.

JICAMA AND AVOCADO APPETIZER

Entremés de Jícama con Aguacate   *8 servings*

JICAMA IS A RATHER SWEET, WHITE ROOT VEGETABLE with a brown skin, similar in shape to a turnip. When ripe and juicy, the brownish peel has a little bit of a shine and it is firm to the touch; the peel is easily removed in sections. If they are not quite ripe, a potato peeler or a small knife will remove the peel. Over-ripe jicamas looks rough and blemished. Jicamas are usually eaten raw.

In particularly hot weather, street vendors are found all over Mexico City selling jicama and cucumbers, served with lots of lime juice, salt and ground piquín chile, the small red chile that is graded as one of the hottest chiles available.

This exciting recipe is a perfect example of cosmopolitan Mexico's nouvelle cuisine. The jicama and the avocado, two ingredients indigenous to Mexican soil, are combined to make a unique and very tasty appetizer. This recipe also calls for ketchup, which is used often in Mexican food as a quick substitute for tomato sauce. This may be served as an appetizer or as a first course, with good crackers.

1 MEDIUM JICAMA, PEELED

¼ CUP HOMEMADE MAYONNAISE
(PAGE 147)

¼ CUP KETCHUP

4 RIPE, FIRM AVOCADOS, UNPEELED

JUICE OF 1 SMALL LIME

LETTUCE LEAVES

SALT

Using a cheese grater, grate the jicama and, if it is juicy, place it in a colander, preferably a plastic one, to drain for about an hour. In a small bowl, mix the mayonnaise with the ketchup.

Slice the avocados in half lengthwise, discarding the pit. Sprinkle each half with the lime juice. Mix the jicama with the dressing and mound about 1 heaping tablespoon in each avocado half.

Serve the avocados on a bed of lettuce sprinkled with a few drops of lime juice and salt.

HARD-BOILED EGGS
WITH AVOCADO

Entremés de Huevos Duros con Aguacate   *12 servings*

THIS IS A GOOD ENTREMÉS *(APPETIZER) that is easy to prepare and looks quite attractive on a table. It saves time if the eggs are boiled a day in advance. The eggs are easier to shell if you cool them under cold running water until completely cold, and then shell them. Place the eggs in a plastic container and refrigerate until you are ready to prepare the appetizer.*

6 HARD-BOILED EGGS, SHELLED

1 LARGE RIPE AVOCADO, PEELED AND PITTED

JUICE OF 1 LIME

2 TEASPOONS OLIVE OIL

1 TO 2 SERRANO CHILES, FINELY CHOPPED

1 SMALL HEAD LETTUCE, WASHED

SALT AND PEPPER

10 MANZANILLA OLIVES, CHOPPED

Slice the eggs in half lengthwise. Place the yolks in a small bowl and chop them. In another bowl, mash the avocado with a fork then add the lime juice, olive oil, chile, and salt and pepper to taste.

Arrange a bed of lettuce on a serving platter. Fill each halved egg with the avocado mixture and place on the lettuce. Garnish with the chopped egg yolks and olives.

BOLOGNA APPETIZER

Entremés de Mortadela   *6 to 8 servings*

BOLOGNA AND CHILE IS AN UNUSUAL COMBINATION; however, the serrano chile provides flavor, and not a lot of piquancy. If the chile happens to be too hot, half of it will do the trick, and the cilantro with the lime juice will bring up the flavor of the bologna.

½ SMALL ONION, THINLY SLICED

¼ CUP CIDER VINEGAR

1 LB (500 G) BOLOGNA, IN ONE PIECE

¼ CUP CHOPPED FRESH CILANTRO

1 SERRANO CHILE, CHOPPED

2 TABLESPOONS LIME JUICE

½ CUP MAYONNAISE

SALT

Marinate the onion in the vinegar for at least 1 hour. Drain. Cut the bologna into bite-size cubes and mix with the onion, cilantro, chile, lime juice, mayonnaise, and salt to taste.

Serve with crackers.

POLLOCK APPETIZER

Cangrejo Frío   *6 to 8 servings*

Authentic Mexican ingredients mixed with pollock, a relative newcomer, reflect the new trends in Mexico City. Needless to say, crab can be used instead of pollock. However, the freshness provided by the shredded pollock combined with the lime juice, tomato, chile, and parsley is almost unbeatable. Nouvelle cuisine at its best!

1 LB (500 G) POLLOCK

JUICE OF 1 LIME

SALT AND PEPPER

$^1/_2$ CUP HOMEMADE MAYONNAISE (PAGE 147)

2 LARGE TOMATOES, SEEDED AND CHOPPED

2 TO 4 SERRANO CHILES, MINCED

$^1/_2$ CUP FINELY CHOPPED ONION

$^1/_2$ CUP CHOPPED FRESH FLAT-LEAF PARSLEY OR CILANTRO

1 LARGE AVOCADO, PEELED, PITTED, AND SLICED

In a mixing bowl, shred the pollock with your fingers. Stir in the lime juice, and salt and pepper to taste. Add the mayonnaise, tomatoes, chiles, onion, and parsley, and mix well. Transfer the appetizer to a serving bowl, garnish with the avocado slices, and serve with crisp toasted bread or good crackers.

PRAWN CEVICHE

Ceviche de Camarón   *4 servings*

CEVICHE IS VERY POPULAR all over Mexico. Traditionally it is made with red snapper or sierra (mackerel) fillets. Chefs throughout the country have created a variety of ceviches by combining other fish, octopus, and scallops; a lobster ceviche was recently created in Acapulco. In some recipes, fish is marinated in lime juice overnight; in others, only two to four hours are recommended. Some chefs favor the serrano chile over the jalapeño chile and others use both in the same recipe. It is difficult to choose one since they all are as refreshing and tasty as can be. Once ceviche is prepared, it can be refrigerated for up to three days.

24 TO 26 PRAWNS, HEADS REMOVED

⅓ CUP LIME JUICE

SALT AND PEPPER

2 LARGE TOMATOES, SEEDED AND CHOPPED

½ CUP FINELY CHOPPED ONION

2 TO 4 SERRANO CHILES, FINELY CHOPPED

½ CUP CHOPPED FRESH CILANTRO OR ¼ CUP CHOPPED FRESH FLAT-LEAF PARSLEY

1 TEASPOON MAGGI SAUCE

3 TABLESPOONS OLIVE OIL

2 RIPE AVOCADOS, PEELED, PITTED, AND SLICED

Blanch the prawns in salted boiling water for only 3 to 4 minutes. Remove the prawns from the heat, drain, and immerse in cold water. Shell the prawns and transfer to a glass or nonreactive metal bowl. Combine the prawns with the lime juice and refrigerate, covered, for at least 2 hours, or until firm to the touch.

Drain and, in a separate bowl, combine the prawns with the tomatoes, onion, chiles, cilantro or parsley. In a separate small bowl, mix the Maggi sauce and the olive oil, and season with salt and pepper. Add the sauce to the prawns, gently combining all the ingredients. Refrigerate until ready to serve.

Divide the ceviche among four chilled cocktail glasses, garnish with the avocado slices, and serve with your favorite crackers.

BAKED OYSTERS ON TOAST

Tostada de Ostiones al Horno   *2 entrée servings or 8 appetizers*

OYSTERS MAKE WONDERFUL APPETIZERS. *Today most bakeries sell mini-loaves of bread, sometimes already toasted, which makes it easier to serve this elegant dish. The toasts are also good for a light supper, or as a main dish preceded by a green salad.*

If you buy shelled oysters in a jar, make sure that they do not have any bits of broken shell, and that the liquid is clear, not cloudy.

2 SLICES BACON, CHOPPED

¼ CUP CHOPPED ONION

1 TOMATO, CHOPPED

1 TABLESPOON TOMATO SAUCE

1 TO 2 SERRANO CHILES, FINELY CHOPPED

1 TABLESPOON CHOPPED FRESH FLAT-LEAF PARSLEY

1 DOZEN FRESH OYSTERS, SHELLED

SALT AND PEPPER

2 REGULAR SLICES OR 8 MINI SLICES BREAD, TOASTED AND BUTTERED

¼ CUP GRATED MOZZARELLA CHEESE

Preheat the oven to 350°F. In a small saucepan, fry the bacon for a few minutes, until cooked through, but not crisp, then add the onion, tomato, tomato sauce, chile(s), and parsley, and cook for 5 to 8 minutes, or until the sauce has thickened slightly. Add the oysters, season with salt and pepper, and continue cooking 2 to 4 minutes longer, or until the oysters are cooked.

Divide the oysters between the slices of buttered toast and sprinkle the grated cheese over them. Bake for 5 to 8 minutes, or until the cheese is melted and serve hot.

OYSTERS WITH CHIPOTLE ADOBO

Ostiones Capeados con Chipotle   *4 servings*

Oysters are edible at any time of the year and are the freshest when bought in their shell. Immediately discard oysters that are open and do not close quickly when handled. Oysters with broken shells should be discarded as well.

Oyster lovers will be delighted with the piquancy that the adobo (the vinegar that comes with the canned chiles) lends to the oysters, without overpowering their natural flavor.

Chipotle chiles are very popular these days. They are used not only in salsas, but also in salad dressings, pestos, and so on. Canned chipotles in adobo sauce may be found in major supermarkets as well as at specialty stores. Store chipotles in a small glass jar and keep refrigerated. Because of the vinegar they last up to two months, however once you discover their many uses, this is not likely.

Keep in mind that fish, and shellfish in particular, benefit tremendously from marinating before cooking. Lime juice is wonderful to bring up the flavors.

24 FRESH OYSTERS, SHELLED

JUICE OF 1 LIME

SALT AND PEPPER

¼ CUP PLUS 1 TABLESPOON
   ALL-PURPOSE FLOUR

2 EGGS, SEPARATED

OIL FOR DEEP-FRYING

1 TEASPOON CHIPOTLE ADOBO

½ CUP CHOPPED FRESH FLAT-LEAF
   PARSLEY

1 LIME, SLICED, FOR GARNISH

Wash the oysters under running water and drain on paper towels. Sprinkle the lime juice over the oysters, and add salt and pepper to taste. Marinate the oysters in the lime juice for about 30 minutes, then coat them with ¼ cup of the flour and set aside.

Beat the egg whites with an electric mixer until stiff, add the egg yolks, and continue beating until well blended. With a wooden spoon, stir in the remaining 1 tablespoon of flour and season with salt and pepper.

In a cast iron frying pan, heat the oil almost to the point of smoking. Carefully dip each oyster into the batter and deep-fry in hot oil until golden brown. Transfer the fried oysters to paper towels to drain the excess oil. Keep them warm.

Sprinkle the chipotle adobo over the oysters and serve them hot, garnished with the parsley and the lime slices.

SOUPS

SOPA AGUADA
SOPA SECA

I FEEL COMPELLED TO EXPLAIN a little bit about the old Mexican custom of having first a *sopa agua-da* (liquid soup) and then a *sopa seca* (dry soup) before the main course. In a *sopa aguada*, pasta, rice, tortillas, or vegetables are served in the broth they were cooked in. In a *sopa seca*, on the other hand, the liquid is absorbed completely and the soup is served dry. The best example of a *sopa seca* is rice.

When I was growing up, my mother always served two soups. The *sopa aguada* was a pasta soup or a vegetable soup. The *sopa seca*, depending on what kind of *sopa aguada* had been served, was either pasta, tortilla, or rice in a color of the Mexican flag, red, white, or green. But again, this is also determined by the main course. You do not want to serve tortilla soup when the main dish calls for tortillas as well.

I myself find that a dry soup is not as filling as a liquid soup. Fortunately, this custom has changed and these days, only one soup is served. I say fortunately, because we really do not need to eat more than we absolutely have to. However, in those days, nobody ever thought any-thing of it if we happened to be a little overweight. In fact mothers worried if you looked too thin. I even heard my aunts tell their marrying daughters things like, "Men do not like thin women." Times have certainly changed!

BASIC TOMATO SAUCE

Caldillo de Jitomate   *Yields about 2 cups*

THE WORD TOMATO COMES FROM THE NÁHUATL TERM xictómat, *formed by the words* xictli *(belly button) and* tómatl *(tomato). Literally, it means a tomato with a navel. The tomato is another gift to the world from Mexican soil.*

When the tomato plant was taken to Europe, it was baptized with the name pomadoro *in Italy (golden apple) and* poma amoris *(love apple) in the rest of Europe. The exact date when the tomato reached Europe is unknown, but it was already widely used in the mid-eighteenth century. It obtained even more names in Europe: the southern Italians called it* pummarola; *the Austrians,* paradeis; *the Germans,* Liebesapfel *or* Goltoaffel. *And finally, the Anglo-Saxons industrialized the amazing tomato and made it into canned juice.*

This sauce is the base for many soups, both dry and liquid. For a more flavorful sauce to be served with chiles rellenos *(stuffed chiles), for example, stir in a dash of cinnamon and of ground cloves before adding the chicken bouillon, which is used for flavor. If you feel the bouillon is too salty, you may add salt and pepper instead.*

2 LARGE RIPE TOMATOES, SEEDED

¼ MEDIUM ONION

2 LARGE CLOVES GARLIC

1 TABLESPOON VEGETABLE OIL

¼ CUP TOMATO SAUCE

2 PACKETS (1 TABLESPOON EACH)
  INSTANT CHICKEN BOUILLON MIX

In a blender or food processor, combine the tomatoes, onion, and garlic, and process until puréed. In a large saucepan, heat the oil over medium heat and add the tomato mixture, tomato sauce, and chicken bouillon. Bring the sauce to a boil, lower the heat, and simmer for 5 to 8 minutes, or until the sauce thickens slightly.

Adjust the seasonings and add ¼ cup of water if the sauce is too thick.

CACTUS PAD SOUP

Sopa de Nopales   *4 servings*

THIS RECIPE IS FROM MY GOOD FRIEND *Araceli Martin del Campo. Our friendship dates back about thirty years. We actually met through our husbands, who have been friends since college and, even though I have lived in Canada more than twenty-five years now, we still remain in contact. During one of my yearly visits to Mexico City, Araceli invited a group of mutual friends to a Mexican-style comida (dinner) in my honor.*

It was such a delight to visit Araceli and her family. Their home in Pedregal de San Angel is one of the most beautiful houses I have ever been to. Designed by her architect husband in a Mexican style, the house is surrounded by a lush garden of bougainvilleas, magnolias, and lemon and orange trees, among other plants. Both the main dining room and the less formal breakfast table, face beautiful fountains reminiscent of the old haciendas. Needless to say, dining in such an atmosphere is a real pleasure. She served this delicious soup, and shared the recipe with me for you to enjoy as much as we all did.

Unused chipotle chiles can be stored in a glass jar and refrigerated for later use.

1 CUP BASIC TOMATO SAUCE (PAGE 29)

4 CUPS CHICKEN OR BEEF BROTH

4 LARGE CACTUS PADS, PEELED AND COOKED, (PAGE 171)

1 CUP CORN KERNELS, FRESH OR CANNED AND DRAINED

1 TO 2 CHIPOTLE CHILES, SEEDED AND CHOPPED

1 TEASPOON CHIPOTLE ADOBO (THE SPICED VINEGAR FROM THE CANNED CHILES)

1 CUP CUBED MANCHEGO OR MONTEREY JACK CHEESE

Heat the Basic Tomato Sauce in a saucepan, add the broth, and correct seasoning. Add the cactus pads, corn kernels, chipotle chiles, and the adobo. Simmer for 3 to 4 minutes, and serve hot with the cubed cheese.

CORN SOUP

Sopa de Elote   *4 to 6 servings*

THIS DELICIOUS SOUP IS ONE OF THE MANY DISHES that my good friend, Paquita Maguey, owner of the Salón Estrella in Mexico City, offers to her clientele. The Salón Estrella is a party hall that is rented for weddings, anniversaries and birthdays, first communions, and other celebrations.

This recipe might seem a bit complicated, however I believe it is worth the time involved, especially when fresh corn is available.

2 LARGE POBLANO CHILES, ROASTED AND PEELED (SEE PAGE 111)

1 CUP MILK

4 TO 5 CUPS HOMEMADE CHICKEN BROTH (PAGE 59)

$\frac{1}{2}$ CUP PLUS 2 TABLESPOONS BUTTER

$\frac{1}{2}$ LARGE ONION, SLICED

3 CLOVES GARLIC, CHOPPED

1 TURNIP, CHOPPED (1 CUP)

1 LEEK, CHOPPED (1 CUP)

2 TABLESPOONS FLOUR

2 CUPS FRESH CORN KERNELS

SALT AND PEPPER

1 CUP MANCHEGO OR MONTEREY JACK CHEESE, CUBED

$\frac{1}{2}$ CUP MEXICAN CREAM OR CRÈME FRAÎCHE (PAGE 148)

In a food processor or blender, process one of the poblano chiles with $\frac{1}{2}$ cup of the milk until puréed, and stir into the broth. Cut the remaining chile into thin strips and set aside.

In a soup pot, melt the $\frac{1}{2}$ cup of butter and add the onion, garlic, turnip, and leek. Sauté the vegetables until the onion is translucent. Add the flour, stirring to avoid burning the vegetables. Add the chicken broth mixture, little by little, stirring, until any lumps are completely dissolved. Bring the mixture to a boil, lower the heat, and simmer until the vegetables are thoroughly cooked. Transfer the broth to another pot, mashing the vegetables through a colander and into the broth.

In a separate pot, cook the corn kernels in salted boiling water with the remaining 2 tablespoons of butter until soft, and drain. In a food processor or blender, process half of the corn with the remaining milk and add it to the soup. Season the corn mixture with salt and pepper. Bring the soup to a boil, lower the heat, and simmer for only 5 to 8 minutes for all the flavors to blend. Keep warm.

Just before serving, add the reserved chile strips and corn kernels to the soup, top with the cheese and crème fraîche, and serve at once. The soup should not boil again.

CREAM OF CORN SOUP

Sopa Crema de Elote   *4 to 6 servings*

ANOTHER CORN SOUP RECIPE, this one from my niece Claudia, a housewife and mother of "high-maintenance" twins who keep her busy; however, she enjoys cooking and makes time to prepare easy but hearty meals for her family.

2 CORN TORTILLAS

OIL FOR FRYING

3 LARGE EARS OF CORN OR 2 CUPS FROZEN OR CANNED AND DRAINED CORN KERNELS

1 CUP 2% MILK

1 TABLESPOON BUTTER

2 PACKETS (1 TABLESPOON EACH) INSTANT CHICKEN BOUILLON MIX

1 CUP CUBED MANCHEGO OR MONTEREY JACK CHEESE

Cut the tortillas into small squares. Heat the oil over medium to high heat, and fry the squares until browned and crisp. With a slotted spoon, drain the tortilla squares and transfer them to paper towels to remove excess oil.

Slice the kernels off the cobs and cook in salted boiling water for about 5 minutes. Reserving 3 tablespoons of the kernels, transfer the remaining corn to a food processor or blender, and process with 1 cup of water and the milk.

In a pot, melt the butter and sauté the corn mixture, stirring, before adding the reserved corn kernels and the bouillon. Bring the soup to a boil and simmer just a few minutes longer to blend the flavors.

Serve hot in soup bowls, topped with the cubed cheese. Pass the tortilla squares at the table to be added at the very last minute.

CORN TORTILLA
DRY SOUP

Sopa Seca de Tortilla   *4 servings*

"THE POOR AS WELL AS THE RICH PEOPLE HAVE A SPECIAL GUSTO *for corn tortillas and beans," observed Countess Paula Kolonitz, one of the ladies who accompanied Empress Carlota during her brief stay in Mexico (1864–67).*

She described tortillas as "flat round slices made of corn flour, as big as a plate, soft and flavorless." She wrote to her husband's family in Austria that the people of Mexico ate tortillas the way they ate bread and that sometimes these were used as spoons to eat beans.

It is not hard to believe that in the present day, tortillas are not only known around the world but have become a favorite in dishes like tacos, nachos, and enchiladas.

If the main dish does not call for tortillas, this homey soup is a must.

OIL FOR FRYING

6 TO 8 CORN TORTILLAS, CUT INTO
   STRIPS

1 RIPE FRESH TOMATO

½ CUP CHOPPED ONION

1 CLOVE GARLIC, CHOPPED

2 TABLESPOONS TOMATO SAUCE

1 CUP CHICKEN BROTH

SALT AND PEPPER

1 CHIPOTLE CHILE, SEEDED AND MINCED

½ CUP *QUESO FRESCO* OR CRUMBLED
   FETA CHEESE

In a saucepan, heat the oil over medium to high heat, and quickly fry batches of tortilla strips until golden brown. Drain excess oil on paper towels and set aside. Remove all but one teaspoon of oil from the saucepan.

In a blender or food processor, purée the tomato, onion, and garlic with just enough water to run the motor. In the same saucepan used for frying the tortilla strips, reheat the oil and sauté the tomato mixture for about 2 minutes. Add the tomato sauce, chicken broth, chipotle chile, and the tortilla strips. Season with salt and pepper, and simmer until liquid is reduced completely.

Divide the soup among four bowls, top with a generous amount of cheese, and serve at once.

CREAM OF CAULIFLOWER SOUP WITH POBLANO CHILE AND CORN

Sopa Crema de Coliflor con Chile Poblano y Elote   *4 servings*

THE SUBTLE FLAVOR OF THE CAULIFLOWER combined with the poblano chile makes this elegant soup a favorite for entertaining.

1 LARGE POBLANO CHILE, ROASTED, PEELED AND SEEDED (PAGE 111)

1 SMALL CAULIFLOWER, CUT INTO FLORETS

1 TABLESPOON BUTTER

2 TABLESPOONS MINCED ONION

2 PACKETS (1 TABLESPOON EACH) INSTANT CHICKEN BOUILLON MIX

DASH OF WHITE PEPPER

1 CUP BUTTERMILK

1 CUP CORN KERNELS

Slice the poblano chile into thin strips about $\frac{1}{2}$ inch wide and set aside.

In salted boiling water, cook the cauliflower for 5 to 7 minutes, or until tender. Drain the florets, reserving the cooking liquid, and cool. In a blender, process the cauliflower with 1 to $1\frac{1}{2}$ cups of the reserved liquid, until puréed.

In a saucepan, melt the butter and sauté the onion until translucent. Add the cauliflower mixture, the chicken bouillon, and white pepper. Bring to a boil and simmer for 2 or 3 minutes before adding the buttermilk. Adjust the seasoning, add the poblano strips and the corn kernels, and continue simmering a few minutes longer to allow the flavors to blend.

Serve hot with crackers or crusty buttered bread.

CREAM OF CUCUMBER SOUP

Crema Fría de Pepino   *Makes 4 servings*

SOMEHOW, CUCUMBERS ARE NOT FREQUENTLY ASSOCIATED *with soups; however, this recipe, once discovered, will become a summer favorite. Cucumbers contain about 96 percent water, which accounts for their refreshing quality. They also contain nutrients, like calcium, potassium, and magnesium, all necessary for a healthy diet.*

2 MEDIUM CUCUMBERS, PEELED AND
   SEEDED

JUICE OF 1 LIME

$^1\!/_2$ CUP 2% MILK

$1^1\!/_4$ CUPS BUTTERMILK

SALT AND WHITE PEPPER

1 TABLESPOON FRESH DILL OR
   1 TEASPOON DRY

OLIVE OIL

In a blender or food processor, purée the cucumber, lime juice, milk, buttermilk, and salt and pepper to taste. Correct the seasoning and add more liquid if necessary. Chill the soup before serving.

Transfer the soup to a tureen, add the dill, and drizzle with olive oil. Serve with good crackers.

CREAM OF CUCUMBER SOUP WITH WHITE WINE

Sopa de Pepino   *6 servings*

MORE OFTEN THAN NOT, IN MEXICO cucumbers are eaten raw as a snack, sprinkled with lots of lime juice and piquín chile. In this recipe, however, they are cooked, and their subtle flavor combined with cream, egg yolks, and wine makes an absolutely superb soup.

2 LARGE CUCUMBERS, PEELED AND SEEDED

$\frac{1}{2}$ SMALL ONION

3 TABLESPOONS BUTTER

2 TABLESPOONS FLOUR

$\frac{1}{2}$ CUP MILK

SALT AND PEPPER

1 CUP CREAM

$\frac{1}{2}$ CUP DRY WHITE WINE

2 EGG YOLKS

DASH OF NUTMEG

Cut the cucumbers into chunks and cook with the onion in 3 cups of salted boiling water, for 5 to 8 minutes, or until barely cooked. Purée in a blender or food processor.

In a soup pot, melt the butter, stir in the flour, and sauté for 2 minutes, before adding the milk and the cucumber mixture. Season with salt and pepper. Bring the soup to a boil and simmer gently for 3 to 5 minutes, or until slightly thickened. Remove from the heat.

While the soup is still hot, mix it in a soup tureen with the cream, egg yolks, wine, and nutmeg. Stir well and serve very hot.

BREAD SOUP WITH GARLIC AND ANCHO CHILE

Sopa de Migas con Chile Ancho   *4 servings*

THIS RECIPE IS A SLIGHT VARIATION *of the famous Spanish* migas *(bread soup), which uses* pimentón *(paprika) for flavor. Ancho chile provides this soup with a sweet and at the same time pungent taste that is most delicious. The secret lies mainly in using good homemade chicken broth, though canned chicken broth may be used too, lots of garlic, and preferably stale bread as it absorbs less oil. Baguettes works very well, as the slices are quite small and at least four fit in a soup bowl or plate. If you are counting calories, the bread can be browned in the oven without oil.*

1 SMALL DRIED ANCHO CHILE

16 ($\frac{1}{2}$ INCH THICK) SLICES OF BAGUETTE

EXTRA-VIRGIN OLIVE OIL FOR FRYING

6 TO 8 LARGE CLOVES GARLIC, SLICED

6 CUPS HOMEMADE CHICKEN (PAGE 59) OR BEEF BROTH

SALT AND PEPPER

$\frac{1}{2}$ CUP GRATED PARMESAN CHEESE

Stem the ancho chile and shake out the seeds. Under running water, wash the chile and let it soak in $\frac{1}{2}$ cup of warm water for about 30 minutes, or until soft. In a blender, purée the chile with the soaking liquid and set aside.

In a soup pot, heat the oil over medium heat and quickly fry the bread in batches, until browned on both sides. Divide the bread among four soup bowls.

In the same soup pot, remove all but 1 tablespoon of oil and sauté the sliced garlic until soft. Add the chile mixture and simmer for a few minutes before adding the broth. Bring the soup to a boil, season with salt and pepper to taste, and simmer for about 5 minutes. Add the hot broth to each soup bowl and serve at once with a generous amount of cheese.

MUSHROOM SOUP WITH EPAZOTE

Sopa de Hongos con Epazote   *6 servings*

THE AROMATIC HERB EPAZOTE is one of the most important staples to achieve authentic Mexican flavors. I do find that it has to be fresh. Dry epazote, in my opinion, does not lend the desired flavor. Outside of Mexico, however, it is not easy to find fresh epazote, because it grows best in warmer climates. Friends who have been successful in growing other products like jalapeños, tomatillos, and serranos, find that epazote grows well but has very little flavor. Fresh cilantro may be used instead of the epazote.

¼ CUP BUTTER

1 SMALL ONION, CHOPPED

4 CUPS SLICED MUSHROOMS

1 EPAZOTE SPRIG, CHOPPED, OR
    ¼ CUP CHOPPED FRESH CILANTRO

2 SERRANO CHILES

2 TABLESPOONS FLOUR

5 CUPS HOMEMADE CHICKEN BROTH
    (PAGE 59)

SALT AND PEPPER

In a pot, melt the butter and sauté the onion until tender. Stir in the mushrooms, epazote and chiles, and fry until the mushrooms are barely cooked and still firm. Stir in the flour and add the chicken broth. Season with salt and pepper. Bring the mixture to a boil and simmer for about 5 minutes.

With a ladle, scoop out about a cup of the mushrooms with some liquid and process in a blender until puréed. Pour the mushroom mixture back into the pot, bring to a boil, and simmer for a few minutes more. Adjust the seasoning, if necessary, and serve very hot.

ZUCCHINI BLOSSOM SOUP

Sopa de Flor de Calabaza   *4 servings*

ZUCCHINI BLOSSOMS ARE AVAILABLE DURING THE SUMMER when people are harvesting zucchini. The blossoms are widely used in Italy where they cook them in all sorts of ways. They are usually big enough that can be filled with other vegetables, breaded, and then fried. In Mexico, they are available all year round, smaller in size than in Italy, and are usually served in soups, quesadillas, budines (casseroles), and crepes.

Zucchini blossoms are also available in cans at specialty stores.

1 POBLANO CHILE, ROASTED, PEELED
    AND SEEDED (PAGE 111)

12 FRESH ZUCCHINI BLOSSOMS OR
    1 (7 OZ / 220 G) CAN

2 TABLESPOONS BUTTER

1 CLOVE GARLIC, CHOPPED

1/3 CUP CHOPPED ONION

4 CUPS CHICKEN BROTH

1 ZUCCHINI, CHOPPED

1 CUP FRESH OR CANNED AND DRAINED
    CORN KERNELS

SALT AND PEPPER

1 CUP CHIHUAHUA OR MONTEREY JACK
    CHEESE, CUBED

Cut the chiles into 1/2 inch strips and set aside. Carefully remove and discard the pistil from the zucchini blossoms and, under running water gently wash the blossoms. Pat dry with paper towels and chop.

In a saucepan, melt the butter and sauté the garlic, onion, poblano strips, and zucchini blossoms until the vegetables are cooked and the onion is translucent. Add the chicken broth, zucchini, corn, and salt and pepper to taste. Bring to a boil and simmer for about 5 to 8 minutes, or until the vegetables are cooked but still firm.

Divide the soup among four bowls and top each one with cubed cheese. Serve hot.

OATMEAL SOUP

Sopa de Avena   *4 to 6 servings*

OFTEN ENOUGH, I FIND MY GLASS CEREAL CONTAINER overflowing with oatmeal bought with the intention of baking cookies. This recipe is a marvelous way to use it before it goes stale.

My mother-in-law, who was quite a creative cook, made this soup whenever someone in the family had a cold and consequently was feeling quite miserable. Pitita, as my son Ralph used to call her, served this soup piping hot with buttered crusty bolillos or French bread. It is definitely a winter soup and it is good, even when you do not have a cold!

4 SLICES BACON, CHOPPED

1 LARGE TOMATO, CHOPPED

2 LARGE CLOVES GARLIC, CHOPPED

¼ CUP CHOPPED ONION

¼ CUP CANNED TOMATO SAUCE

6 TABLESPOONS QUICK-COOKING
   ROLLED OATS

3 TO 4 CUPS CHICKEN BROTH

PEPPER

In a heavy saucepan, fry the bacon until crisp. Meanwhile, process the tomato, garlic, and onion in a blender or food processor until well puréed.

Remove all but one tablespoon of bacon fat from the saucepan, add the tomato mixture, and sauté for a few minutes before adding the tomato sauce. Simmer for about 3 to 5 minutes. Stir in the oatmeal, broth, and pepper to taste.

Simmer the soup for another 5 minutes, or until the oatmeal is cooked. Check the seasoning and adjust the liquid for a lighter soup if desired.

SEAFOOD SOUP

Sopa de Mariscos   *6 to 8 servings*

MEXICO HAS MORE THAN FIVE THOUSAND MILES OF SHORELINE, so it is not surprising that we Mexicans are very fond of fish and shellfish and cook both in the most imaginative ways.

This Sopa de Mariscos *is flavorful without the addition of the chile, however the chile provides just the right amount of piquancy making this soup a marvelous treat and a whole meal in itself. Good French bread is a must.*

1 LARGE RIPE TOMATO

1 SMALL ONION, QUARTERED

1 TABLESPOON EXTRA-VIRGIN OLIVE OIL

2 LARGE CLOVES GARLIC, CHOPPED

1/2 CUP CANNED TOMATO SAUCE

2 PACKETS (1 TABLESPOON EACH) INSTANT CHICKEN BOUILLON MIX

1 LB (500 G) RED SNAPPER FILLETS, CUT INTO CHUNKS

8 LARGE PRAWNS, HEADS REMOVED

8 FRESH OYSTERS WITH LIQUID

10 CLAMS, WELL SCRUBBED

3 TO 4 SERRANO CHILES, MINCED

SALT AND PEPPER

1/2 CUP DRY WHITE WINE

1/2 CUP CHOPPED FRESH FLAT-LEAF PARSLEY

2 LARGE LIMES, QUARTERED

In a blender, combine the tomato and one quarter of the onion until well processed. Chop the remaining onion.

In a soup pot, heat the olive oil and sauté the chopped onion and the garlic, until the onion is translucent. Stir in the tomato mixture and tomato sauce, and sauté for 2 to 3 minutes before adding 4 cups of water, the bouillon, red snapper, prawns, oysters, clams, and chiles.

Season the soup with salt and pepper, bring to a boil, and simmer for about 5 to 8 minutes, or until the prawns are firm and red. Stir in the wine and the parsley and serve, very hot, with the limes for everyone to add to their own bowls.

RICE AND PASTA

ARROZ Y PASTA

I HAVE TO ADMIT THAT I AM FUSSY when it comes to choosing pasta. I strongly recommend Italian or Spanish (Gallo) brands. The excellent quality of the durum wheat grown in certain regions of Italy and Spain makes their pasta absolutely unique in flavor and texture. Pasta, when properly cooked, should be slippery, slightly tough and chewy, and definitely not sticky. Crusty bread and a glass of wine go hand-in-hand with any pasta dish.

In Mexico, rice is as versatile as is pasta in Italy. It is usually cooked with chicken broth and garlic and served separately as a dry soup. It is never simple, and always presented colorfully: It could be red rice with tomatoes, green rice with cilantro or poblano chiles, or yellow rice with saffron and tomatoes. Fried plantains and guacamole or slices of avocado are the most common garnishes. Rice is also served topped with mole sauce, a good way to use up any leftovers. White rice with black beans, *Moros con Cristianos* (Moors with Christians), is a favorite dish in Mexico as well as in the Caribbean. For a *merienda* (light supper), rice is sometimes served with fried eggs on top.

Rice is always rinsed, drained and then sautéed before adding the rest of the ingredients. The best quality rice comes from the state of Veracruz, and it is the long-grained variety that is most commonly used.

I find that the rice we get in Canada is not as starchy as Mexican rice, and does not need to be rinsed or sautéed. For sweet puddings, I use jasmine rice; for any other dish, basmati or arborio work very well. Rarely, if ever, do I use long-grained rice.

VALENCIA-STYLE PAELLA

Paella Valenciana   *6 to 8 servings*

FOR *MANY YEARS, THE BEST PAELLA was served at the Spanish Casino in downtown Mexico City, a building with a handsome façade of rose-color stone reminiscent of a Renaissance palace. Built at the beginning of the nineteenth century, it serves as a meeting place for the Spanish community. Abundant Spanish-style comidas are served in the magnificent central courtyard, from which you can admire the palatial staircase. On its landing, the coat of arms of Spanish King Charles V attracts tourists and locals alike; and on the lower part is a magnificent painting of Christopher Columbus on his deathbed.*

It is undeniable that if the locals favor a restaurant, it must be good. The Spanish Casino is no exception, since the whole colonia española went to savor the delicious callos de hacha (scallops in tomato sauce), fabada Asturiana (white beans in tomato sauce with sausage, chorizo, and ham), and other specialties.

In Spain, paella is traditionally cooked outside over a charcoal fire. Even prepared inside on a stove, however, it is a festive dish, colorful and full of surprises. A green salad as a first course will complement this tempting dish.

Saffron is available at most grocery stores. For paella, it is best to buy small chicken pieces such as drumsticks and thighs.

2 TEASPOONS SAFFRON THREADS

2 CUPS CHICKEN BROTH, HOT

12 CLAMS, WELL SCRUBBED

SALT AND PEPPER

6 TO 8 PIECES OF CHICKEN

1/2 LB (250 G) BONELESS PORK, CUBED

1 TEASPOON VEGETABLE OIL

2 TABLESPOONS OLIVE OIL

12 PRAWNS, HEADS REMOVED

1/2 CUP CHOPPED ONION

4 LARGE CLOVES GARLIC, CHOPPED

2 LARGE RIPE TOMATOES, CHOPPED

1 LARGE RED BELL PEPPER

1 TABLESPOON PAPRIKA

1/2 CUP CHOPPED FRESH FLAT-LEAF
   PARSLEY

1 1/2 CUPS ARBORIO RICE

1/2 LB (250 G) CHORIZO SAUSAGE, CUT
   INTO SMALL CHUNKS

Soak the saffron in the broth. Meanwhile, bring about 3 cups water to a boil in a sauce pan and steam the clams to open, about 4 to 5 minutes. Remove from heat, discarding any unopened clams.

Sprinkle salt and pepper on the chicken and the pork. In a wide, shallow pan, heat the oil and sauté the chicken and pork until golden brown. Remove from the pan, skin the chicken, and keep it warm. Discard all but 1 tablespoon of the drippings. Add the olive oil to the remaining drippings and sauté the prawns with the onion and garlic until the onion is translucent. Remove the prawns from the pan, add the tomatoes and red pepper, and sauté until all the vegetables are softened. Stir in the paprika, parsley, and rice. Pour the saffron liquid into the rice, add the meats, clams, prawns, and the sliced chorizo. Season with salt and pepper.

Bring the rice mixture to a boil, cover the pan, lower the heat, and simmer for approximately 15 to 20 minutes, or until the liquid is almost completely absorbed. Turn off the heat and let the paella sit, covered, for 5 to 8 minutes before serving. This allows the rice to finish cooking and the flavors to blend. Paella should not be served very hot.

MESÓN DEL ANGEL RICE

Arroz Estilo "Mesón del Angel"   *4 to 6 servings*

THE MESÓN DEL ANGEL IS A HOTEL in the city of Puebla that was very new when I lived there in the 1970s. It had a very good restaurant that was extremely popular among the local residents. We used to go there for Sunday brunch with friends or family visiting from Mexico City. The brunch would usually turn into the comida (lunch) in the late afternoon, after which the whole crowd would enjoy a drink in the beautiful gardens before supper.

Puebla is quite close to the port of Veracruz, making it easy to bring the freshest and most succulent fish and shellfish to La Victoria market, a beautiful two-story building erected around 1913 and the main market in the city. The prawns, served in a tomato and chipotle chile sauce, were out of this world and one of my husband's favorite dishes; red snapper a la Veracruzana was another one. Needless to say, traditional dishes like mole poblano or tinga, shredded beef smothered with pineapple vinegar in a tomato sauce that boiled for hours, were enjoyed by everyone. Their rice was always a must. The Mesón del Angel is still there, still beautiful and certainly worth visiting.

1 LARGE POBLANO CHILE, ROASTED, PEELED, AND SEEDED (PAGE 111)

1 TEASPOON VEGETABLE OIL

2 TABLESPOONS CHOPPED ONION

1 LARGE CLOVE GARLIC, CHOPPED

1 CUP LONG-GRAIN RICE

2 CUPS CHICKEN BROTH

1 CUP UNCOOKED FRESH OR CANNED AND DRAINED CORN KERNELS

1/2 CUP CHOPPED FRESH CILANTRO

SALT AND PEPPER

1 LARGE RIPE AVOCADO, PEELED AND SLICED

Slice the chile into 1/2-inch-wide strips, cut these in half, and set aside.

In a saucepan, heat the oil over medium heat and sauté the onion, garlic, and chile, until the onion is translucent. Add the rice, chicken broth, corn, cilantro, and salt and pepper to taste. Bring to a boil and simmer for about 15 minutes, or until the rice is cooked and the liquid is completely absorbed.

Serve at once, as a dry soup, garnished with the avocado slices.

ANDALUSIAN-STYLE RICE SALAD

Ensalada de Arroz a la Andaluza   *6 servings*

CAN YOU THINK OF A BETTER SUMMER buffet dish than this? It reminds me of the warm temperatures in southern Spain and of all the good things from that region, like saffron, olives, almonds, and pimientos. Going south from Madrid, as you cross the Sierra Nevada into Andalusia, the olive trees form a wide and beautiful spectacle, especially when you think of the precious olive oil coming from those wonderful trees.

Mexico is proud of its Spanish heritage and it shows in many popular dishes like this colorful rice salad.

1 CUP BASMATI RICE

1 TEASPOON SALT

6 TO 8 TABLESPOONS EXTRA-VIRGIN
    OLIVE OIL

3 TABLESPOONS WINE VINEGAR

1 LARGE CLOVE GARLIC, MINCED

1 SMALL ONION, CHOPPED

SALT AND PEPPER

2 TO 3 CANNED ROASTED RED PIMIENTOS,
    SLICED INTO STRIPS

12 GREEN OLIVES, PITTED AND SLICED

12 BLACK OLIVES, PITTED AND SLICED

2 TABLESPOONS CHOPPED FRESH
    FLAT-LEAF PARSLEY

Bring 2 cups of salted water to a boil. Add the rice, cover, and cook over low heat for about 15 minutes, or until the rice is cooked and fluffy, and the water is completely absorbed.

While the rice is cooking, make a vinaigrette by combining the olive oil, vinegar, garlic, onion, and salt and pepper to taste. Reserving six to eight pimiento strips for garnish, finely chop the remaining pimientos.

Cool the rice slightly and add the vinaigrette, chopped pimientos, olives, and parsley. Toss gently.

Spoon the rice into a serving bowl and garnish with the reserved pimiento slices. Cover and chill thoroughly. This rice salad can be prepared 3 to 4 hours in advance, and served at room temperature.

CREAMY RICE WITH POBLANO CHILE STRIPS

Arroz Blanco con Rajas de Poblano   *6 servings*

THIS CAN BE EASILY TURNED INTO A GOOD BUFFET DISH. *Layer the cooked rice and poblano chile strips in a casserole dish, finishing with cream and cheese. Just before serving, bake the casserole at 350°F for eight to ten minutes, or until it is heated through and the cheese is melted. The baking time may be reduced if the rice is already warm. Serve with piping hot tortillas.*

4 POBLANO CHILES, ROASTED, PEELED, AND SEEDED (PAGE 111)

2 TEASPOONS VEGETABLE OIL

⅓ CUP CHOPPED ONION

½ CUP SOUR CREAM

½ CUP GRATED MANCHEGO OR MONTEREY JACK CHEESE

SALT

1 CLOVE GARLIC, CHOPPED

1 CUP BASMATI OR LONG-GRAIN RICE

2 CUPS CHICKEN BROTH

2 SPRIGS CILANTRO

Discarding the stems, slice each chile into ½-inch-wide strips. In a small saucepan, heat 1 teaspoon of the oil over medium heat and sauté the onion and chile until the vegetables are cooked. Remove the *rajas* from the heat and add the sour cream, cheese and a dash of salt. Set aside and keep warm.

In a separate saucepan or a frying pan with a lid, heat the remaining teaspoon of oil over medium heat and lightly sauté the garlic, then add the rice, chicken broth, cilantro, and salt to taste. Bring the rice to a boil, lower the heat, and simmer covered for 12 to 15 minutes, or until the rice is cooked and fluffy, and the water has evaporated completely. Let the rice sit for a few minutes.

Transfer the rice to a round serving platter with the *rajas de poblano* in the middle, and serve at once.

RICE WITH
CHORIZO TACOS

Arroz Blanco con Taquitos de Chorizo   *4 servings*

It can be difficult to find plantains that are ripe and sweet precisely when we need them. If they are not quite ready, place them in a warm place, wrapped in newspaper, or better still in a place where they can get some sun. They are sweetest when the peel is almost black and the flesh is soft. This sweetness lends a very pleasing flavor to the rice and, when served with guacamole and chorizo, you have a winner.

Good chorizo is essential for the taquitos. Specialty stores and some delicatessens are a good source of quality chorizo. If you want to skip the added step of making the taquitos and still have the flavor of the chorizo, this can be fried along with the onion and garlic and added directly into the rice; however, I do recommend the chorizo taquitos.

1 TEASPOON VEGETABLE OIL PLUS OIL
    FOR FRYING

1 LARGE CLOVE GARLIC, MINCED

2 TABLESPOONS CHOPPED ONION

1 CUP LONG-GRAIN RICE

2 PACKETS (1 TABLESPOON EACH)
    INSTANT CHICKEN BOUILLON MIX

SALT AND PEPPER

1 RIPE PLANTAIN, PEELED

½ LB (250 G) CHORIZO SAUSAGE,
    PEELED

12 CORN TORTILLAS

1 CUP GUACAMOLE (PAGE 149)

In a heavy saucepan, heat 1 teaspoon of oil over medium heat and sauté the garlic and onion until the onion is translucent. Stir in the rice until well coated with oil. Add 2 cups of water, the bouillon, and salt and pepper to taste. Bring the rice to a boil and simmer for about 12 to 15 minutes, or until the rice is cooked and the liquid is completely absorbed.

While the rice is cooking, cut the plantain in half and slice it lengthwise, into four to five thin slices. Fry the plantain in oil until golden brown. Drain on paper towels and keep warm. Reserve the pan for frying the tacos.

In a separate, dry pan, lightly cook the chorizo until it crumbles completely. Good chorizo usually crumbles easily. Set aside.

In another dry pan, warm the corn tortillas until they are pliable and fold without breaking. Fill each one with about 2 tablespoons of the chorizo and roll very tightly. Using the same pan used for frying the plantain, fry the *taquitos* until very crisp. Drain on paper towels and keep warm.

Place the *taquitos* on a serving platter and serve immediately with the rice, topped with the plantain slices and, pass the guacamole at the table.

GREEN HERB SPAGHETTI

Spaghetti Verde   *Makes 4 servings*

A GREEN HERB SPAGHETTI SAUCE makes for a distinctive dish and it is certainly a good way to use all those leftover greens in your fridge and maybe an open package of pasta. This sauce can also be served with other shapes of pasta like fettuccine, spaghettini, or penne.

8 OZ (250 G) SPAGHETTI

½ CUP CHOPPED FRESH CILANTRO

½ CUP CHOPPED FRESH FLAT-LEAF
PARSLEY

½ CUP CHOPPED CELERY LEAVES

½ CUP PLUS 1 TABLESPOON MILK

½ CUP SOUR CREAM

1 TABLESPOON BUTTER

SALT AND PEPPER

½ CUP FRESHLY GRATED PARMESAN
CHEESE

In salted boiling water, cook the spaghetti according to the package directions, or until al dente. In the meantime, using a blender or food processor, purée the cilantro, parsley, and celery leaves with ½ cup of the milk. Separately, beat the sour cream with the remaining tablespoon of milk and set aside.

In a saucepan, melt the butter and sauté the herb mixture for 3 to 4 minutes. The sauce should be a light green color. Add the drained pasta, season with salt and pepper, and serve at once, topped with the sour cream mixture and a generous amount of cheese.

SPAGHETTI WITH ANCHO CHILE AND BASIL

Spaghetti al Chile Ancho   *4 servings*

THE VERY MEXICAN ANCHO (WIDE) CHILE with its mild and bittersweet flavor, combined with basil, used extensively in Italian recipes, results in an intriguing flavor in this pasta recipe. Refer to the glossary for more information about the ancho chile.

2 DRY ANCHO CHILES, STEMMED

1/2 CUP WINE VINEGAR

8 OZ (250 G) SPAGHETTI

4 TO 6 TABLESPOONS EXTRA-VIRGIN
   OLIVE OIL

3 CLOVES GARLIC, CHOPPED

2 TABLESPOONS CHOPPED FRESH BASIL,
   OR 1 TEASPOON DRY

SALT AND PEPPER

1/2 CUP CRUMBLED *QUESO FRESCO* OR
   FETA CHEESE

Break the chiles in half and discard the seeds. Wash them under running water and pat dry. Soak the chiles in the vinegar for about 10 minutes, or until soft. Drain and slice the chiles into thin strips and discard the vinegar.

Cook the spaghetti in salted boiling water with a few drops of oil, according to the package directions, or until al dente. Drain.

While the spaghetti is cooking, heat the olive oil in a pan and sauté the garlic and chile strips for a few minutes, being careful not to burn the garlic. Toss the spaghetti with the olive oil mixture. Add the basil and season with salt and pepper. Serve the pasta at once, topped with a generous amount of cheese.

FUSILLI WITH AVOCADO CREAM AND RICOTTA

Tornillos con Crema de Aguacate y Queso Fresco   *4 servings*

My husband and I owned a dairy farm in Chipilo, Puebla, southeast of Mexico City, and we produced, what people used to call, the best queso fresco *in the region. We had Canadian Holstein registered cows that produced very good milk so the cheese, made in a very simple way was absolutely delicious. It got to be so popular that our friends and family in Mexico City asked us to expand the business and sell our cheese in the big city, which we eventually did for a few years before moving to Canada.*

Queso fresco *is perfect for this pasta recipe. It is moist and blends very well with the avocado to make a delectable, creamy sauce.*

8 oz (250 g) FUSILLI PASTA

½ TEASPOON OLIVE OIL

2 LARGE RIPE AVOCADOS, PEELED

JUICE OF ½ LIME

½ CUP *QUESO FRESCO* OR RICOTTA
    CHEESE

1 TO 2 SERRANO CHILES, MINCED

2 TO 3 TABLESPOONS CHOPPED FRESH
    CILANTRO

2 TO 3 TABLESPOONS MILK

Bring a large pot of salted water to a boil and cook the pasta with the oil, according to the package directions, or until al dente.

While the pasta is cooking, mash the avocados with the lime juice. Stir in the cheese and mash together until well blended. Add the chile, cilantro, and enough milk to soften the mixture to a smooth paste. Add to the drained hot pasta and mix thoroughly.

Serve at once as a first course or as a side dish with meat or chicken.

ZUCCHINI BLOSSOM LASAGNA

Lasagna de Flor de Calabaza   *6 to 8 servings*

IN THIS RECIPE, PASTA IS COMBINED with typically Mexican ingredients such as zucchini blossoms, chiles, and epazote. If this aromatic herb is not available, cilantro can be used instead. The filling can be prepared a day in advance and refrigerated until you are ready to bake it.

2 TABLESPOONS EXTRA-VIRGIN OLIVE OIL

1 SMALL ONION, CHOPPED

2 LARGE CLOVES GARLIC, FINELY
  CHOPPED

1 SMALL SERRANO CHILE, MINCED

2 POBLANO CHILES, ROASTED, PEELED,
  AND SEEDED (PAGE 111)

2 CUPS FRESH CORN KERNELS

2 SMALL ZUCCHINI, CHOPPED

SALT

2 CUPS FRESH ZUCCHINI BLOSSOMS OR
  2 (7 OZ / 220 G) CANS

1 SPRIG FRESH EPAZOTE, CHOPPED OR
  2 TABLESPOONS CHOPPED FRESH
  CILANTRO

9 STRIPS LASAGNA-STYLE PASTA

½ CUP CRÈME FRAÎCHE (PAGE 148)

¾ CUP CRUMBLED *QUESO FRESCO* OR
  FETA CHEESE

Preheat the oven to 350°F.

Heat the olive oil and sauté the onion and garlic, until the onion is translucent. Stir in the serrano and poblano chile, corn, and zucchini. Lower the heat and simmer for about 6 to 8 minutes, stirring occasionally, until the vegetables are cooked but still crisp. Season with salt to taste.

Wash the zucchini blossoms, removing and discarding the pistil, and chop them. Add the chopped zucchini blossoms (including the liquid if using canned) and the epazote to the chile mixture, and simmer for 2 or 3 minutes, until the liquid has evaporated.

Meanwhile, cook the pasta in salted boiling water according to the package instructions or until al dente, and drain. Cover the bottom of a 9 x 12-inch rectangular baking dish with three strips of lasagna pasta, cover the pasta with a third of the vegetable mixture, and top with a third of the crème fraîche and cheese. Continue layering in the same order until all the ingredients have been used. Cover the dish with aluminum foil and bake for about 15 to 20 minutes, or until the lasagna is heated through. Be careful not to overbake, or the pasta will be dry. Serve the lasagna with a green salad, garnished with tomato slices.

CHICKEN
POLLO

IN MEXICAN CUISINE, chicken is generally served in stews with a simple sauce of chopped onion, garlic, tomatoes, and green chiles; or baked in a creamy poblano chile sauce. In other dishes, chicken breasts are poached and shredded for casseroles, tostadas, tacos, or enchiladas and the broth is used in soups and sauces.

In Mexican cuisine, homemade chicken broth is the base for most soups, stews, and moles. I remember with great nostalgia the chicken broth my mother used to prepare for me when I was sick. She would cook the chicken with the vegetables I liked the most: chayote squash, zucchini, pieces of corn on the cob, and carrots. And, unbeknownst to me at that time, also with chicken feet! These, of course, never made it to my plate; however, I now know that they provided most of the flavor in the broth. Sometimes she would also add a little bit of rice, making the broth a meal in itself.

I had not had a soup like the one I am describing above, until a few months ago, when I happened to be sick and my good friend Elena Lewis kindly brought what she referred to as "just some chicken broth." Well, to my surprise, her soup immediately brought back those memories. She still makes chicken broth like *her* mother, with chicken feet she buys at Chinese supermarkets. Needless to say, I was very grateful.

CHICKEN BREASTS IN ORANGE JUICE

Pechugas de Pollo en Jugo de Naranja   *4 servings*

CHICKEN CAN BE TIRESOME AND BORING; *however, this is not the case with the following recipe. Fresh orange juice gives the chicken a tangy flavor, and the bread crumbs mixed with Parmesan cheese form a splendid crust. Bear in mind that chicken is very easy to overcook, and the end result could be a dry piece of meat that has lost its flavor and texture if you are not careful.*

2 WHOLE BONELESS CHICKEN BREASTS, HALVED

¾ CUP FRESH ORANGE JUICE

SALT AND PEPPER

¾ CUP FINE DRY BREAD CRUMBS

½ CUP GRATED PARMESAN CHEESE

OIL FOR FRYING

Open each chicken breast and press between two pieces of plastic wrap. With a rolling pin, flatten the breasts until almost double in size. In a bowl, cover the chicken with the orange juice and marinate for 2 to 3 hours. Drain the chicken, and sprinkle salt and pepper on both sides.

In a separate bowl, mix the bread crumbs with the Parmesan cheese. Coat the chicken breasts on both sides with the bread crumb mixture.

In a heavy frying pan, heat the oil over medium heat and quickly fry the chicken breasts on both sides until golden brown. Remove the chicken with a slotted spoon to drain as much oil as possible. Drain on paper towels to remove excess oil.

Serve hot, with a green salad or enchiladas.

CHICKEN BREASTS WITH MOLCAJETE SALSA

Pechugas en Salsa de Molcajete   *4 servings*

WHEN I MOVED TO CANADA, I left my molcajete behind. It was just too heavy to carry and, at the time, I thought that I would never use it here. Years later, returning from one of my trips to visit my family, I decided to bring my mother's molcajete with me to continue the tradition of using it for cooking and to serve guacamole and salsas at the table.

The three-legged stone mortar and pestle is always a good piece of conversation in my cooking classes, although it is not used as frequently as a blender. For this recipe, in particular, I always use my molcajete. It reminds me very much of my grandmother's kitchen, with the aromatic essence of cloves mixed with garlic and that special flavor the stone provides. A blender or a small food processor can also be used.

2 WHOLE BONELESS CHICKEN BREASTS, HALVED

2 LARGE CLOVES GARLIC

2 TABLESPOONS CHOPPED ONION

2 TO 3 WHOLE CLOVES

¼ CUP CHICKEN BROTH

SALT AND PEPPER

¾ CUP FINE DRY BREAD CRUMBS

OIL FOR FRYING

Open each chicken breast and press it between two pieces of plastic wrap. With a rolling pin, flatten the chicken until almost double in size. Set aside.

In a mortar and pestle or in a *molcajete*, mash the garlic, onion, and cloves to a paste. Stir in the chicken broth, little by little, and mix until completely blended. If the sauce is too thick, add a little more broth and season with salt and pepper. Coat each chicken breast in the sauce and then roll in bread crumbs to cover completely.

In a nonstick frying pan, heat the oil over medium heat and fry the chicken breasts until golden brown.

Serve hot, with mashed potatoes and a green salad.

MEXICAN CULINARY TREASURES

CHICKEN IN CHEESE AND CHIPOTLE CHILE SAUCE

Pollo en Salsa de Queso y Chipotle   *4 to 6 servings*

IN THIS RECIPE, THE COMBINATION OF THE CHIPOTLE chile's piquancy with the cheese makes a very palatable dish. I strongly recommend mild Cheddar cheese. Chipotle chiles can be found in the Mexican food aisle of major supermarkets, usually in small (7 oz / 199 G) cans.

Serve this chicken with a green salad, topped with avocado strips and tomato slices. Once the chicken is poached, the remaining liquid is a Homemade Chicken Stock.

1 SMALL RED POTATO, PEELED AND
  CHOPPED

1 STALK OF CELERY WITH LEAVES,
  CHOPPED

1 SMALL CARROT, PEELED AND CHOPPED

¼ SMALL ONION

1 CHICKEN (2 LB / 1 KG), CUT INTO
  PIECES

SALT

¾ CUP MILD CHEDDAR CHEESE, CUBED

½ CUP MEXICAN CREAM OR CRÈME
  FRAÎCHE (PAGE 148)

½ CUP 2% MILK

1 LARGE CHIPOTLE CHILE, SEEDED AND
  STEMMED

1 TEASPOON CHIPOTLE ADOBO

In a soup pot, bring 4 to 5 cups of water to a boil. Add the vegetables, chicken, and a dash of salt. Reduce the heat, skim off the foam that forms at the top, and simmer until the chicken and vegetables are cooked, about 10 to 12 minutes. Drain the chicken pieces, cool, and remove the skin. Reserve the chicken broth for homemade soups. (Once cold, the chicken broth can be frozen in a plastic container to be used at a later date.)

Preheat the oven to 350°F. Place the chicken pieces in a baking dish. In a blender or food processor, blend the cheese with the cream, milk, chile, and the *adobo*, to a smooth paste. Cover the chicken with the cream sauce and bake for 8 to 10 minutes, or until heated through. The sauce should be thick and of a light yellow color. Serve at once.

LOS GUAJOLOTES CHICKEN IN MOLE POBLANO

Pollo en Mole Poblano Los Guajolotes   *Yields 10 to 12 cups of mole sauce*

DURING ONE OF MY ANNUAL VISITS TO MEXICO CITY, *my uncle Arturo and his wife invited my father and me out for dinner. He told me that I was going to have "the best mole in town." I took this statement with three grains of salt, since I had lived in Puebla for several years where mole originated. I knew however, that I was going to have a good mole. Los Guajolotes is one of the most traditional restaurants in the city, where families and businessmen alike get together, and it is always full. But not even in my wildest dreams had I imagined such a delicious flavor, somewhat different from other moles I had tried before, good as they might have been.*

My visit to Los Guajolotes, turned out to be memorable, not only because I was able to visit with my uncle whom I had not seen in more than twenty years, but because, knowing my love for cooking, my uncle sent for the owner, introduced me as a cookbook author and asked him to package two kilos of the mole for me to take back to my family in Canada (which, by the way, I do every year now). Needless to say, I was elated, and after praising this magnificent mole, I asked him if there was a slight chance of getting the recipe from him to include in this book. I knew at that moment that the worst was for him to say no. There was a moment of silence in our table. He looked at me very seriously and turned around to look at my uncle and said: "Yes, only because you are the niece of my lawyer and friend of so many years, about fifty or so." I still cannot believe that he actually obliged!

I was to leave Mexico in a couple of days and was afraid the recipe would not be ready in time. Again, to my surprise, the manager of the restaurant called to let me know that the recipe was ready. He was sorry it could not be faxed; I had to pick it up personally. And so I did.

If you compare this recipe with other mole poblano *recipes, you will find that this one contains perhaps a few more ingredients and, instead of using granulated sugar, which most of the others use, the sweetening agent here is prunes. In all this lies the secret of its distinctive and delectable flavor. It is indeed a unique recipe, never before published.*

After this rather long introduction to an already long recipe, I hope I have stimulated your curiosity enough to either visit Los Guajolotes Restaurant on Avenida Insurgentes Sur in Mexico City, or to try the recipe at home. Serve this magnificent mole sauce with cooked chicken or turkey, on top of rice, or with enchiladas.

Before leaving the topic of moles, I should also mention that there are many other kinds of moles. To name a few: mole de oaxaca *or* mole negro, mole verde, mole de olla colorado, mole de olla verde, mole de chipotle, mole de barbacoa, *and many more.*

OIL OR LARD FOR FRYING

16 DRY *MULATO* CHILES

3 TO 4 DRY PASILLA CHILES

8 DRY ANCHO CHILES

1 TO 2 DRY CHIPOTLE CHILE(S)

4 TO 6 CUPS BOILING WATER

1 LARGE TOMATO

1 MEDIUM HEAD GARLIC

2 LARGE ONIONS, QUARTERED

10 TO 12 TOMATILLOS, HUSKED

2 CORN TORTILLAS

¾ CUP SESAME SEEDS

2 TABLESPOONS LARD OR OIL

1 SMALL PLANTAIN, PEELED

½ CUP BLANCHED ALMONDS

½ CUP SHELLED PEANUTS

½ CUP PITTED PRUNES, CHOPPED

½ CUP RAISINS

2 (2-INCH) CINNAMON STICKS

1 TEASPOON CORIANDER SEEDS

1 TEASPOON ANISE SEEDS

2 CUPS CHICKEN BROTH

1 TABLET (2 OZ/60 G) MEXICAN CHOCOLATE, CHOPPED

Heat the oil and sauté the *mulato*, pasilla, ancho, and chipotle chiles in oil or lard. Stem and shake out their seeds. Rinse the chiles under running water and place in a large bowl. Cover the chiles with the boiling water, and soak for about 30 minutes, or until they are soft and the liquid is reddish. Drain the chiles and reserve the soaking liquid. In a blender or food processor, purée the chiles in batches with 2 cups of the soaking liquid. Strain the chile mixture into a bowl, discarding the residue of the pods. Set aside. Preheat the oven to 400°F.

Place the tomato, garlic, onions, tomatillos, and tortillas on a cookie sheet, and bake, turning frequently, until the vegetable peels are charred and the tortillas have dark brown spots and edges. Remove from the oven and peel the vegetables when cool. Discard the peels. Purée the vegetables in a blender or food processor, adding about 1 cup of the chile soaking liquid. Strain and discard the residue. Set the purée aside.

In a large frying pan, over medium heat, dry-roast the sesame seeds for about 3 to 4 minutes. Remove the seeds from pan. Add oil or lard to the same pan and lightly fry the plantain slices, almonds, peanuts, prunes, raisins, cinnamon sticks, coriander, and anise seeds, stirring constantly until browned. Purée the fried ingredients in a blender or food processor with ¼ cup of the sesame seeds and the remaining chile-soaking liquid.

In a large *cazuela* or saucepan, combine the puréed chiles, vegetables, and seasonings with the chicken broth. Bring the mixture to a simmer over medium heat. Cover and continue simmering for 1 to 1½ hours, stirring frequently with a wooden spoon. Stir in the chocolate and mix well until the chocolate is melted. Serve the mole sauce sprinkled with the remaining sesame seeds.

CHICKEN IN
CHORIZO SAUCE

Pollo en Salsa de Chorizo   *4 to 6 servings*

ALMOST EVERY STATE IN MEXICO *has its own version of chorizo, a pork sausage seasoned with a variety of spices that depend on the region where it is made. Cumin, cinnamon, oregano, cloves, garlic, and dried ancho chile or* pimentón dulce *are the most common spices. Particularly good is the chorizo made in Toluca, the capital of the state of Mexico, and the only place where they make red and green chorizo. My favorite however, was made in Chipilo, Puebla, by descendants of northern Italians who immigrated to Mexico in the 1920s.*

These Italian immigrants were mostly farmers. Through the years, and with hard work, they formed a dairy cooperative. Their butter, queso fresco *and* queso de Oaxaca, *were sold across the country under the brand name Chipilo. As I remember, their chorizo was wonderfully seasoned and not as aromatic, but equally as delicious as those in other parts of the country. On Sundays, Chipilo was full of visitors from the Big City who were willing to make the trip to Puebla in order to buy the Chipilo products freshly made. Good chorizo can be found in Portuguese and Italian delicatessens.*

1 (3 LB/1½ KG) CHICKEN, CUT INTO
    PIECES

1 CELERY STALK, WITH LEAVES

¼ SMALL ONION PLUS 2 TABLESPOONS
    CHOPPED

1 CARROT, PEELED AND CHOPPED

1 POTATO, PEELED AND CHOPPED

1 LARGE RIPE TOMATO

1 CLOVE GARLIC, CHOPPED

2 SERRANO CHILES, STEMMED AND
    CHOPPED

1 CHORIZO SAUSAGE
    (ABOUT ¼ LB/125 G), PEELED

¼ CUP TOMATO SAUCE

½ CUP CHICKEN BROTH

1 TABLESPOON CIDER VINEGAR

SALT AND PEPPER

In salted boiling water, cook the chicken pieces with the celery stalk, quarter onion, carrot, and potato for about 10 to 12 minutes, depending on the size of the chicken pieces, or until cooked but still tender. Drain the chicken, and when cool enough to handle, remove the skin. Set the chicken aside.

While the chicken is cooking, roast the tomatoes in a dry frying pan until the peel is charred. Cool. Peel the tomatoes and remove the seeds. In a blender or food processor, blend the tomatoes with the garlic, chopped onion, and chiles, until well blended. Set aside.

In a dry frying pan, crumble the chorizo with a fork and sauté for 2 to 4 minutes. Remove the chorizo from the pan. Using the same pan, fry the tomato mixture in the chorizo drippings for 3 to 4 minutes. Add the tomato sauce, chicken broth, chicken pieces, chorizo, vinegar, and salt and pepper to taste. Bring to a boil and simmer for an additional 5 to 8 minutes, or until the sauce has thickened.

CHICKEN IN PRUNE AND RED WINE SAUCE

Pollo con Ciruelas y Vino Tinto   *4 to 6 servings*

MEXICAN CUISINE BOASTS MANY SOPHISTICATED DISHES *in which fruit is combined with tomatoes and red wine. This prune sauce is equally good served with a loin of pork.*

10 TO 12 PRUNES, PITTED

2 LARGE PLUM TOMATOES, ROASTED AND PEELED

2 TABLESPOONS CHOPPED ONION

1 TABLESPOON VEGETABLE OIL

1 (2 LB/1 KG) CHICKEN, CUT INTO PIECES

1 CUP DRY RED WINE

SALT AND PEPPER

In a small bowl, cover the prunes with 1 cup water and soak for about 10 minutes, or until soft. Drain the prunes, reserving the soaking liquid. Process the prunes with the ½ cup of the reserved liquid and set aside.

In the same blender or food processor, process the tomatoes and onion with the remaining soaking liquid until well blended.

In a large pan, heat the oil over medium heat and fry the chicken pieces on both sides until golden brown. Remove the chicken from the pan and skin. Discard all but 1 teaspoon of the fat.

Transfer the tomato mixture to the pan and sauté for 3 to 4 minutes in the chicken drippings, stirring occasionally. Add the prune sauce, wine, and chicken. Sprinkle with salt and pepper to taste. Bring the chicken to a boil, reduce the heat, and simmer for 12 to 15 minutes, depending on the size of the chicken pieces, or until the chicken is thoroughly cooked and the sauce has thickened.

Serve at once with French bread.

XOCHITL CASSEROLE

Budín Xóchitl   *4 to 6 servings*

I AM THE TYPICAL MEXICAN who likes to make certain dishes, such as enchiladas, at the very last minute. This is not always easy when you have ten or more people for dinner, so a budín *comes to the rescue. A* budín *is a type of casserole whose ingredients are assembled beforehand and then baked just before serving time. The sauce is usually prepared a day ahead and warmed before the assembling of the dish.*

Keep in mind that tomatillos can be a bit acidic. If this is the case, add a dash of sugar.

1 LARGE CHICKEN BREAST, HALVED

¼ SMALL ONION

½ CELERY STALK WITH LEAVES

TOMATILLO SAUCE:

12 TOMATILLOS, HUSKED AND WASHED

2 TO 4 SERRANO CHILES

¼ CUP CHOPPED ONION

1 CLOVE GARLIC

½ CUP CHOPPED FRESH CILANTRO

1 TEASPOON VEGETABLE OIL

SALT

SUGAR (OPTIONAL)

BUDÍN:

VEGETABLE OIL FOR FRYING

8 TO 10 CORN TORTILLAS, SLICED INTO
   STRIPS

⅔ CUP SOUR CREAM

2 TABLESPOONS MILK

½ CUP CRUMBLED *QUESO FRESCO* OR
   FETA CHEESE

In salted boiling water, cook the chicken breast with the onion and celery for about 12 minutes, or until the chicken is barely cooked. Remove the chicken from the broth and let it cool. When it is cool enough to handle, remove the skin and the bones, and using your fingers, shred the chicken. Use the chicken broth for homemade soups, rice, or stews.

FOR THE TOMATILLO SAUCE: While the chicken is cooking, process the tomatillos, chiles, onion, garlic, cilantro, and ½ cup water in a blender or food processor until puréed. In a small saucepan, heat the oil over medium heat, add the tomatillo sauce and season with a dash of salt and a dash of sugar if necessary. Bring the sauce to a simmer, and continue simmering for 8 to 10 minutes, or until it thickens slightly. Set the sauce aside.

FOR THE BUDÍN: In a heavy frying pan, heat the oil almost to the point of smoking and quickly fry the tortilla strips until crisp. Drain the tortillas on paper towels to remove the excess oil. Preheat the oven to 350°F.

Using the same pan, lightly sauté the chicken and then add the tomatillo sauce. Bring the sauce to a gentle simmer for 2 or 3 minutes to allow the flavors to blend. Keep warm.

TO ASSEMBLE THE BUDÍN: In a rectangular baking dish, alternately layer the tortilla strips, chicken mixture, cream, and cheese until all the ingredients are used up, ending with the cream and cheese. Bake the *budín* for about 10 to 12 minutes, or until it starts to bubble, the cheese is melted, and it is heated through.

Serve immediately with refried beans.

AZTEC CASSEROLE

Budín Azteca   *4 to 6 servings*

Planning a Sunday family brunch? This budín *is an easier and faster way of preparing the traditional* chilaquiles rojos. *The salsa and the chicken can be cooked and shredded the day before, leaving only the assembly for the very last minute. Please refer to* Budín Xóchitl *(page 64) for instructions on cooking chicken breasts, as well as assembling* budines. *This dish can also be prepared without the chicken and served with scrambled eggs and refried beans.*

For a scrumptious brunch, and while the Budín Azteca *is baking, start the meal with fresh seasonal fruit, like pineapple, cantaloupe, papaya, and/or watermelon. A steaming hot cup of coffee with* bizcochos *(sweet rolls) would be a memorable ending.*

2 LARGE TOMATOES, ROASTED AND PEELED

2 TO 4 SERRANO CHILES

1/4 CUP CHOPPED ONION

2 CLOVES GARLIC

VEGETABLE OIL FOR FRYING

SALT AND PEPPER

1/2 CUP CANNED TOMATO SAUCE

8 TO 10 CORN TORTILLAS, LIGHTLY FRIED

2/3 CUP SOUR CREAM

2 TABLESPOONS MILK

1 LARGE CHICKEN BREAST, COOKED AND SHREDDED (SEE PAGE 66)

1/2 CUP CRUMBLED *QUESO FRESCO* OR FETA CHEESE

Preheat the oven to 350°F. In a blender or food processor, purée the tomatoes, chiles, onion and garlic. In a small saucepan, heat 1 teaspoon of oil over medium heat and fry the tomato mixture for 3 to 4 minutes, stirring occasionally, before adding 1/2 cup water and the tomato sauce. Season the sauce with salt and pepper and bring to a boil, lower the heat, and simmer for 8 to 10 minutes, or until thickened. Set aside, keeping the sauce warm.

Mix the sour cream with the milk. In a round baking dish, alternately layer the tortillas, chicken, tomato sauce, sour cream mixture, and cheese, until all the ingredients are used up, ending with tortilla, sour cream mixture, and cheese. Bake the casserole for 8 to 10 minutes, or until the sauce starts to bubble, the cheese is melted, and the *budín* is heated through.

Serve at once as a main course, with refried beans.

MOLE CASSEROLE

Budín de Mole   *6 to 8 servings*

Use LEFTOVER MOLE SAUCE *in this splendid casserole. It's easy to make when you have the chicken cooked in advance and the mole sauce already prepared. The assembling of the* budín *does not take very long.*

Please note that mole sauce tends to get dry very fast and tortillas absorb liquid very quickly. It is always a good practice to reserve about half a cup of the mole sauce to spoon over each serving, if necessary.

Outside of Mexico, mole poblano is available in jars in major supermarkets and specialty stores. Good brands to look for are La Costeña and Doña María. Mole sauce, once prepared, freezes very well.

1 LARGE WHOLE CHICKEN BREAST

¼ SMALL ONION

1 SMALL CARROT

½ CELERY STALK WITH LEAVES

VEGETABLE OIL FOR FRYING

10 TO 12 CORN TORTILLAS

2 CUPS MOLE SAUCE, WARMED (PAGE 61)

1 CUP CORN KERNELS, FROZEN OR CANNED AND DRAINED

1 CUP MEXICAN CREAM OR CRÈME FRAÎCHE (PAGE 148)

1 CUP SHREDDED OAXACAN OR MOZZARELLA CHEESE

Preheat the oven to 350°F and lightly grease a round baking dish. In salted boiling water, cook the chicken breast with the onion, carrot and celery for about 8 to 10 minutes, or until the chicken is cooked but still tender. Drain the chicken and cool, reserving the broth to thin the mole sauce if necessary. (Use the remaining broth for homemade soups or freeze it for later use.) When cool enough to handle, shred the chicken with your fingers and set aside.

In a frying pan, heat the oil almost to the point of smoking and lightly fry the tortillas. Drain each tortilla on a paper towel. In the prepared dish, alternately layer the tortillas, shredded chicken, mole sauce, corn, cream, and cheese, ending with cream and cheese. Bake the casserole for about 8 to 10 minutes, or until heated through. Be careful not to overbake the *budín*.

Serve at once with a lettuce salad.

BAKED CHICKEN IN ACHIOTE SAUCE

Pollo al Horno en Achiote   *4 to 6 servings*

THE CONDIMENT ACHIOTE, WIDELY USED IN SOUTHERN MEXICO, *comes already prepared with garlic and vinegar, and is a hard paste that is diluted before use with the juice of the* naranja agria *(bitter orange), a type of orange grown mainly in Chiapas and Yucatán. In other parts of Mexico where this juice is not available, grapefruit or orange juice combined with vinegar is used instead. Please refer to the Glossary (page 233) for more information about this condiment.*

Unused achiote can be stored in a dry place, covered with plastic wrap. It will keep for several months and does not need to be refrigerated. Achiote is usually available in specialty stores.

1 (2 LB/ 1 KG) CHICKEN, CUT INTO PIECES

SALT AND PEPPER

1 CLOVE GARLIC

¼ TEASPOON BLACK PEPPERCORNS

¼ TEASPOON GROUND CUMIN

¼ TEASPOON GROUND OREGANO

¼ TEASPOON GROUND CINNAMON

1 BAY LEAF

¼ TO ⅓ ACHIOTE SQUARE

¾ CUP GRAPEFRUIT JUICE OR FRESH ORANGE JUICE

¼ CUP CIDER VINEGAR

1 MEDIUM RED ONION, SLICED

ROMAINE LETTUCE LEAVES, WASHED AND DRAINED

Wash the chicken pieces, drain, and pat dry with paper towels. Transfer the chicken to a rectangular baking dish and sprinkle with salt and pepper. Set aside. In a molcajete or mortar, mash the garlic with the peppercorns, cumin, oregano, cinnamon, and bay leaf until completely crushed. Preheat the oven to 350°F.

In a small bowl, mix the achiote with the grapefruit juice and the vinegar, and mash until completely dissolved. Add the crushed spices and mix well. Reserve.

Cover the chicken with the achiote sauce and red onion slices, and bake 45 minutes to 1 hour, or until the chicken is tender and thoroughly cooked. Serve hot, with 2 or 3 lettuce leaves and white rice on the side. It can also be served with good crusty bread or warm corn tortillas.

RED POSOLE WITH CHICKEN

Pozole Rojo   *6 to 8 servings*

In Mexico City, where Paseo de la Reforma and Bucareli intersect, in an area known as El Caballito (little horse), the equestrian statue of Carlos IV of Spain stood for many years. This statue is considered comparable to that of Marcus Aurelius on the Capitoline Hill in Rome for its beauty, and it is one of the best examples of neoclassical equestrian sculpture in Mexico. It was cast by the famous Valencian architect Manuel Tolsá. Through the years, the statue has been moved to different places, from the Plaza Mayor (the main square) to the courtyard of the old university building, and in 1982 was moved outside the National Art Museum, just across from one of Tolsá's masterpieces, the magnificent Palacio de Minería. This plaza is now called Plaza Manuel Tolsá in his honor.

Going back to El Caballito, there used to be dozens of small restaurants and cafés listing every dish served from the northern state of Chihuahua to the Yucatán Peninsula in the south. One of them was this heartening soup called pozole, a favorite dish for people coming out late in the evening from the theater or a nightclub or, better, to cure a terrible hangover. The spicy combination of the ancho and guajillo chiles with the tomato, oregano, and cloves turns an ordinary chicken broth into the most flavorful broth for the hominy corn. It is really what we call a plato fuerte (main dish), when served with lots of chicken and all its trimmings.

Pozole originated in the state of Jalisco, where they use pork instead of chicken, or both, and have two versions of this hearty soup: white with no tomatoes, and red. Hominy corn can be found in specialty stores and sometimes in major supermarkets. Please refer to the Glossary (page 233) for more information about hominy corn.

1 WHOLE CHICKEN BREAST

1 CHICKEN BACKBONE

2 CHICKEN WINGS

3 DRIED *GUAJILLO* CHILES

2 DRIED ANCHO CHILES

2 LARGE TOMATOES

2 CLOVES GARLIC

¼ CUP CHOPPED ONION

½ TEASPOON OREGANO

½ CUP CANNED TOMATO SAUCE

1 TEASPOON VEGETABLE OIL

4 TO 5 CUPS CHICKEN BROTH

2 (30 OZ/900 G) CANS HOMINY CORN, DRAINED

SALT

6 TO 8 CORN TORTILLAS, FRIED UNTIL CRISP (TOSTADAS)

GARNISHES:

CHOPPED RADISHES, FINELY CHOPPED LETTUCE, FINELY CHOPPED ONION, AVOCADO SLICES, GROUND PIQUÍN CHILE, AND QUARTERED LIMES

In 6 cups of salted boiling water, cook the chicken breast and backbone for 10 to 12 minutes, or until the chicken breast is tender. Reserving the broth, drain, remove the skin and bone, and shred the chicken breast with your fingers. Set aside, discarding the backbone and the wings.

While the chicken is cooking, stem the chiles, shake out the seeds, and wash them under running water. Soak the chiles in 1 cup of the reserved chicken broth for about 15 minutes, or until soft. Transfer the chiles with the soaking liquid to a blender and process with the tomatoes, garlic, onion, and oregano until puréed.

In a soup pot, heat the oil over medium heat and fry the chile mixture for 3 to 4 minutes before adding the tomato sauce, the remaining chicken broth, hominy corn, salt to taste, and the shredded chicken. Bring the soup to a boil and simmer for 5 to 7 minutes longer to allow the flavors to mix. Divide the *pozole* between soup bowls and serve hot, with the tostadas. Let everyone add their choice of garnish to their own bowl.

ZACATECAS-STYLE ROASTING HEN

Gallina Rellena Estilo Zacatecas   *6 to 8 servings*

THIS IS A CHERISHED RECIPE that my grandmother, Mamá Jesusita, used to cook for the whole family. She was born in the state of Zacatecas, and met and married my grandfather there when she was just fifteen. At that time, Papá Gustavo was a widower with children, and they went on to have thirteen children of their own.

My grandfather, a well-known teacher in the city, decided to move to the capital with his family to try a new way of life. I am sure they never imagined how big Mexico City was going to be! First, they lived in what is now the old downtown, where my father and his brothers and sisters grew up. Raising thirteen children was, I am sure, not an easy task. However, their children grew up to be lawyers, doctors, and teachers. They eventually moved to the suburbs where my first memories of my grandparents' house begin, in the Colonia Roma, where we also lived and where we were still living until I got married.

I remember with great nostalgia those Sunday afternoons and the huge meals in their house and the garden surrounded by fruit trees. Before the comida was served, I played with my cousins in the garden and hid in the rooms designated for Teresa, the old maid who eventually became part of the family and who was especially close to my father's younger brothers, having helped Mamá Jesusita in raising them. Teresa did not particularly like us rummaging through her quarters, but that only made it more exciting and we did it every Sunday, and each time she chased us out and into the garden. We had a lot of fun making Teresa lose her patience.

Finally the call would come: "La comida está lista!" ("Dinner is ready!"). We were all served in shifts, in the main dining room. The children were served first and, while our parents chatted in the living room, Papá Gustavo sat with us to make sure we behaved. It was hard not to; his stern presence dominated the room, he did not have to do anything else.

During our meal, Mamá Jesusita was constantly coming and going for at least two to three hours, trying to accommodate everybody. Somehow, she always remembered what each of us liked and she would order the cook to make exactly what we wanted and how we wanted it; not an easy thing, since we are talking of at least fifteen grandchildren.

To start the meal, there always was a succulent chicken broth served with corn, zucchini, carrots, fresh cilantro and lots of lime juice; then red rice, as the middle dish. Other dishes were Pierna de Puerco Enchilada, *leg of pork smothered in ancho chile sauce,* served with fresh corn tortillas that the maids would be making right then and there. Those tortillas were heavenly, nothing like those we now get in supermarkets. We also had Arroz con Mole (*Red Rice with Mole*), prepared Zacatecas-style, of course, meaning that not a lot of garlic or chiles were used, confirming one more time that Mexican cuisine is extremely regional.

Later in the afternoon, my aunt Sara, at that time principal of a big school, would offer to take me and my cousins Rosita and Margarita to a movie. These two cousins and I were exactly the same age, and for many years were quite close. My parents would pick us up from the movie and take us out for a merienda (light supper). This was how every Sunday ended, for many, many years. Even when we were teens and had invitations from friends, we were expected to visit with Mamá Jesusita on Sunday.

She died in 1970, a widow. By that time, most of my cousins were married and I was already expecting my second child. I have been living in Canada for more than twenty years, and every year while I am in Mexico, we organize a gathering of all the cousins. It is quite amazing, the fond memories we all have about those Sundays!

If you are ready for a change, try Mamá Jesusita's recipe for Christmas dinner.

1 (5 TO 6 LB / 2.5 K) ROASTING CHICKEN

3 TABLESPOONS LARD OR BUTTER

DASH OF SALT

DASH OF PEPPER

DASH OF CINNAMON

DASH OF CUMIN

MARINADE:

¼ CUP WHITE WINE VINEGAR

1 CUP DRY SHERRY OR DRY WHITE WINE

1 LARGE ONION, SLICED INTO RINGS

2 BAY LEAVES

1 TEASPOON WHOLE PEPPERCORNS

¼ TEASPOON GROUND CUMIN

STUFFING:

2 SLICES CRUSTY BREAD

½ CUP 2% MILK

2 TABLESPOONS VEGETABLE OIL

1½ CUP CHOPPED ONION

2 LARGE TOMATOES, PEELED, SEEDED,
AND CHOPPED

¼ CUP CANNED TOMATO SAUCE

1 CUP PEELED AND CHOPPED APPLE

½ CUP RAISINS

½ CUP ALMONDS, BLANCHED AND
TOASTED

½ CUP PIMIENTO-STUFFED GREEN
OLIVES, CHOPPED

1 LB (500 G) GROUND PORK

1 EGG, LIGHTLY BEATEN

¼ TEASPOON GROUND CUMIN

¼ TEASPOON GROUND CINNAMON

SALT AND PEPPER

Rinse the chicken thoroughly, inside and out, pat dry with paper towels, and place in a large bowl or directly into the roasting pan. Sprinkle salt and pepper inside and out. In a bowl, combine the vinegar, sherry, onion, bay leaves, peppercorn, and cumin, and pour over the chicken. Cover the chicken with aluminum foil and marinate, refrigerated, for at least 8 hours, turning once and basting with the marinade as often as possible.

FOR THE STUFFING: Soak the bread in the milk until most of the milk is absorbed. Meanwhile, heat the oil over medium heat and sauté the onion until translucent. Add the tomatoes, tomato sauce, apple, raisins, almonds, and olives, and sauté for about 2 minutes. Remove from the heat. Stir in the ground pork, the bread, and the egg. Sprinkle with the cumin and cinnamon, and season with salt and pepper to taste. Set aside.

Preheat the oven to 350°F. Drain the chicken, reserving the marinade, and pat dry with paper towels. Rub the bird with the lard and sprinkle salt, pepper, cumin, and cinnamon inside and out. Fill the cavity with the stuffing and truss loosely. (Bake any remaining stuffing separately for additional servings.)

Using a baster with an injector, inject about ¾ cup of the marinade into the breasts and thighs, and bake the chicken for about 1½ hours, depending on the weight, basting the bird as often as possible and turning it for an even roasting.

Serve with the drained pan juices in a gravy boat, with lettuce and chopped radishes on the side.

To reheat, cover the chicken with aluminum foil and bake for 10 to 15 minutes, or until heated through.

BAKED CHICKEN WITH FRUIT AND VEGETABLES

Tapado de Pollo   *4 to 6 servings*

THIS DISH IS SURPRISINGLY GOOD and quite easy to make. The chicken skin is left on for flavor and to keep the meat from breaking apart. However, if you are counting calories, the skin may be removed before baking. It is better not to cut the fruit too small or it will disintegrate while cooking. If you are not a sweet-and-sour fan, try this chicken without the fruit.

1 (2 LB/1 KG) CHICKEN, CUT INTO PIECES BUT NOT SKINNED

2 LARGE RIPE TOMATOES, CHOPPED

1 MEDIUM SPANISH ONION, SLICED INTO RINGS

2 LARGE ZUCCHINI, CUBED

1 CUP FRESH PEAS

2 FRESH PINEAPPLE SLICES, CUBED

2 GOLDEN APPLES, PEELED, CORED, AND CUBED

2 LARGE BANANAS, UNPEELED, SLICED INTO ROUNDS

1/4 CUP EXTRA-VIRGIN OLIVE OIL

SALT AND PEPPER

Preheat the oven to 350°F. Place the chicken in a large baking dish, and cover with the vegetables and fruit. Drizzle the olive oil over the dish and add salt and pepper to taste. Cover the baking dish with aluminum foil and bake for 45 minutes to 1 hour, or until the chicken is done and the vegetables and fruit are cooked but still crisp.

Serve hot, with rice.

BEEF AND PORK
CARNE

It is said that we Mexicans *somos de buen comer*, meaning that we enjoy eating. Judging by the diversity of Mexican cuisine, the hundreds of recipes that vary from one region to another, or even from one family to another, some of them following the established patterns of the most traditional dishes, and others influenced by specific historic events, this statement must be true.

The phrase "*somos de buen comer*" may be interpreted more in the sense that we enjoy eating almost everything. Seafood in the coastal states is favored for obvious reasons, and beef and pork, in simple or sophisticated dishes, in the central states.

The well known Mexican poet and writer José Vasconcelos, referring to the northern part of Mexico, said that "civilization ends where the *carne asada* (roasted meat) begins." In the northern states such as Sonora, Chihuahua, Coahuila and Nuevo León good pastures mean that beef is usually served in a very simple way, whereas in the Bajío or the central states, beef is served with more elaborate sauces, such as the various moles. A perfect example is the famous cold dish from San Luis Potosí, *fiambre*, a combination of slices of beef tongue, pork feet, chicken breast with potatoes, carrots, onions, peas and chiles.

In Mexico, pork is often served fried as the popular *carnitas* complemented by a variety of salsas, guacamole, and *chicharrón* (pork rind).

A very popular Sunday outing is to one of the many restaurants that offer *carnitas* as their specialty. These establishments usually serve fresh hot tortillas as well, and the experience of *tacos de carnitas* is a very special one.

The first establishment to go this route was a restaurant called Arroyo in the Tlalpan area, south of Mexico City. Once the restaurant became the favorite place for a *comida dominguera* (Sunday dinner), Mr. Arroyo provided Mariachi music. This addition to an already scrumptious meal was the best he could have done for his business. The Arroyo restaurant is today one of the most successful enterprises in the city.

Carnitas are usually served preceded by a hot chicken broth and a plate of red rice and accompanied by good Mexican beer.

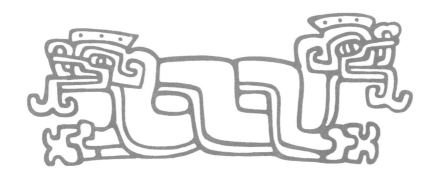

ROUND ROAST IN VINAIGRETTE

Cuete a la Vinagreta   *8 to 10 servings*

MY MOTHER LIKED TO COOK and used to do most of the cooking, even though help in the kitchen was available. I was always busy at school and after that at work, so my experience with cooking really started when I got married. And it so happened that the family I married into was full of amazing cooks.

I had been married for just a few years when we had to host a dinner for important people: a famous eye surgeon, a well-known architect, and a talented writer, with their respective wives. As it is customary in these types of events, the meal consisted of at least five dishes, so my mother-in-law suggested this recipe as the plato fuerte *(main dish) not only for its delicious flavor and splendid presentation but because it could be prepared well in advance. Thanks to her suggestion, my first experience in serious cooking was a big success. At the end, everybody was using the crusty bread to soak up the olive oil left on their empty plates.*

1 LB (500 G) EYE OF ROUND ROAST

SALT

1 MEDIUM ONION

1 CLOVE GARLIC

DASH OF DRIED THYME

2 FRESH BASIL LEAVES

1 CUP JULIENNED GREEN BEANS, ENDS
   REMOVED

1 CUP JULIENNED CARROTS, PEELED,
   ENDS REMOVED

¾ CUP EXTRA-VIRGIN OLIVE OIL

⅓ CUP CIDER VINEGAR

SALT AND PEPPER

½ CUP CANNED PEAS

1 (4½ OZ/128 ML) JAR RED PIMIENTOS

In salted boiling water, cook the roast with one quarter of the onion, the garlic, and the herbs for about 45 minutes, or until tender when tested with a fork. Thinly slice the remaining onion and set aside. Drain the meat and cool to room temperature. Reserve the broth for a future use.

Steam the green beans and the carrots for approximately 6 to 8 minutes or until vegetables are barely cooked and still crisp. Drain. In the same saucepan, mix the olive oil and the vinegar, bring to a boil, and add the green beans, carrots, onion slices, and salt and pepper to taste. Lower the heat and gently simmer the vegetables for about 2 minutes more. Remove the saucepan from the heat.

Once the meat is cool enough to handle, slice it as thinly as you can with a very sharp knife, paper thin if possible. Arrange the slices of meat on a serving platter and pour the vegetable mixture over them, making sure the vinaigrette covers every slice of meat. To finish off this attractive beef platter, top it with the peas and the pimiento strips.

Cover the platter with aluminum foil and let the meat marinate for 4 to 6 hours in the refrigerator, before serving. Serve at room temperature.

BREADED BEEF ROULADE

Milanesas   *4 servings*

THE UNPRETENTIOUS FONDAS IN MEXICO *are small restaurants, usually family run as well as very family oriented. This means that their menus are simple and homey, almost always consisting of a pasta soup, rice, and a* plato fuerte *(main dish).*

This plato fuerte *can be a chicken or a beef stew;* bisteces encebollados *(sirloin steaks with lots of onions); or a* milanesa, *breaded pork or beef, served with a* guarnición *(side dish) of mashed potatoes and a green salad. All would be served with a fiery salsa or marinated jalapeños. For a change,* milanesas *or* bisteces *are also served with a side dish of* enfrijoladas, *fried corn tortillas, smothered in beans and topped with Mexican cream and cheese, and other times with* enchiladas verdes *or* entomatadas.

Beef roulade is a very thinly sliced steak cut from the inside round, the bigger the piece the better the steaks will be. I have noticed that not all butcher shops have roulade readily available; however, you can ask the butcher to cut it for you.

SALT AND PEPPER

1 LB (500 G) BEEF ROULADE

1 EGG

2 TABLESPOONS MILK

¾ CUP FINE DRY BREAD CRUMBS

SALT AND PEPPER

OIL FOR FRYING

1 CUP SALSA VERDE WITH AVOCADO
  (PAGE 157)

Sprinkle salt and pepper on both sides of each beef roulade. In a medium-size bowl, beat the egg with the milk, and salt and pepper to taste. Dip a steak in the egg mixture and then coat completely with the bread crumbs. Repeat the same procedure with the remaining steaks.

In a frying pan, heat the oil over medium heat and quickly fry each beefsteak on both sides. Transfer the steaks to paper towels to drain the excess oil, and serve at once with salsa.

BAJIO-STYLE SHREDDED BEEF

Salpicón Estilo Bajío   *4 to 6 servings*

THE RECENT CRAZE IN WRAPS *was dreamed up by four Americans vacationing in Mexico, who were inspired by none other than the flour tortilla extensively used in northwest Mexico, mainly the states of Sonora, Sinaloa, and Chihuahua.* Machaca, *shredded beef in a dry chile sauce, cooked with eggs, is a very old and traditional dish from this area, usually served with warm, homemade flour tortillas. Nobody would even think of eating* machaca *without them.*

On the other hand, in the central states, or Altiplano, shredded beef dishes like this salpicón *are always served with corn tortillas. Use either kind of tortilla; both go well with this recipe. Serve the* salpicón *at room temperature.*

1 LB (500 G) FLANK STEAK

½ CUP OLIVE OIL

2 TABLESPOONS CIDER VINEGAR

SALT AND PEPPER

½ MEDIUM ONION, THINLY SLICED

1 TO 2 PICKLED JALAPEÑO CHILE(S)
(PAGE 159), STEMMED, SEEDED, AND
CHOPPED PLUS 1 TABLESPOON
PICKLING LIQUID

1 CUP CHOPPED LETTUCE

1 LARGE TOMATO, SLICED

1 LARGE RIPE AVOCADO, SLICED INTO
THIN WEDGES

Cut the flank steak into small chunks and boil in salted water for about 12 to 15 minutes, or until tender. Cool and drain the beef with a slotted spoon. When it is cool enough to handle, finely shred the beef with your fingers and set aside. Reserve the broth for a future use.

Meanwhile, prepare the vinaigrette by combining the olive oil, vinegar, and salt and pepper to taste. Stir in the onion slices and let them marinate in the vinaigrette for about half an hour.

In a medium-size bowl, combine the vinaigrette and the onions with the jalapeño and the pickling liquid. Mix in the shredded beef until it is well coated with the vinaigrette. Adjust the seasoning and transfer the *salpicón* to a serving platter. Garnish with the lettuce, tomato slices, and avocado wedges.

AUNT GEOR'S
BEEF TARTARE

Carne Tártara de Tía Geor   *6 servings*

THIS WAS ONE OF MY HUSBAND'S FAVORITE *recipes that his aunt Geor, short for Georgina, used to whip up when he showed up unexpectedly for a visit. Somehow, she always managed to have the finest and the freshest ingredients on hand. The ground beef had to be from her butcher in the market of San Angel, one of the best markets in the southern part of Mexico City, and it had to be ground* aguayón *(rump roast), and not any other part of the animal that would render more fat than necessary or not have the right flavor. She was very demanding when it came to food; needless to say, having a meal cooked by her was a superb experience, and this recipe is nothing less than superb.*

PLEASE NOTE: *The use of lime juice reduces the risk of bacterial growth as long as meat is refrigerated before and after preparation.*

1 LB (500 G) LEAN GROUND BEEF

1 EGG

¼ CUP LIME JUICE

2 TABLESPOONS MINCED ONION

1 TABLESPOON WORCESTERSHIRE SAUCE

¼ CUP EXTRA-VIRGIN OLIVE OIL

2 TABLESPOONS CAPERS

SALT AND PEPPER

Combine all the ingredients until completely mixed, and refrigerate until ready to serve.

Serve the tartar meat with dark brown bread or good French bread. Since it is quite filling, you might just serve it with a simple green salad and red wine.

LEG OF PORK IN ANCHO CHILE SAUCE

Pierna de Puerco Enchilada   *8 to 10 servings*

THIS IS YET ANOTHER OF THE MEMORABLE RECIPES *from my grandmother Mamá Jesusita, as her grandchildren called her. I say "memorable"because, in my nostalgia, it brings back so many good memories of my father's side of the family inevitably intertwined with the evocative aromas from her kitchen.*

As I mentioned before, the cuisine of Zacatecas, where my father's family is from, does not favor spicy food; however, in this recipe, the ancho chile lends a rather sweet and, at the same time spicy flavor to the pork turning an ordinary dish into a memorable one.

One of the traditional dishes from our Sunday family gatherings, this leg of pork was always served preceded only by a piping hot chicken consommé. The freshly made corn tortillas kept coming at a steady pace and at the end a bowl of Frijoles de la Olla *(page 164), complemented the meal.*

A pork roast would also work well with this recipe. Keep in mind that slow cooking is best for pork.

4 DRY ANCHO CHILES

2 TABLESPOONS VEGETABLE OIL

4 LARGE CLOVES GARLIC

½ CUP CIDER VINEGAR

SALT

1 LEG OF PORK (6 LB/3 K)

1 HEAD ROMAINE LETTUCE

Stem the chiles and shake out the seeds. With a small knife, cut open each chile and wash under running water to remove all the seeds. In a small bowl, cover the chiles with hot water and soak until soft, about 20 minutes. Drain the chiles, reserving the soaking liquid, and pat dry.

In a small frying pan, heat the oil over medium heat and quickly fry the chiles. Remove from the heat and drain on paper towels to remove the excess oil. Transfer the chiles to a blender or food processor, add the reserved soaking liquid, garlic, and vinegar, and purée. Add salt to taste.

Place the leg of pork in a roasting pan, and spread the chile sauce over the meat, covering all sides of the leg well. Cover the pan with aluminum foil and refrigerate for 24 hours before baking.

Preheat the oven to 350°F. Add 2 cups of water to the pork and bake for 30 minutes. Lower the heat to 200°F and continue baking until the pork is very tender, about 3 hours. Serve the pork, sliced, with romaine lettuce leaves on the side.

PORK CHOPS IN SPICY TOMATO SAUCE

Chuletas en Salsa de Jitomate   *2 servings*

A SIMPLE BUT TASTY WAY to cook pork chops. Keep in mind that the cooking time may vary, depending on the thickness of the chops.

White rice and hot corn tortillas at the table are in order for these pork chops.

4 PORK CHOPS

SALT AND PEPPER

1 TEASPOON VEGETABLE OIL

2 LARGE TOMATOES, PEELED
   AND SEEDED

¼ SMALL ONION

1 LARGE CLOVE GARLIC

3 TO 4 SERRANO CHILES

¼ CUP TOMATO SAUCE

2 (1 TABLESPOON EACH) PACKETS
   INSTANT CHICKEN BOUILLON

1 CUP PEELED COOKED POTATOES,
   CUBED

Season the pork chops with salt and pepper. In a saucepan, heat the oil and brown the pork chops on both sides.

Meanwhile, in a blender or food processor, purée the tomato, onion, garlic, and chiles with ½ cup of water. Add the tomato mixture to the browned pork chops, bring to a boil, and simmer for 3 to 5 minutes. Stir in the tomato sauce and bouillon and continue simmering for about 5 minutes more, or until the chops are tender and the sauce has thickened. Add the potatoes and serve hot.

PORK WITH GREEN MOLE SAUCE

Caldillo de Cerdo en Mole Verde   *4 to 6 servings*

IN MEXICO, MORE AND MORE WOMEN *work outside the homes. In Mexico City, the problem is compounded by the distance between home and place of work. The busy life of a big city has definitely affected the pace of working women, making it necessary to find ways to feed our families in less time than our own mothers had. Fortunately, we are able to take advantage of good quality prepared foods such as the moles.*

Markets in any city display an array of different moles available in a paste form, usually made by the vendor at home. The moles are of an excellent quality and it certainly cuts down the time involved in the preparation of a meal.

Mole verde *is a concoction of pumpkin seeds ground with peanuts, onion, garlic, tomatillos, cilantro, serrano chiles, and sesame seeds. Outside of Mexico, moles are also available in jars in major supermarkets made by such Mexican companies as La Costeña, Herdez, and Doña Maria.*

After a full day's work, my niece Julieta, a mother of two children, serves this Caldillo de Cerdo *with warm corn tortillas and a bowl of beans.*

1 TABLESPOON VEGETABLE OIL

1 LB (500 G) PORK, CUBED

1/2 CUP *MOLE VERDE*

6 TOMATILLOS, HUSKED, WASHED, AND CHOPPED

1 SMALL EAR OF FRESH CORN, CUT INTO 3/4 INCH PIECES

1 CUP PEELED, CUBED POTATOES

SALT

In a deep, heavy saucepan, heat the oil over medium heat and fry the pork until browned. Stir in the *mole verde* and sauté for 2 minutes before adding the tomatillos, corn, potatoes, about 3/4 cup water, and salt to taste. Bring the mole to a boil, lower the heat, and simmer for another 12 to 15 minutes, or until the pork is cooked and the potatoes are tender.

PORK LOIN WITH CHIPOTLE CHILES

Tinga Estilo "Pitita"   *4 to 6 servings*

LIVING IN PUEBLA GAVE ME A VERY GOOD INSIGHT into one of the best cuisines in Mexico, la cocina poblana *(the cuisine of Puebla). Located southeast of Mexico City, this state, with its two magnificent volcanoes, the Popocatépetl and the Iztacíhuatl, boasts an amazing array of dishes, including the traditional* Tinga Poblana, *a most delectable beef stew made with homemade pineapple vinegar, smothered in tomatoes, garlic, onion, and chipotle chiles and then cooked for hours.*

Mole poblano *is another well-known regional dish. Puebla is also famous for its* camotes, *or sweet potato candies. In the downtown part of the city, there is a row of candy stores selling these* camotes, *as well as many other sweets and cookies.*

This is my mother-in-law's version of the famous but very elaborate Tinga Poblana. *I must say that hers is a much easier dish and almost as enjoyable as more elaborate versions. Keep in mind that chipotles are always quite hot, usually one chipotle and its adobo is quite enough for this amount of meat. Serve the remaining chiles in a* salsera *at the table so people can have more if desired. Chipotles keep very well refrigerated in a glass jar with a tight lid.*

1½ LB (750 G) PORK LOIN, CUT INTO 6
   TO 8 CHUNKS

1 CLOVE GARLIC

¼ CUP CHOPPED ONION

SALT

1 TABLESPOON VEGETABLE OIL

1 RIPE PLANTAIN, PEELED

1 CHIPOTLE CHILE IN ADOBO, SEEDED
   AND CHOPPED, PLUS 1 TABLESPOON
   ADOBO

1 LARGE RIPE AVOCADO, PEELED AND
   SLICED INTO STRIPS

In a saucepan, cook the pork in salted boiling water with the garlic and onion for 12 to 15 minutes, or until soft. With a slotted spoon, drain the pork and cool. Reserve the broth. Once the pork is cool enough to handle, shred it with your fingers and set aside.

Slice the plantain lengthwise. In a frying pan, heat the oil over medium heat and fry the plantain until golden brown. Drain on paper towels and keep warm. In the same frying pan, quickly fry the shredded pork with the chile and the adobo sauce. Add more oil if the pork starts to stick to the pan. Season with salt to taste. The tinga should be almost the color of the chipotle chiles, but not very hot. Add some of the reserved broth if the tinga begins to dry out.

Serve at once with the fried plantain slices on top, and garnish with the avocado strips.

SPARE RIBS IN ADOBO SAUCE

Costillas de Puerco Adobadas   *6 servings*

DRY CHILES ARE AVAILABLE AT SPECIALTY STORES *and major supermarkets, usually in small cellophane bags clearly marked by name. Although dry chiles may look alike, they have very different flavor and will give a different color to a mole when used separately.*

Dry and fresh chiles are not interchangeable. If the recipe calls for fresh chiles, you can substitute another fresh chile, but in the case of dry chiles, things become a bit more complicated, since each particular one provides not only a distinct flavor but a different color and sometimes even a different texture.

These tempting costillitas, *as we Mexicans call them, are also good grilled on your barbecue.*

6 TO 8 COUNTRY-STYLE SPARE RIBS

2 DRY ANCHO CHILES

1 DRY PASILLA CHILE

1 DRY MULATO CHILE

2 LARGE CLOVES GARLIC

2 TABLESPOONS CIDER VINEGAR

DASH OF OREGANO

DASH OF SALT

2 TABLESPOONS VEGETABLE OIL

Place the ribs in a baking dish, preferably one large enough to hold them all in one layer. Wash the dry chiles under running water, stem, and shake out the seeds. In a blender or food processor, blend the chiles with the garlic, vinegar, oregano, and salt until puréed. Pour the chile mixture over the ribs and let them marinate for 1 to 2 hours, covered with aluminum foil or plastic wrap. Keep refrigerated.

Just before serving, heat the oil in a heavy frying pan and slowly sauté the ribs on both sides. Serve at once with mashed or new potatoes, and greens.

PORK PICADILLO
EMPANADAS

Empanadas de Picadillo de Puerco   *10 to 12 empanadas*

Picadillo is a term that applies to both pork and beef, the ingredients may vary, depending on the region, especially the chiles. In Puebla, the picadillo is made with chipotles; whereas in Mexico City and the central part of the country, the pickled serrano or jalapeño are favored. This pork picadillo can also be served as a taco filling topped with the salsa of your choice.

There is a difference between an empanada, or turnover, and a fried quesadilla. Simple quesadillas are warmed tortillas with a queso *(cheese) filling, thus the name. Fried quesadillas are made with* masa *(corn dough) formed into a tortilla; then stuffed with a filling, which could be poblano rajas with cheese, mushrooms, zucchini blossoms, or* cuitlacoche, *for example. The tortilla is then folded over, sealing the edges, and deep-fried in hot oil.*

Empanadas, on the other hand, are made with wheat flour dough. Those filled with meat or fish are the most popular. There are also sweet empanadas with a filling of pumpkin or sweet potato sweetened with brown sugar, cinnamon, and cloves.

Savory empanadas make a great light supper when served with fresh greens.

1 TABLESPOON VEGETABLE OIL

2 CLOVES GARLIC, CHOPPED

$^1/_2$ CUP CHOPPED ONION

1 LB (500 G) LEAN GROUND PORK

3 TABLESPOONS CHOPPED FRESH FLAT-LEAF PARSLEY

2 TOMATOES, SEEDED AND CHOPPED

$^1/_4$ CUP CANNED TOMATO SAUCE

8 MANZANILLA OLIVES, PITTED AND CHOPPED

1 TO 2 PICKLED JALAPEÑO CHILES, STEMMED, SEEDED AND CHOPPED, PLUS 2 TABLESPOONS OF THE PICKLING LIQUID

2 TABLESPOONS RAISINS

10 BLANCHED ALMONDS, CHOPPED

SALT AND PEPPER

1 (1 LB/500 G) PACKAGE FROZEN PUFF PASTRY

1 EGG, LIGHTLY BEATEN

In a saucepan, heat the oil over medium heat and sauté the garlic and onion, then add the pork, breaking it up with a fork, and cook until no longer pink. Drain the fat, if any, before adding the parsley, tomatoes, tomato sauce, and $^1/_4$ cup water. Add the olives, chiles, pickling liquid, raisins, and almonds. Season the picadillo with salt and pepper, and bring to a boil. Lower the heat and simmer for about 10 minutes, or until the sauce is thickened. Let the picadillo cool.

Preheat the oven to 400°F and grease a baking sheet. Roll the dough out into a rectangle just under $^1/_4$ inch thick and cut into 6-inch squares. Spoon about 2 tablespoons of the picadillo onto each square and fold over to form a triangle, sealing the edges with a fork. Glaze the empanadas with the beaten egg, transfer them to the prepared baking sheet, and bake for about 12 to 15 minutes, turning once, or until the pastry is cooked and golden brown.

Let cool for a few minutes before serving the empanadas with a fresh green salad.

CORN TORTILLA AND PORK CASSEROLE

Budín de Tortilla con Carne de Puerco   *4 to 6 servings*

I FIND THAT TOMATOES GROWN IN TEMPERATE CLIMATES do not provide the flavor, color, or consistency I am used to. Generally, Mexican tomato sauces are quite robust and thick, so I have introduced the practice of adding canned tomato sauce whenever I use fresh tomatoes, especially during the winter months.

This is a good company dish and, to save some time, the tomato sauce and the chiles can be prepared the day before. Serve in wedges with a hot bowl of pinto or black beans.

1 LB (500 G) PORK LOIN, CUT INTO 2-INCH CHUNKS

2 LARGE RIPE TOMATOES

1 TABLESPOON VEGETABLE OIL

2 CLOVES GARLIC, CHOPPED

1/4 CUP CHOPPED ONION

1/4 CUP CANNED TOMATO SAUCE

1 CUP UNCOOKED CORN KERNELS

2 MEDIUM POBLANO CHILES, ROASTED, PEELED, AND SEEDED (PAGE 111)

6 TO 8 CORN TORTILLAS, LIGHTLY FRIED IN OIL

1 CUP SOUR CREAM

2 TABLESPOONS 2% MILK

3/4 CUP GRATED CHIHUAHUA OR FARMER CHEESE

In a deep saucepan, cook the pork in salted boiling water for 12 to 15 minutes, or until tender. Drain and cool, set aside 1/2 cup of the broth, reserving the rest for a future use. When cool enough to handle, shred the pork with your fingers and set aside.

In a saucepan, cover the tomatoes with water, bring to a boil, and simmer for 3 to 4 minutes, or until they start to peel. Drain the tomatoes, peel, seed, and transfer to a blender or food processor. Add 1/2 cup of the cooking liquid and process until puréed. Reserve 1/2 cup of the tomato sauce to use on top of the casserole.

Preheat the oven to 350°F. In the same saucepan, heat the oil over medium heat and sauté the garlic and onion until the onion is translucent. Stir in the shredded pork and lightly sauté for 2 minutes before adding the puréed tomato sauce, canned tomato sauce, and the 1/2 cup of reserved broth. Add the corn and chile. Season with salt and pepper and simmer for 4 to 5 minutes, or until the chile and corn are cooked and the stew has thickened.

In a 9-inch (23-cm) round baking dish, alternately layer the tortillas, pork stew, sour cream, and cheese. Continue to layer using all the tortillas and the stew. Cover the last layer with a tortilla topped with the reserved tomato sauce, sour cream, and cheese.

Bake the casserole for about 10 minutes, or until it is heated through and the cheese is melted.

SEAFOOD

PESCADO Y MARISCOS

FRIDAY, IN CATHOLIC COUNTRIES, was traditionally the designated day of the week to fast, and my mother and everyone else of her generation were quite observant of this day by cooking fish. Meat was out of the question on Fridays, and for some people it still is. The Holy Week was a week of mourning, and Thursday and Good Friday were also days of fasting. I continued this tradition and it was not until I moved to Canada that, because of the circumstances, the day of having fish became more erratic. However, it has always been part of my family's diet, at least once a week.

La Marinera, a restaurant on Avenida Chapultec, was always, no matter the day of the week nor the time of the day, full of customers eager to have a scrumptious *campechano*, a ceviche made with red snapper, octopus, scallops, chopped tomato, cilantro, lime juice in abundance, and fiery serrano chiles. Shellfish cocktails were also a specialty, served in tall glasses with their own tomato-chile sauce, slices of avocado, and lime wedges on the side. Fried fish fillets, or fish in tomato sauce with olives and capers, were other dishes served in this popular restaurant. The owners were always proud of the fact that only the best and the freshest fish was served to their customers.

The variety of fish consumed throughout Mexico is quite large. Just to name a few, in the south, the *pejelagarto* (gar), a very tasty fish, native to the state of Tabasco, is grilled, shredded, and served as a taco filling with chiles and limes. *Tiburón* (baby shark) is very popular in the Yucatán Peninsula, in a dish called *pan de cazón*, in which it is shredded and served between corn tortillas, with black beans and a red salsa on top. The state of Michoacán, is renowned for *blanco de Pátzcuaro* (white fish), from the Pátzcuaro Lake, famous for its delicate flavor, similar to flounder. In the rest of the *bajío* (the center of the country), the *mojarra* (a silvery tropical fish of the Gerridoe family) and *trucha de mar* (trout) are cooked with lots of garlic and olive oil and a few chiles; the *robalo* (sea bass), *mero* (grouper), and *sierra* (mackerel), usually filleted, are dipped in an egg batter or dredged in flour, fried until crisp, and served with lime wedges and a fresh green salad. These are also cooked in a tomatillo and chile sauce, or in a well seasoned tomato sauce. Red snapper, very popular in Mexico City, is often cooked in olive oil with tomatoes, olives, and capers; baked with olive oil and orange juice; or in a tomatillo sauce with cilantro, serrano chiles, onion, and garlic.

All through the country, from the most humble little *fonda* to the most sophisticated restaurant, fish and shellfish are part of the menu.

SEA BASS WITH PICKLED CHILES

Robalo al Horno   *4 to 6 servings*

ROBALO *(SEA BASS) IS A POPULAR fish in Mexico. This is a simple recipe and at the same time distinctive, because of its combination of orange juice and chiles. Please keep in mind that the baking time depends very much on the thickness of the fillets. Red snapper, halibut, or any other firm, white-fleshed fish fillets are good choices for this dish.*

Transfer any unused pickled chiles to a glass jar with a tight lid and keep refrigerated for later use. Pickled chiles are very handy in the absence of a good salsa and they are available in cans at major supermarkets.

4 TO 6 (6 OZ / 180 G) SEA BASS FILLETS

JUICE OF ½ LIME

SALT AND PEPPER

1 SMALL ONION, SLICED INTO RINGS

1 LARGE TOMATO, SLICED

1 CUP ORANGE JUICE, WARMED

2 TO 4 PICKLED JALAPEÑO CHILES
(PAGE 159) PLUS 2 TABLESPOONS
PICKLING LIQUID

Preheat the oven to 350°F. Sprinkle the fish with the lime juice and season with salt and pepper to taste. In a baking dish, layer the fish, onion, and tomato, and bake for about 8 to 10 minutes before adding the warmed orange juice, chiles, and pickling liquid. Continue baking for another 5 to 8 minutes, or until the fish is cooked or firm to the touch, and the flavors are blended.

Serve hot with rice and green vegetables.

CHRISTMAS COD

Bacalao de Navidad   *8 to 10 servings*

BACALAO *PREPARED FROM DRIED, SALTED COD, and cooked Spanish-style is customarily served for Christmas* along with Romeritos, *a very Mexican dish in a mole sauce, accompanied by shrimp patties. Again, here you can see the perfect marriage of the Spanish and Indian cuisines.* Bacalao *is served with bread and* Romeritos *with tortillas, of course. These two incredibly flavorful dishes are followed by* Ensalada de Nochebuena, *or Christmas Eve Salad, a cold salad made with slices of jicama, orange, peanuts, and cooked beets, and garnished with chopped lettuce. Various Spanish desserts, like* buñuelos, *marzipan* turrones *from Alicante or Gijona, dry fruit, and all sorts of nuts, are available for the taking.* Rompope *(Mexican eggnog) (page 202), and a fruit punch for the children are served afterward, until it is time to go to Misa de Gallo (Midnight Mass). Finally comes the opening of presents in a house full of* flores de Nochebuena *(poinsettias).*

Every year, early in the morning, a few days before Nochebuena *(Christmas Eve), my mother headed to the San Angel market and, after some deliberation, decided which* flores de Nochebuena *were the most appropriate for the space she had in mind: huge ones in gorgeous clay pots for the main entrance, smaller ones for the bottom of the stairs, dining and living room areas, and one for the upstairs family room, usually in a special pot.*

After my two brothers and I married, the tradition continued, since my mother bought the flowers not only for her home but for the three of us, even if Christmas Eve dinner was being celebrated somewhere else that year.

The flor de Nochebuena *is originally from Mexico. The Aztecs called it* cuetlaxóchitl. *It is a shrub, and in certain parts of Mexico, such as the state of Jalisco, the bushes can be quite tall. Today, of course, they are grown in greenhouses in order to meet the demand of the market.*

Of the many legends that tell about its origin, one is particularly beautiful. It concerns a little boy who wanted, more than anything, to visit the manger in his village church. He felt sad because he was very poor and had no gift to bring the Christ Child. Along the way to see the Child, he noticed a bush growing beside the dusty road, and thought he could at least take a few of its green branches to present to the newborn Jesus. As soon as he cut them, they sprouted scarlet, star-shaped flowers! The boy had a lovely gift for the infant Jesus, after all. He ran to the church and laid the flowers by the manger, over which the Virgin Mother raised her hand in a gesture of love.

It is indeed a beautiful story. It is believed, however, that the name came about when people noticed that the bush bloomed only in December and associated it with the birth of Christ.

In the 1830s, Mr. Joel Poinsett, the first American ambassador to Mexico, was so impressed with the beauty of this Christmas flower that he sent some cuttings to his home in South Carolina. Soon, the beautiful flower was grown in greenhouses in the United States and, not long after that, it was being exported throughout the world. It is now used to decorate Nativity scenes and homes around the globe. It is too bad, however, that botanists renamed the flower with Mr. Poinsett's last name; I think that Christmas Eve Flower would have been so much prettier!

Salt cod is available at Portuguese and Italian delicatessens. Some major supermarkets are now beginning to carry it as well, around Christmastime. We usually cook Bacalao *during the first week of December, and freeze it in a plastic container. This is one of those dishes that gets better every time you reheat it. In this case, I recommend adding the baby potatoes on the day you are serving it.*

2½ LBS (1.25 K) SALT COD, BONED

½ CUP EXTRA-VIRGIN OLIVE OIL

6 TO 8 LARGE CLOVES GARLIC, CHOPPED

1 CUP TOMATO SAUCE

3 LARGE TOMATOES, CHOPPED

1 (4½ OZ / 128 ML) JAR RED PIMIENTOS

1 LARGE ONION, CHOPPED

2 TABLESPOONS DRAINED CAPERS

20 MANZANILLA OLIVES, CHOPPED

¾ CUP CHOPPED FRESH FLAT-LEAF
PARSLEY

½ LB (250 G) BABY POTATOES, COOKED
AND PEELED

8 TO 10 CANNED *CHILES LARGOS* OR
ITALIAN PEPERONCINI PEPPERS PLUS 4
TABLESPOONS PICKLING LIQUID

Chop the cod into chunks and soak in water for about 24 hours, changing the water twice to remove excess salt. Drain the cod, pat dry with paper towels, and shred into a bowl with your fingers. Be sure to remove any bones. Set aside.

In a large saucepan, heat the olive oil over medium heat and sauté the garlic until cooked but not brown. Transfer the garlic to a blender or food processor, add ½ cup of the tomato sauce, 1 tomato, and half the pimientos, and process until puréed.

In the same pan in which the garlic was fried, add the onion and sauté until translucent. Stir in the remaining 2 tomatoes, remaining tomato sauce, and the garlic mixture. Cook the sauce for 5 to 8 minutes and stir in the shredded cod. Bring to a boil, lower the heat, and simmer the mixture for 10 to 12 minutes, or until the liquid has slightly reduced. Stir in the capers, olives, and parsley, and continue simmering for 5 minutes. Add the potatoes, the remaining pimientos, the chiles, and the pickling liquid, and simmer for just 3 or 4 minutes to allow the flavors to blend. Serve the *bacalao* with warm crusty bread.

FISH FILLETS IN ADOBO

Filetes de Pescado en Adobo   *4 to 6 servings*

IN PRE-COLUMBIAN TIMES, THE EMPEROR *Moctezuma, an epicure in his own right, had his people bring fresh fish every day from the port of Veracruz, to augment his already abundant meal.*

In the True History of the Conquest of New Spain, *Bernal Díaz del Castillo reported to King Ferdinand and Queen Isabella that the emperor of the Aztecs had at least thirty elaborate dishes prepared for him every day. These included* guisados—*stews containing hens, partridges, pheasants, duck, venison, pork, rabbit, birds, and doves. A great variety of fruit was also presented and, at the end of the meal, the servers would bring a beverage made of cacao, in beautiful golden cups.*

Díaz del Castillo also described small green and red vegetables that the Aztecs included with all their meals. Some they ate fresh, and others were left to dry in the sun for several days, he wrote. It is safe to assume that he was referring to chiles. The Spaniards quickly incorporated the tasty chiles into their diets, combining them with ingredients brought from the Old Country, like oil and garlic.

1 DRY ANCHO CHILE

¹⁄₂ CUP CHICKEN BROTH

1 TEASPOON DRY OREGANO

6 (6 OZ / 180 G) RED SNAPPER FILLETS

SALT AND PEPPER

2 TABLESPOONS VEGETABLE OIL

4 MEDIUM TOMATOES

2 CLOVES GARLIC

¹⁄₄ CUP CHOPPED ONION

¹⁄₂ CUP ORANGE JUICE

LETTUCE LEAVES

RADISHES

Stem the chile and shake out the seeds. Wash it under running water, pat dry with a paper towel, and soak in the chicken broth for about 10 minutes, or until soft. Set aside.

Sprinkle salt, pepper, and oregano on both sides of the fish. In a nonstick frying pan, heat the oil over medium heat and fry the fish until golden brown. Drain the fillets on paper towels to remove excess oil.

In a blender, purée the tomatoes, garlic, onion, and ancho chile with its soaking liquid. Reheat the oiled pan used to fry the fish, add the tomato mixture, and quickly sauté for about 2 minutes. Add the orange juice and season with salt and pepper. Bring the sauce to a simmer and continue cooking for about 5 minutes. Carefully add the fillets and continue to simmer for just 1 minute more, to allow the flavors to blend.

Serve at once, with lettuce leaves and radishes cut into florets.

FRIED FISH FILLETS IN TOMATO SAUCE

Pescado Rebozado en Caldillo de Jitomate   *4 to 6 servings*

BATTER-FRIED FISH FILLETS ARE VERY COMMON *in Mexico. A green salad with tomato slices drizzled with olive oil is a good accompaniment, providing a fresh and light counterpoint to the heavier fish.*

Chiles, like salsas, are usually served in a salsera *so people can add more to their plates according to their taste. Salseras come in different shapes, some are similar to gravy boats, in either wood or colorful ceramics and others more sophisticated, in pewter the shape of a very small* molcajete. *Refrigerate any unused chiles in a glass jar with a lid. Chiles keep very well for weeks, if properly stored.*

SALT AND PEPPER

JUICE OF 1 LIME

4 TO 6 (6 OZ / 180 G) RED SNAPPER FILLETS

2 EGGS, SEPARATED

⅓ CUP ALL-PURPOSE FLOUR

OIL FOR FRYING

2 CUPS BASIC TOMATO SAUCE (PAGE 29)

4 TO 6 PICKLED JALAPEÑO CHILES PLUS 2 TABLESPOONS PICKLING LIQUID

Sprinkle salt, pepper, and lime juice on the fish (cut the fillets in half if they are too big to handle).

In the bowl of an electric mixer, beat the egg whites until stiff, add the egg yolks, and beat until well blended. Stir in salt and pepper, and 1 tablespoon of flour. Set aside.

Heat the oil in a large skillet, over medium heat. Coat each fillet with the remaining flour, and then carefully dip in the egg batter. Fry the fillets until golden brown on both sides. Drain on paper towels to remove the excess oil and keep warm.

Just before serving, heat the tomato sauce. Add the fish, jalapeños, and the pickling liquid, and serve hot.

FISH WITH AVOCADO AND TOMATO SAUCE

Pescado con Salsa de Aguacate y Jitomate   *4 to 6 servings*

THE AZTECS CONSIDERED THE AVOCADO TREE to be sacred and believed that its fruit gave potency to men. This *exquisite fruit is very rich in vitamins, calcium, phosphorus, and iron.*

The tomato, one of the many gifts Mexico gave to the world, is also an essential part of Mexican cuisine. The Spaniards took it back to Spain and from there it traveled to Italy, where it is widely used in delicious pastas and pizzas.

I find Mexican oregano much more aromatic and flavorful, giving the tomato and avocado sauce a very pleasing flavor.

1 LARGE TOMATO

1 LARGE RIPE AVOCADO, PEELED AND PITTED

1 TABLESPOON CIDER VINEGAR

JUICE OF ½ LIME

½ CUP FINELY CHOPPED ONION

2 TABLESPOONS OLIVE OIL

OREGANO

SALT

½ CUP FLOUR

1 TEASPOON CORNSTARCH

PEPPER

4 TO 6 (6 OZ/180 G) RED SNAPPER FILLETS

OIL FOR FRYING

4 LARGE CLOVES GARLIC, HALVED

2 TO 4 PICKLED JALAPEÑO CHILES (PAGE 159), SLICED

½ CUP MANZANILLA OLIVES, CHOPPED

In a small, dry frying pan, cook the tomato on all sides until the peel is charred. When cool enough to handle, remove and discard the peel and seeds. In a small bowl, mash the tomato and then the avocado with a fork, while at the same time adding the vinegar and lime juice. Combine well, stir in the onion and olive oil, and season with oregano and salt to taste. Set aside.

Combine the flour and the cornstarch. Sprinkle salt and pepper on the fillets, and dredge in the flour mixture. Heat the oil in a large frying pan, add the garlic, and quickly fry each fillet until golden brown on both sides. Drain on paper towels to remove the excess oil and keep warm. Discard the garlic.

Place the fish on a serving platter, cover with the avocado and tomato sauce, and garnish with the jalapeños and olives.

PICKLED FISH

Pescado en Escabeche   *2 servings*

ESCABECHE IS A TERM USED TO DESCRIBE A MIXTURE *of sliced onions cooked in a vinaigrette with an assort-*
ment of spices and herbs, sometimes with carrots and peas, served hot or at room temperature. Escabeche can
be prepared ahead of time and warmed just before serving.

Pickled chiles, either jalapeños or serranos, can be found in small cans. They are usually quite hot, very
flavorful, and very addictive, and instantly add flavor to any dish. Some people might find these so hot that
adding only the pickling liquid from the chiles is enough. Refrigerate the unused chiles in a glass jar with
a tight lid. They keep very well for weeks.

SALT AND PEPPER

2 (6 TO 8 OZ / 225 G) HALIBUT STEAKS

$^1\!/_2$ CUP FLOUR

2 LARGE CLOVES GARLIC

1 TEASPOON GROUND CUMIN

6 WHOLE BLACK PEPPERCORNS

$^1\!/_2$ CUP PLUS 2 TABLESPOONS CIDER
VINEGAR

$^1\!/_4$ CUP EXTRA-VIRGIN OLIVE OIL

1 MEDIUM ONION, SLICED INTO RINGS

1 (2-INCH) CINNAMON STICK

3 BAY LEAVES

2 MEDIUM PICKLED JALAPEÑO CHILES,
SLICED (PAGE 159), OR
1 (7 OZ / 220 ML) CAN CHILES EN
VINAGRE

2 ROMAINE LETTUCE LEAVES, WASHED

2 AVOCADOS, PEELED, PITTED, AND
SLICED

Sprinkle the fish with salt and pepper on both
sides and dredge in the flour. Set aside.

In a *molcajete* or mortar, grind the garlic, cumin,
and peppercorns with 2 tablespoons of the vinegar. In a small saucepan, heat 2 tablespoons of
olive oil and sauté the onion until translucent. Add
the remaining vinegar, the garlic mixture, the cinnamon stick, the bay leaves, and the chiles.
Sprinkle with salt to taste. Bring the mixture to a
boil, lower the heat, and simmer the escabeche for
3 or 4 minutes to allow the flavors to blend.

Meanwhile, in a frying pan, heat the remaining 2
tablespoons olive oil over medium heat and fry the
fillets until golden brown, turning them once.
With a slotted spoon, remove the fillets from the
oil and transfer them to paper towels to remove
the excess oil. Serve at once with the sliced avocados. Serve this pickled fish on a bed of lettuce,
topped with the escabeche and garnished with the
avocado slices.

RED SNAPPER FILLETS WITH GUACAMOLE

Filetes de Huachinango con Guacamole   *4 to 6 servings*

In this recipe, the ever-popular red snapper fillets are cooked in milk to help the fish keep its own juices and to provide an unusual tenderness. A spicy guacamole adds to the flavor of the fish.

SALT AND PEPPER

6 (6 OZ/180 G) RED SNAPPER FILLETS

1 CUP 2% MILK

4 WHOLE BLACK PEPPERCORNS

2 BASIL LEAVES

1/2 SMALL ONION, SLICED

PEEL OF 1/2 LIME

1 CUP GUACAMOLE (PAGE 149)

Sprinkle salt and pepper on both sides of the fillets and place them in a large saucepan. Pour the milk over the fish, and add the peppercorns, basil, onion, and lime peel. Bring the fish to a boil, lower the heat, and simmer, depending on the thickness of the fillets, about 5 to 7 minutes, or until the fish is no longer red but still firm and in one piece.

Drain the fish from the milk mixture, place on a platter, and serve at once, topped with the guacamole.

BAKED PRAWNS WITH CHEESE AND JALAPEÑOS

Camarones al Queso   *4 servings*

PRAWNS ARE DEFINITELY THE FIRST CHOICE for this dish, however, shrimp may be used, too (adjust the cooking time and slice the red pepper and jalapeño chile into smaller strips). Serve hot with good crusty bread—a good start to a fancy dinner!

20 TO 24 PRAWNS, SHELLED

JUICE OF 1 LIME

SALT

2 TABLESPOONS EXTRA-VIRGIN OLIVE OIL

¼ CUP CHOPPED ONION

2 CLOVES GARLIC, CHOPPED

1 SMALL RED BELL PEPPER, SLICED INTO STRIPS

1 JALAPEÑO CHILE, SLICED INTO STRIPS

BLACK PEPPER

½ CUP SHREDDED MOZZARELLA CHEESE

Preheat the oven to 375°F. Sprinkle the prawns with the lime juice and salt. Set aside.

In a frying pan, heat the oil over medium heat and sauté the onion and garlic. Add the red pepper and jalapeño, and cook for about 3 minutes. Sprinkle with salt and pepper to taste. Stir in the prawns, and continue cooking for about 5 minutes more, or until the prawns are red and firm. Adjust the seasoning.

Divide the prawns and vegetables among four ovenproof bowls or ramekins. Cover with the cheese, and bake until the cheese is melted and the mixture is heated through, about 5 to 8 minutes.

TAMALES AND STUFFED CHILES

TAMALES Y
CHILES RELLENOS

ABOUT TAMALES

LEGEND HAS IT THAT FOR TAMALES TO BE GOOD, they must be made in jovial camaraderie in a partylike setting. The story must have something to it, because tamales are almost always served at birthdays, first communions, or baptisms—celebrations that are not as substantial as a wedding banquet or a Christmas dinner, but certainly more ordinary than an everyday snack. Tamales are one of Mexico's most truly characteristic dishes.

The word in Náhuatl, the Aztec language means "bundle." They are thus called because tamales consist of small (four- or five-inch) elongated mounds of corn dough with a stuffing that can range from incredibly tasty bits of pork or chicken to candylike marmalades or dry fruit. Each tamale is wrapped in corn leaves and then steamed, usually in large pots, a few dozen at a time. Their preparation is time-consuming and labor-intensive (thus the party-cooking approach). But the rewards are most remarkable.

Tamales are ordinarily classified into red, green, or sweet, depending on whether the stuffing is cooked in tomato sauce, tomatillo sauce, mole, or a sweet sauce. Sweet tamales are traditionally served alongside a mug of thick hot chocolate, *atole* (a corn beverage), or *champurrado* (a chocolate and corn drink), either as a brunch or a *merienda* (light supper). In more sophisticated forms, tamales also are incorporated into formal meals, usually as a side dish to meats or even beans. The choices are endless, as is to be expected from a foodstuff dating back thousands of years.

In 1565, Bernardino de Sahagún, the wise Dominican friar who dedicated his life to studying the habits and traditions of the Meshica Indians, reported the existence of tamales. He described them as "bundles, not quite round nor square, with different fillings, wrapped in leaves." In the south, for instance, tamales are wrapped in banana leaves and the filling is contained in the dough itself; whereas in other regions, tamales are made with a variety of fillings and are wrapped in dry cornhusks. The size varies according to each region.

It is not surprising that tamales have survived since pre-Hispanic times. Legend has it that they were invented by women who needed to provide their men with a nutritious and practical way of sustenance, and what better way of doing this than wrapping the corn dough in leaves for easy carrying. Many things have changed since pre-Hispanic times, however. In the same lands where those men fought wars, it is now easy to spot a *tamalero* (tamale vendor) selling piping hot tamales out of huge pots, to customers on their way to work early in the morning and again in the evening for people to take home for a nice *merienda*.

Worth mentioning here is a family restaurant in the Colonia Condesa neighborhood of Mexico City that has been in existence since I was a child, La Flor de Lys. The story of this restaurant is indeed a success story. The first owner started selling tamales out of her house, mainly to her neighbors, since her production was modest. Demand grew, little by little, and in a few years her house was converted into what is now the restaurant.

The menu has expanded as well as the house to meet demand, and she now serves a variety of tamales accompanied by enchiladas, guacamole, and refried beans, among other antojitos. Combos can be quite exciting there, especially for people who want to savor the real thing in an authentic atmosphere. Quality and service are as good as they have always been. It is no small wonder that Mexican families have frequented La Flor de Lys since time immemorial.

BASIC TAMALES

Tamales   *Yields 25 to 30 medium-size tamales*

MY MOTHER ALWAYS MADE TAMALES *to celebrate my father's birthday. Friends, aunts, uncles, and their children were invited and everybody enjoyed the chile and sweet tamales with a steaming hot cup of strawberry, guava, and/or pecan* atole, *a thick corn-based beverage made with milk and cornstarch and flavored with seasonal fruit. Unfortunately, my mother's secret recipe for this delicious beverage was lost and I have not been able to reproduce it exactly the way I remembered it.*

The celebration of my father's birthday really began the day before, when my mother's sisters arrived to help in the preparation of the tamales. My mother and the cook prepared the various fillings the day before and started to beat the dough. The cornhusks were soaked in water in a big tub. Everybody was in a festive mood; after all, it was my father's birthday! They sat around a big table, chatting about who was or was not coming to the brunch. At some point my mother would ask, "Who wants to do the green mole ones, or the red mole ones, or the sweet ones?"

When I was old enough to help, the sweet tamales are the ones I always chose. It was fun to count the raisins and the chopped dried fruit, although I think that what I liked the most was being in the middle of that partylike atmosphere, especially because my favorite aunt, my mother's younger sister Juanita, was there and I knew I could get away with a lot of things.

When the process of wrapping the tamales began, the cook maintained a steady flow of cornhusks, while everybody was busy in the assembly line. By dusk, the tamales were wrapped, steamed, and stored for the next day. The festive mood continued, and the preparation of the different atoles *and* champurrado *(a mixture of* atole *and chocolate) started.*

By the time my mother called it a day, it was midnight. The next day we had to have an early start. Guests arrived around nine o'clock in the morning and everything had to be ready by then. The cook would also start her day early, preparing fresh fruit cocktail, served in beautiful stemmed, doubled glasses, the ice water in the outer glass tinted with color; setting the tables; and so on.

My mother supervised every detail and, by the time the guests arrived, everything was ready. This brunch was planned well in advance every year, and everybody enjoyed my mother's tamales so much that they became a tradition in our family.

The gathering was usually extended until about noon. At that time, one of my uncles who was ready to leave would get an old cup from the kitchen and everybody, including the children, would form a circle. My uncle would start the throwing of the cup around, from one person's hand to the next.

Nobody could leave until the game was over. Eventually somebody would drop the cup, and the saying "Aquí se rompió una taza y cada quien para su casa" (very loosely translated, "A cup is broken and it's time for all to go home") would end the birthday party. Another family tradition!

INGREDIENTS AND RECIPE ON NEXT PAGE

BASIC TAMALES

1 TO 2 (8 OZ) BAGS CORN HUSKS

1¼ CUPS LARD

4 CUPS Maseca CORN FLOUR

3 CUPS CHICKEN BROTH

1 TABLESPOON SALT

2 TABLESPOONS BAKING POWDER

Soak the corn husks in water for about 30 minutes, or until soft and pliable. Drain the husks and pat dry with a kitchen towel or with paper towels. Discard any corn silks. Set aside.

With a standing electric mixer (the dough is too heavy for most hand mixers), beat the lard for 6 to 8 minutes, or until light and very fluffy. Set aside. In a large mixing bowl, combine the flour with the chicken broth, add the salt and lard, and mix well. If you are doing more than one batch, you may have to use your hands. To verify that the *masa* (corn dough) is ready, place a small ball, the size of a marble, in a glass filled with cold water. If it immediately floats to the top, the dough is ready. Beat 2 to 3 minutes more, if necessary. Stir in the baking powder and mix well.

Hold a damp corn husk open, smooth side up, and spoon 2 to 3 tablespoons of *masa* into the center. Spread the *masa* evenly to the sides, leaving about a 1-inch margin at the top and about 2 inches at the bottom of husk. Add 1 or 2 heaping teaspoons of filling, and fold the two sides of the husk in to cover the filling with the *masa*. If the husk does not quite meet to enclose the filling, patch it with a piece of another husk. Fold the remaining bottom part of the husk to form the tamal. Repeat this procedure with the remaining *masa*. Please refer to pages 103–110 for the various *rellenos* (fillings) for tamales.

Insert a footed metal rack in a steamer, soup pot, or roasting pan, to cover the bottom of the pot and pour in about 2 inches of water or just less than the height of the rack. At the same time, place a coin in the water (it doesn't have to be a Mexican coin!)—if the water cooks dry, the coin will start rattling, alerting you to add more water. Cover the rack with a bed of corn husks and stack the tamales tightly together in layers folded-side down, to fill the container horizontally and vertically. Cover the tamales with more husks and then with a damp tea towel to preserve the heat.

Cover the pan and simmer for about 35 to 40 minutes, depending on the size of the tamales. Add water to the bottom of the pan, if necessary. The tamales are ready when the *masa* no longer sticks to the husks. Serve hot with salsa and refried beans.

NOTE: One batch of this recipe is enough for 2 different fillings.

CHICKEN PICADILLO FILLING

Picadillo de Pollo

Filling for 15 to 20 tamales

THE COMBINATION OF OLIVES, ALMONDS AND RAISINS *goes hand in hand with chiles. This* picadillo *is the perfect example of the sweet and spicy combined to perfection.*

A picadillo cooked specially for filling tamales should be almost dry. On the other hand, if it is to be served as a main dish, then picadillo can be a little runny and served with warm tortillas or good bread.

1 LARGE CHICKEN BREAST, HALVED

1 TABLESPOON VEGETABLE OIL

2 CLOVES GARLIC, CHOPPED

$1/2$ MEDIUM ONION, CHOPPED

2 LARGE TOMATOES, SEEDED AND CHOPPED

$1/4$ CUP TOMATO SAUCE

$1/2$ CUP CHICKEN BROTH

$1/2$ CUP RAISINS

$1/2$ CUP CHOPPED ALMONDS, TOASTED

12 MANZANILLA OLIVES, PITTED AND CHOPPED

SALT AND PEPPER

1 TABLESPOON CIDER VINEGAR

In salted boiling water, poach the chicken breast for about 12 minutes, or until cooked but still tender and juicy. While the chicken is cooking, skim away the brown foam that forms at the top to obtain a clear broth. With a slotted spoon, remove the chicken, and reserve the broth. When cool enough to handle, shred the chicken with your fingers.

In a saucepan, heat the oil over medium heat and sauté the garlic and onion until the onion is translucent and the garlic is barely cooked. Add the tomatoes, tomato sauce, and broth. Bring the sauce to a boil, lower the heat, and simmer for a few minutes, or until slightly thickened. Add the raisins, almonds, olives, and the shredded chicken. Season with salt and pepper, and simmer for 5 to 8 minutes more. Adjust the seasoning and the liquid if necessary. Add the vinegar to bring out the flavors.

TOMATILLO CHICKEN FILLING

Chile Verde para Relleno   *Filling for 15 to 20 tamales*

CHILE VERDE *IS BEST* when the tomatillos are an even bright-green color. Tomatillos can sometimes be a bit acidic. If this is the case, add a little bit of sugar and let the sugar dissolve while the sauce is boiling.

1 CHICKEN BREAST, HALVED, OR 1 LB
(500 G) PORK LOIN, CUT INTO
CHUNKS

1 SMALL ONION

1 SMALL CELERY STALK

12 TOMATILLOS, HUSKED AND WASHED

4 TO 6 SERRANO CHILES

2 SMALL CLOVES GARLIC

1 TEASPOON VEGETABLE OIL

SALT

In a deep saucepan, cover the chicken or pork with salted water. Add ¼ of the onion and the celery stalk with its leaves. Bring the water to a boil, lower the heat, and simmer for about 10 to 12 minutes for chicken and 12 to 15 minutes for pork. Remove from the heat and drain, reserving ¼ cup of broth; save the rest for another use. When cool enough to handle, shred the meat with your fingers and set aside.

In a small saucepan, cover the tomatillos with water, add the chiles, and cook for 4 to 6 minutes, or until the tomatillos have become lighter in color. Cool, reserving ½ cup the cooking liquid.

In a blender or food processor, purée the tomatillos, chiles, remaining onion, and garlic with the reserved cooking liquid.

In the same saucepan, heat the oil over medium heat and sauté the tomatillo mixture for 2 to 3 minutes before adding the shredded meat, the reserved broth, and salt to taste. Bring the sauce to a boil and simmer for another 2 to 4 minutes, or until it has thickened slightly. Cool the *chile verde* before you start filling the tamales.

MOLE POBLANO CHICKEN FILLING

Relleno de Pollo con Mole   *Filling for 15 to 20 tamales*

THE MOLE CAN BE PREPARED IN ADVANCE and frozen; add the cooked chicken the day you assemble the tamales. However, if time is of the essence, you might consider buying the mole poblano *sauce. There are several brands available in the market, all of them relatively good, especially if you doctor them a little by adding tomato sauce and a bit of sugar.*

1 CHICKEN BREAST, HALVED

¼ SMALL ONION

1 SMALL RED POTATO, PEELED AND
   CHOPPED

½ CELERY STALK WITH LEAVES

1 SMALL CARROT, PEELED AND CHOPPED

2 CUPS *MOLE POBLANO* (PAGE 61)

Cook the chicken breast in salted boiling water with the onion, potato, celery, and carrot, for about 10 to 12 minutes. While chicken is boiling, skim off the foam that forms on top of the broth. Drain the chicken from the broth and set aside, reserving the broth for the mole sauce.

When cool enough to handle, shred the chicken with your fingers. In a saucepan, heat the mole sauce over medium heat and add the shredded chicken, plus some of the chicken broth, if the mole is too thick. Set aside to cool.

If you are using ready-made mole sauce, follow the directions on the label, using only about 2 cups of mole. Stir in ¼ cup of tomato sauce, and the shredded chicken. You may add a bit of sugar to the sauce to counteract the acidity of the chiles.

RED CHILE
CHICKEN FILLING

Chile Rojo para Relleno   *Filling for 15 to 20 tamales*

EN LA VARIEDAD ESTÁ EL GUSTO *(variety is the spice of life). Here is yet another filling for tamales. In this recipe, the chiles and tomatoes are roasted, removing the normal acidity in the tomato and sweetening the chile sauce.*

CHICKEN:

1 WHOLE CHICKEN BREAST

1 SMALL CARROT, PEELED AND CHOPPED

1 SMALL CELERY STALK WITH LEAVES

1/4 SMALL ONION

SAUCE:

2 LARGE TOMATOES

2 TO 4 SERRANO CHILES

1/2 CUP ONION, CHOPPED

1 LARGE CLOVE GARLIC

1 TEASPOON VEGETABLE OIL

In salted boiling water, cook the chicken breast with the carrot, celery, and onion for about 10 to 12 minutes, or until cooked, but still tender. For a clear broth, skim away the foam that forms on top while the chicken is boiling. Remove the chicken from the broth and drain, reserving 1/2 cup of broth for the sauce and the rest for a future use. When cool enough to handle, shred the chicken with your fingers.

In a dry pan, roast the tomatoes and serrano chiles until blistered. Cool and remove the charred peel. Transfer to a blender or food processor, add the onion and garlic, and blend until well processed.

In a saucepan, heat the oil over medium heat and fry the tomato mixture for 2 minutes. Add the 1/2 cup of reserved broth and the shredded chicken, and season with salt and pepper. Bring the mixture to a boil and simmer for about 6 to 8 minutes, or until the sauce has thickened. Cool the *chile rojo* before filling the tamales.

ZUCCHINI BLOSSOM AND POBLANO CHILE TAMALES

Tamales de Flor de Calabaza   *Yields 25 to 30 regular-size tamales*

A FEW YEARS AGO, A MAJOR EVENT CALLED LA MERIENDA DEL TAMAL took place during the culinary festival of the Centro Histórico in Mexico City. La Merienda was held in the central patio of the Palacio del Arzobispado (Palace of the Arbishopric), a striking building with a baroque facade dating back to 1743.

This prestigious event, brought together major personalities from Mexico's culinary world to resurrect old recipes of the myriad varieties of tamales from the different regions, Zacatecas, Jalapa, Guerrero, Oaxaca, and Totonaca, to name a few; as well as a taste of the traditional corn-based beverage called atole, *which was mixed with such tidbits as strawberries, pineapple, chocolate, almonds, and walnuts.*

This old recipe was one of many featured at this event. In this recipe, the filling is mixed right into the masa, *so no stuffing is required. Beautiful, bright yellow zucchini blossoms can be found fresh in some markets or canned in Latin American stores. They are usually lightly fried with either epazote or cilantro, and chiles.*

▼▼▼▼▼▼▼▼▼▼▼▼▼▼▼▼▼▼▼▼▼▼▼▼▼▼

2 LARGE POBLANO CHILES, ROASTED,
   PEELED, AND SEEDED (PAGE 111)

1 TEASPOON VEGETABLE OIL

2$\frac{1}{2}$ CUPS FRESH ZUCCHINI BLOSSOMS,
   CHOPPED OR 2 (8 OZ/250 G) CANS
   ZUCCHINI BLOSSOMS, DRAINED AND
   CHOPPED

$\frac{1}{4}$ CUP CHOPPED ONION

2 LARGE CLOVES GARLIC

1 SPRIG EPAZOTE OR $\frac{1}{2}$ CUP CHOPPED
   FRESH CILANTRO

SALT

3 EGG YOLKS

1 RECIPE BASIC TAMALE DOUGH
   (PAGE 102)

1 (8 OZ) BAG CORN HUSKS

Slice the poblano chiles into $\frac{1}{4}$-inch strips. In a small saucepan, heat the oil and sauté the onion, garlic, blossoms, epazote, and chile strips. Season with salt and set aside.

Stir the egg yolks into the tamale dough, then add the zucchini mixture and mix well. Please refer to the Basic Tamales recipe (see page 102) for assembling and steaming the tamales.

VERACRUZ-STYLE
BAKED TAMAL

Tamal de Cazuela Estilo Veracruz   *6 to 8 servings*

CENTÉOTL, AS SHE WAS KNOWN IN AZTEC MYTHOLOGY, was not only considered the Goddess of Corn but also the Goddess of Fertility, since the noble corn represented the fertility and vitality of the soil, offering men a daily sustenance.

The Aztecs celebrated the first harvest of the year with ritual dances accompanied by a small drum, a slim flute made out of reed-grass, and a few jingle bells. This ritual still takes place in small towns and villages throughout Mexico. Modern times of course, have modified the ritual. In the valley of Toluca, near Mexico City, the Mazahua Indians dress in very brightly colored costumes for what is now called the Dance of Centéotl, which also includes chants in Náhuatl.

Few people are aware that this wonderful grain, which sprouted from a prehistoric Mexican grass, evolved into many varieties and has influenced modern economies as no other cereal has. Research has revealed that, six to eight thousand years ago, the corn cob was very similar in size and shape to a wheat ear; only through hybridization, has corn become what we know today. Considered at one time a Third World nourishment and used as cattle food, corn now grows on six continents, with an annual harvest that exceeds that of wheat, oats, rice, barley, and sorghum combined.

This casserole is a good company dish and although different from a real tamal, *it is a good introduction to the amazing world of corn.*

1 WHOLE CHICKEN BREAST OR 1 LB (500 G) CUBED PORK

2 DRY ANCHO CHILES

1 DRY CHIPOTLE CHILE, SEEDED

1 LARGE TOMATO, ROASTED AND PEELED

1/4 CUP CHOPPED ONION

2 CLOVES GARLIC

1 TEASPOON VEGETABLE OIL

SALT AND PEPPER

4 MEDIUM EARS OF CORN (TO YIELD ABOUT 4 CUPS OF KERNELS)

1/3 CUP MILK

1/2 CUP BUTTER, MELTED

2 TABLESPOONS LARD

1/4 CUP FLOUR

1/4 TEASPOON SALT

Cook the chicken or pork in salted boiling water for about 10 to 12 minutes, or until cooked. Drain the meat from the broth, reserving the broth, and set aside. When cool enough to handle, shred the meat with your fingers.

Stem the ancho chiles, shaking out the seeds. Wash the chiles under running water and soak in 1 cup of the reserved hot broth for about 10 to 15 minutes, or until soft.

In a blender or food processor, purée the chipotle chile, tomato, onion, garlic, and ancho chiles with the soaking liquid. In a saucepan, heat the oil and fry the tomato mixture, stirring occasionally. Season with salt and pepper, and add the pork or shredded chicken. Simmer the mixture for about 10 to 15 minutes, or until the sauce has thickened. Preheat the oven to 350°F and grease an 8-inch square baking dish or *cazuela*.

Meanwhile, slice the kernels off the corn cobs. In a blender or food processor, process the kernels and the milk, in batches, until puréed. Stir in the butter, lard, flour, and salt, and mix well.

In the prepared baking dish, place a layer of the corn mixture, cover with the stew, and top with another layer of the remaining corn mixture. Bake, covered, for about 30 minutes, and uncovered for an additional 30 to 40 minutes, or until it is browned and the corn is thoroughly cooked. Let the casserole sit for about 10 minutes before serving. A fresh green salad would be a good complement to this dish.

SWEET TAMALES

Tamales de Dulce   *Yields 15 to 20 tamales*

A CHILD'S FIRST COMMUNION is usually celebrated with a festive breakfast that starts with a fresh fruit cocktail, followed by a variety of tamales and a steaming cup of hot chocolate, atole, or champurrado. For the little ones who attend this big celebration, sweet tamales are in order.

Fillings for sweet tamales vary from jam to raisins to candied fruit. The corn flour is made pink by the use of food coloring. These are so good that, even when the festivity is not for children, sweet tamales are always available.

1 (8 OZ) BAG CORN HUSKS

1/2 LB (250 G) LARD OR VEGETABLE
   SHORTENING

2 CUPS MASECA CORN FLOUR

15 DROPS LIQUID RED FOOD COLORING

1 TABLESPOON CORNSTARCH

1 1/2 CUPS CHICKEN BROTH

1 CUP SUGAR

DASH OF SALT

1 1/2 TEASPOON BAKING POWDER

1/2 CUP RAISINS, SOAKED IN WATER

1/2 CUP CHOPPED ALMONDS

1/2 CUP CHOPPED CANDIED CITRON,
   PAPAYA OR PINEAPPLE, OR 1 CUP
   STRAWBERRY JAM

In a large bowl, soak the corn husks in water for about 30 minutes, or until they are soft and pliable. Drain and pat dry with a kitchen towel or paper towels, and set aside. With an electric mixer (the dough is too heavy for a hand mixer), beat the lard for 6 to 8 minutes, or until very fluffy. Set aside.

In a separate bowl, mix the flour with the cornstarch and the chicken broth. Stir in the lard, add the food coloring and beat for about 3 to 4 minutes, or until completely mixed. The mixture should be of a lighter consistency than that of Basic Tamales. Place a small ball of dough, the size of a marble, in a glass filled with cold water. If it immediately floats to the top, the mixture is light enough and is ready for filling. Beat 2 to 3 minutes more if necessary. Stir in the sugar, salt, and baking powder, and mix well.

In a small bowl, combine the drained raisins, almonds and the candied fruit for the filling. If you use jam instead of the fruit, 1 tablespoon in the middle of each tamal is quite enough.

Please refer to the recipe for Basic Tamales (page 102) for instructions on how to assemble and steam tamales.

ABOUT POBLANO CHILES

THE POBLANO CHILE, originally grown in the state of Puebla, is a moderately hot pepper, about five inches long by three inches wide, extensively used in Mexican cookery. It is commonly used for stuffing, for rajas, and blended with milk or cream for chile sauces.

HOW TO ROAST, PEEL, AND SEED POBLANO CHILES FOR STUFFING :

Place the poblano chiles on a hot, dry frying pan, turning them constantly until they are blistered and charred. Seal the chiles in a plastic bag and let them steam until cool enough to handle. Wearing rubber gloves and holding the chile by the stem, carefully remove the charred peel, trying to keep the chile intact. With a small sharp knife, cut a slit in the chile and very gently remove the seeds. Wash the chiles under running water if there are still some seeds adhered to the insides. With a paper towel, pat the chile dry, inside and out, before stuffing.

A second method for roasting the chiles is to place them on a baking sheet, under the broiler for 2 to 3 minutes each side, turning them carefully with tongs. It is a good method as long as you can keep an eye on them, otherwise they burn quite quickly.

FOR *RAJAS DE POBLANO* (STRIPS OF ROASTED POBLANO CHILE):

Roast the chiles according to the procedure outlined above. Once they are cool enough to handle, with a small sharp knife cut a circle around the stem and carefully remove the stem with the seeds attached. Cut the chile open and remove any remaining seeds adhered to the walls of the chile by washing it under running water. With a paper towel, pat dry and slice the chiles into strips.

FOR CHILE SAUCE:

With a small sharp knife, cut a circle around each stem and carefully remove it with the seeds attached. Cut the chile open and remove any seeds adhered to the chile. With a wet paper towel, clean the chile, then chop it. Transfer it to a blender or food processor, add milk and/or cream, and purée. This sauce can be used for pasta, baked chicken, or enchiladas.

POBLANO CHILE
STRIPS FILLING

Rajas de Poblano para Relleno   *Yields about 1 to 1½ cups of filling*

RAJAS DE POBLANO *ARE A VERY POPULAR FILLING for tamales, as well as quesadillas, for use on top of rice, or as an accompaniment to steak, which reminds me of a wonderful restaurant, on La Calle Balderas in down-town Mexico City.*

Carne a la Tampiqueña, *now a very popular throughout Mexico, originated in the Tampico Club Restaurant, where I used to go with my parents just to savor this scrumptious dish. It was served on an oval platter and was a meal in itself. The beefsteak, juicy and very thinly sliced into long strips, was accompa-nied by enchiladas verdes, refried beans, and* rajas de poblano *smothered with cream and Manchego cheese. The Tampico Club was extremely popular in the 1950s and was favored by businessmen as well as families.*

These days, you do not have to go to the Tampico Club to savor Carne a la Tampiqueña, *since this* platillo *is served in most restaurants.*

4 TO 6 LARGE POBLANO CHILES, ROASTED, PEELED, AND SEEDED (PAGE 111)

1 TABLESPOON VEGETABLE OIL

½ CUP CHOPPED ONION

2 LARGE TOMATOES, SEEDED AND CHOPPED

1 TO 2 TABLESPOONS TOMATO SAUCE

SALT

¼ LB (125 G) MANCHEGO OR MONTEREY JACK CHEESE, SLICED IN STRIPS

Slice the poblano chiles into ¼-inch strips. In a small saucepan, heat the oil over medium heat, and sauté the onion, chile strips, and tomatoes for 3 to 4 minutes, or until the vegetables are cooked. Stir in the tomato sauce, add salt to taste, and continue simmering for 5 to 7 minutes, or until the sauce has thickened slightly. Cool.

Add a small slice of cheese to the *rajas* filling, before folding each tamale.

PORK-STUFFED POBLANO CHILES

Chiles Rellenos de Picadillo de Puerco   *4 servings*

EVERY TIME I COOK Pork Picadillo Empanadas (page 84), I end up with leftover stuffing. I usually freeze it in a plastic container until I am ready to use it in this recipe that my family loves.

2 LARGE RIPE TOMATOES, SEEDED

¼ MEDIUM ONION

2 LARGE CLOVES GARLIC

¼ TO ½ CUP CANNED TOMATO SAUCE

SALT AND PEPPER

1 TABLESPOON VEGETABLE OIL

4 POBLANO CHILES, ROASTED, PEELED,
    AND SEEDED (PAGE 111)

1 CUP PORK PICADILLO (PAGE 84)

½ CUP FLOUR

2 EGGS, SEPARATED

OIL FOR FRYING

In a blender or food processor, blend the tomatoes, onion, and garlic until puréed. In a large saucepan, heat the oil over medium heat and add the tomato mixture and the tomato sauce. Season with salt and pepper. Bring the sauce to a boil, lower the heat, and simmer for about 8 to 10 minutes, or until the sauce thickens. Keep hot.

Meanwhile, stuff each chile with about 2 tablespoons of the picadillo and secure the opening with a toothpick. Reserving 2 tablespoons of flour, roll each chile in the remaining flour until well coated.

With an electric mixer, beat the egg whites until stiff, add the egg yolks and beat for 2 minutes, until stiff. Mix in the reserved 2 tablespoons of flour, and salt and pepper.

In a heavy frying pan, heat the oil over medium heat. Holding the chiles by their stems, dip into the batter and fry until golden brown on all sides. Transfer the chiles to paper towels to remove excess oil. Keep warm.

Just before serving, remove the toothpicks and transfer the chiles to the hot tomato sauce. Serve at once, with rice and/or black beans and warmed corn tortillas.

SARDINE-STUFFED
POBLANO CHILES

Chiles de Sardina en Frío   *4 to 6 servings*

WHEN BUYING CHILES, TRY TO PICK *the freshest ones of the lot, with no black spots or blemishes. Poblanos should be thick and firm to the touch. If they are old, they will not withstand a proper roasting and will fall apart easily. Canned poblano chiles are also available in Latin markets and specialty stores.*

These stuffed chiles make a very attractive buffet dish, served at room temperature with good French bread.

¼ CUP CIDER VINEGAR

1 SMALL ONION, SLICED INTO RINGS

2 (3 OZ/90 G EACH) CANS SARDINES IN
    TOMATO SAUCE

4 SMALL CARROTS, SLICED INTO ROUNDS
    AND COOKED

1 CUP DRAINED CANNED PEAS

4 TO 6 POBLANO CHILES, ROASTED,
    PEELED, AND SEEDED (PAGE 111)

¾ CUP SOUR CREAM

¼ CUP 2% MILK

½ SMALL HEAD LETTUCE

SALT

In a small saucepan, bring the vinegar and ¼ cup water to a boil, add the onion, and simmer for 4 or 5 minutes. Drain and set aside.

In a bowl, mix the sardines with half of the carrots and the peas. Stuff the chiles with the sardine mixture and secure the opening with a toothpick. Mix the sour cream with the milk. Arrange a bed of lettuce on a serving platter; place the chiles on the lettuce, and top the chiles with the sour cream mixture. Sprinkle with salt to taste.

Serve the chiles, garnished with the pickled onion, remaining carrots and peas, and additional chopped lettuce.

POBLANO CHILES STUFFED WITH TAMALES

Chiles Rellenos de Tamales   *12 servings*

THIS IS ONE OF MY COUSIN TERE'S *most treasured recipes. She often prepares it for Sunday brunch at her gorgeous home in Pedregal de San Angel in Mexico City. She serves this popular dish preceded by a fresh fruit cocktail. To end the brunch on a high note, a steaming hot cup of* café de olla *(see page 199). Nothing more is needed.*

The tomato sauce and the salsa verde *can be prepared a day in advance and kept refrigerated until needed. The preparation of the chiles can also be done the day before. Any leftover dough may be used to make tamales, filled with a slice of cheese. Tamales freeze very well once they are cool.*

FOR THE DOUGH:

$^1/_2$ POUND (250 G) LARD

2 CUPS MASECA CORN FLOUR

$1^1/_2$ CUPS CHICKEN BROTH

$^1/_4$ TEASPOON SALT

1 TABLESPOON BAKING POWDER

FOR THE CHILES:

12 LARGE POBLANO CHILES, ROASTED
    AND PEELED (PAGE 111)

$1^1/_2$ CUPS *SALSA VERDE* (PAGE 156)

1 (8 OZ) BAG CORN HUSKS

1 TO 2 CUPS BASIC TOMATO SAUCE
    (PAGE 29), HEATED

1 CUP SOUR CREAM

$^1/_4$ CUP 2% MILK

$^1/_2$ CUP CRUMBLED *QUESO FRESCO* OR
    FETA CHEESE (OPTIONAL)

Please follow the instructions given in the Basic Tamales recipe (page 102) to prepare the dough and, later, for the wrapping and steaming procedures.

Wipe the chiles with a damp cloth and very carefully slice off their stems, keeping the stems intact in order to reattach them after the chiles have been stuffed. Set the stems aside. Remove the seeds completely.

Slice each chile open and, hold it open in the palm of your hand, and spoon in about 1 to 2 tablespoons of corn dough, depending on the size of the chile. Place about 1 tablespoon of *salsa verde* in the middle, fold the dough over to cover the salsa, and close the chile. Reattach its stem carefully and wrap the corn husk around the chile as you would with a tamale. Steam the stuffed chiles for about $1^1/_2$ hours, or until the chile is no longer soft but firm to the touch.

Mix the sour cream with the milk. Serve the tamales hot on top of the tomato sauce, garnished with the sour cream mixture and the cheese. Accompany this spectacular dish with *Frijoles de la Olla* (page 115), if desired.

STUFFED POBLANO
CHILES IN WALNUT SAUCE

Chiles en Nogada   *Yields 10 large chiles*

THIS MAGNIFICENT DISH *was created in the city of Puebla to celebrate the triumphant arrival of General Agustin de Iturbide, when independence from Spain was finally attained in 1821. The idea was to create a dish with the colors of the Mexican flag: green, white, and red.*

In Mexico City, Chiles en Nogada *are traditionally served in the fall, when* nueces *(walnuts) for the creamy* nogada *sauce are harvested in northern Mexico.*

The combination of pork and the sweetness of the raisins, almonds, and candied fruit with the spicy heat of the chiles is bound to conquer refined palates anywhere. Serve this festive dish at room temperature, with French bread.

FOR THE FILLING:

1 LB (500 G) PORK LOIN

1 TO 2 TABLESPOONS VEGETABLE OIL

4 LARGE CLOVES GARLIC, CHOPPED

½ CUP CHOPPED ONION

3 LARGE RIPE TOMATOES, SEEDED AND
CHOPPED

½ CUP CANNED TOMATO SAUCE

DASH OF CINNAMON

DASH OF CUMIN

DASH OF CLOVES

½ CUP CHOPPED COOKED HAM

¼ CUP CHOPPED ALMONDS

¼ CUP RAISINS, SOAKED IN WATER

½ CUP CHOPPED, CANDIED CITRON OR
¼ CUP EACH, PEELED, CHOPPED
FRESH APPLE, PEAR, AND PEACH

DASH OF SALT

DASH OF SUGAR

Cook the pork loin in boiling salted water for 12 to 15 minutes, or until tender. Drain and reserve the broth. When the pork is cool enough to handle, shred it with your fingers and set aside.

In a saucepan, heat the oil over medium heat and sauté the garlic and onion until the onion is translucent. Add the chopped tomatoes and tomato sauce, and continue cooking for a few minutes longer. Stir in the pork, ½ to 1 cup of the reserved broth, the cinnamon, cumin, cloves, ham, almonds, drained raisins, and citron. Bring to a boil and simmer for 5 to 8 minutes, or until the sauce has thickened and the fruit is tender. Set aside to cool.

FOR THE *NOGADA* SAUCE:

1 SLICE OF BREAD

½ CUP MILK

1 CUP CHOPPED WALNUTS

1 (4 OZ/125 G) PACKAGE CREAM CHEESE

DASH OF CINNAMON

DASH OF SUGAR

1 TEASPOON DRY SHERRY

10 LARGE POBLANO CHILES, ROASTED,
   PEELED, AND SEEDED (PAGE 111)

1 TO 2 POMEGRANATE(S) OR
   1 (2 OZ/60 G) JAR RED PIMIENTOS

¼ CUP FRESH PARSLEY, CHOPPED

Soak the bread in the milk. In a blender or food processor, half an hour before serving the chiles, blend the walnuts with the cheese, soaked bread, sherry, cinnamon, and sugar. The *nogada* sauce should be thick. Keep at room temperature until ready to serve.

Fill each chile with a spoonful of the pork mixture and carefully place each stuffed chile on a serving platter. Cover the chiles with the *nogada* sauce and garnish with pomegranate seeds and parsley.

STUFFED ANCHO CHILES

Chiles Anchos Rellenos   *4 servings*

Dry ANCHO CHILES should be selected especially for stuffing. As opposed to the ones used for moles, these should be very flat and a bit wider, so it is easy to wipe them clean and to stuff them. In Mexican markets it is very common for vendors to have two different baskets of the chiles, one for moles and the other for stuffing, and even then, discerning customers pick through and choose the best they can find.

Chicken bouillon cubes dissolved in water may be used instead of the chicken broth. Serve these luscious chiles with refried beans on the side

---

1 TABLESPOON VEGETABLE OIL

2 LARGE RIPE TOMATOES, SEEDED AND CHOPPED

¼ CUP CANNED TOMATO SAUCE

½ CUP CHICKEN BROTH

½ MEDIUM ONION, THINLY SLICED INTO RINGS

SALT AND PEPPER

4 DRY ANCHO CHILES

½ LB (250 G) *QUESO FRESCO* OR MILD FETA CHEESE

VEGETABLE OIL FOR FRYING

In a medium saucepan, heat the oil over medium heat and sauté the tomatoes and tomato sauce for 2 minutes, stirring. Add the chicken broth, onion, and salt and pepper to taste. Bring the sauce to a boil and simmer for about 8 to 10 minutes, or until the sauce has thickened. Keep warm.

Clean the chiles with a damp cloth. With a paring knife, cut them open and remove the seeds. After stuffing the chiles with a generous amount of cheese, fold over the openings and secure with a toothpick. In a heavy frying pan, heat the oil almost to the point of smoking and quickly fry the chiles for about 2 minutes, or until they start to puff. Transfer each chile to paper towels to remove excess oil.

Place the chiles in the tomato sauce and serve hot with warm tortillas.

ANTOJITOS

ANTOJITOS, MEANING "LITTLE WHIMS," or "sudden cravings," include such dishes as enchiladas, quesadillas, tacos, tostadas, *tortas*, *enfrijoladas*, *enmoladas*, *entomatadas*, *enjitomatadas*, *gorditas*, *panuchos*, *sincronizadas*, and so on. Despite the name, these are generally nourishing foods, since most of them contain corn, beans, greens, meat, Mexican cream and cheese.

The main component of *antojitos* is the humble tortilla. A well-known fact in Mexico is that native Mexicans whose main staple is corn in tortilla form have beautiful milky-white teeth, even those living in the most remote hamlets where toothpaste is not known. In fact, they use burned corn tortilla to clean their teeth.

North America's love affair with the Mexican tortilla is also well-known. In 2003 alone, sales of corn tortillas totaled 4 billion dollars in the United States, exceeding those of all other ethnic and specialty breads combined, including bagels, croissants and pita.

Antojitos may be served at any time of the day. Even though some people consider these to be street food snacks, tasty *antojitos* are also enjoyed in homes. For a Sunday brunch, for instance, scrambled eggs are served accompanied by enchiladas or *entomatadas*; for a main meal, a steak or a *milanesa* go very well with *enfrijoladas* on the side; and for *merienda*, *tortas* (sandwiches) filled with cold cuts or leftovers are very common.

One can find small establishments of *taquerías* and *torterías*, in any city, big or small. Some have their own specialties. The *tostadas* in the *barrio* of San Francisco in the city of Puebla, were famous. The tacos from Beatricita, in downtown Mexico City were for years and years, the best tacos in town, until El Farolito, a chain of small restaurants serving only tacos with a wide assortment of salsas, came along. The *tostadas* at La Hostería de Santo Domingo, behind the zócalo, were to die for.

More sophisticated restaurants serve *antojitos as botanas* (appetizers), small versions of the dishes. It is safe to say that these addictive *antojitos* are present in Mexicans' everyday life, in one form or another.

ANCHO CHILE MOLE FOR ENMOLADAS

Mole de Chile Ancho para Enmoladas   *4 servings*

For Sunday brunch, my husband's aunt Geor served these enmoladas with scrambled eggs or bisteces de res (thinly sliced steak). The enticing aroma of frijoles de la olla (black beans in the pot) and fresh tortillas made by Petrita, the cook, immediately whetted our appetites. Needless to say, our visits with Aunt Geor and Uncle Rafael were always memorable. More often than not, I left their beautiful house in San Angel with new recipes to try.

These delectable enmoladas are a bit different in that the tortillas are first dipped in mole and then fried. The flavor of the mole fried with the tortilla renders quite a delicious result. Another fabulous recipe from la Tía Geor. Serve these as a side dish or first course.

2 DRY ANCHO CHILES

$^{1}/_{2}$ CUP MILK

1 LARGE EGG

1 LARGE CLOVE GARLIC

SALT

8 CORN TORTILLAS

2 TABLESPOONS VEGETABLE OIL

$^{1}/_{2}$ CUP MEXICAN CREAM OR CRÈME FRAÎCHE (PAGE 148)

$^{1}/_{2}$ CUP CRUMBLED *QUESO FRESCO* OR FETA CHEESE

Clean the chiles with a damp cloth, stem and shake out the seeds. In a small bowl, soak the chiles in the milk for 15 to 20 minutes, or until soft. Transfer the chiles and milk to a blender, add the egg, the garlic, and a dash of salt, and purée. Pour the mole into a wide-mouthed bowl.

In a heavy frying pan, heat the oil over medium heat, dip each tortilla in the mole, and then quickly fry it in the hot oil. Place each tortilla, folded in half, on a serving warm plate. Keep the plate warm in a low oven until all tortillas are made. Garnish the enchiladas with a generous amount of cream and cheese, and serve at once.

BAKED SCRAMBLED EGG TAQUITOS

Taquitos de Huevo al Horno   *2 servings*

These taquitos make a scrumptious Sunday brunch or a tasty merienda *(light supper). They are not too elaborate and certainly very delicious. The tomato salsa can be cooked and the cheese shredded the day before, leaving only frying tortillas, cooking the eggs, and assembling the dish for the last minute.*

½ CUP SOUR CREAM

¼ CUP 2% MILK

1 LARGE RIPE TOMATO, CHOPPED

2 TABLESPOONS CHOPPED ONION

1 CLOVE GARLIC

1 SERRANO OR CHIPOTLE CHILE, SEEDED
   AND CHOPPED

1 TABLESPOON PLUS 1 TEASPOON
   VEGETABLE OIL

¼ CUP CANNED TOMATO SAUCE

SALT

4 EGGS, LIGHTLY BEATEN WITH SALT
   AND PEPPER

6 CORN TORTILLAS, LIGHTLY FRIED

¼ CUP SHREDDED MANCHEGO OR
   FARMER CHEESE

Mix the sour cream with the milk and set aside.

In a blender, process the tomato, onion, garlic, and serrano chile with ½ cup of water until well blended. In a small saucepan, heat 1 teaspoon of the oil over medium heat and, using a colander, strain the tomato mixture into the saucepan and sauté for a few minutes before adding the canned tomato sauce. Season with salt to taste. Simmer the salsa for about 8 minutes, or until it thickens. Adjust the liquid and correct the seasoning. Keep warm. Preheat the oven to 350°F.

In a nonstick frying pan, heat the remaining tablespoon of oil and quickly scramble the eggs until set. Fill each fried tortilla with 1 or 2 tablespoons of the scrambled eggs, and roll up. Place the tacos in a small baking dish, cover with the tomato sauce, and top with the sour cream mixture and a generous amount of cheese.

Bake the taquitos for 6 to 8 minutes, or until they are heated through and the cheese is melted. Do not overbake, or the tomato sauce will dry out.

CHICKEN AND POBLANO CHILE TACOS

Tacos Poblanos   *4 servings*

THIS CHILE SAUCE COMBINES THE POBLANO and chipotle chiles used extensively in the cuisine of the state of Puebla. Poblano chile, often used for stuffing, is also sliced into rajas *(strips) for sauces and stews. Chipotle chiles may be found dry or canned in adobo, a tomato sauce with vinegar, onion and garlic.*

2 POBLANO CHILES, ROASTED AND PEELED (PAGE 111)

1 WHOLE CHICKEN BREAST

1 TABLESPOON VEGETABLE OIL

$\frac{1}{2}$ CUP CHOPPED ONION

8 CORN TORTILLAS

OIL FOR FRYING

1 CUP SALSA VERDE (PAGE 156)

1 CHIPOTLE CHILE, SEEDED AND FINELY CHOPPED

With a sharp knife, cut a slit in the poblano chiles and remove the seeds and stem. Slice the chiles into thin strips and set aside.

Simmer the chicken breast in salted boiling water for about 10 to 12 minutes, or until cooked but still tender and juicy. Remove the chicken from the broth and when cool enough to handle, finely shred it with your fingers.

In a frying pan, heat the oil over medium heat and sauté the onion and poblano strips until the onion is translucent. Add the shredded chicken and sauté for 2 minutes longer. Keep warm.

In a dry pan, warm each tortilla until it softens and becomes pliable, top with about 2 tablespoons of the chicken mixture, and roll up. In a frying pan, heat the oil over medium heat, almost to the point of smoking, and fry until golden brown. For crisper tacos, fry them 1 or 2 minutes longer. Transfer the tacos to paper towels to remove excess oil and keep warm.

Serve immediately, topped with the salsa and the chopped chipotle chile.

FLOUR TORTILLAS FILLED WITH HAM AND CHEESE

Burritas Norteñas   *2 servings.*

I HAVE CONCLUDED THAT THE BURRITO *is the Texas version of our* burrito, *from the northern states of Mexico, but sauced with their "chile con carne." Despite the fact that they are folded like a quesadilla, they are called* burritas, *and are always made with flour tortillas.* Burritas *are served for a light late dinner or a snack with the salsa of one's choice.*

Burritas, *like the traditional quesadillas, are usually heated on a* comal *(flat cast iron griddle), until the cheese melts. In Mexico, this is the traditional method to heat up any kind of tortilla. It works very well because it can be maintained at a relatively high heat for a long period of time, at least one hour, making it easy to maintain a steady supply of hot tortillas during a meal.*

4 SMALL FLOUR TORTILLAS

¼ LB (125 G) COOKED HAM, SLICED

¼ LB (125 G) MONTEREY JACK
   CHEESE, SLICED

½ CUP SALSA

On a hot, dry frying pan or *comal*, warm a flour tortilla slightly and fold it in half. Place a slice of ham and a slice of cheese inside and reheat the *burrita* in the dry frying pan until the cheese melts. Turn the *burrita* as often as necessary to avoid burning the tortilla.

Follow the same procedure with the remaining tortillas and serve warm with the salsa of your choice (see pages 145-160).

NORTHERN-STYLE TAQUITOS

Taquitos Norteños   *2 servings*

THESE TAQUITOS ARE COMMONLY SERVED *for Sunday brunch or for an easy and casual dinner. Prepare the poblano chiles beforehand and keep them refrigerated in a plastic container until ready to use.*

Poblano chiles are readily available in specialty stores and in the fresh produce department of your local supermarket, sometimes incorrectly labeled as pasilla chiles.

2 POBLANO CHILES, ROASTED AND
  PEELED (PAGE 111)

1 TABLESPOON VEGETABLE OIL

½ SMALL ONION, SLICED

4 EGGS, LIGHTLY BEATEN

SALT AND PEPPER

4 SMALL FLOUR TORTILLAS

1 CUP COOKED BLACK BEANS
  (PAGE 164)

With a sharp knife, carefully cut a slit in the chiles remove the seeds and stem. Slice the chiles into thin strips.

In a frying pan, heat the oil over medium heat and sauté the chile strips with the onion until the onion is translucent. Stir in the eggs, and add salt and pepper to taste. Continue stirring the egg mixture until the eggs are barely cooked. Keep warm.

Meanwhile, in a dry frying pan or *comal*, heat a flour tortilla, place 2 to 3 tablespoons of the egg mixture in the middle, and roll up. Repeat with the rest of the tortillas.

Serve immediately with hot black beans.

ZACATECAS-STYLE ENJITOMATADAS

Enjitomatadas Estilo Zacatecas　　　　　　　　　　　*4 servings*

ZACATECAS, THE LAND OF MY ANCESTORS, *is one of the most beautiful cities in northeast Mexico. Built around a magnificent baroque cathedral, it has maintained its wonderful colonial architecture. Zacatecas was originally a mining town with one of the richest silver veins in the world. In fact, in the 1800s, when Mexico was producing two thirds of the world's silver, a large part of it came from this area. It is a pity that silver is not mined in the amounts that were produced then, and that iron and coal mining have now substituted for this industry.*

Just by looking at the government buildings, museums, and theaters, you can still feel the atmosphere of what Zacatecas was in past centuries. One landmark is the steep and rugged hill called La Bufa, which overlooks the city and has become the symbol of the state. In what is called the Crestón de la Bufa (the Crest of the Bufa), a very advanced meteorology observatory was built after the 1910 revolution. The observatory is accessed by land and also by gondolas, which give those lucky enough to ride in them the opportunity to enjoy a magnificent view of the city. There are many ways to reach the top of La Bufa. In my opinion, the most exciting one is through a mine called El Edén.

The Franciscans were one of the very first orders to arrive in Zacatecas and founded the old Church of San Francisco with its beautiful convent, recently turned into the Rafael Coronel Museum, honoring the artist born in Zacatecas. The Goitia Museum is also a must-visit, not only because it holds art from many of the artists born in the state, but also for the architecture of its building.

I vividly remember the times when we took my grandparents to visit my grandmother's sisters, who never followed her to Mexico City. While the adults were visiting with las tías *(the aunts), as we called them, we played, racing up and down those steep and narrow streets. We loved to throw a ball and then race down the steps to get it, something that did not always happen and we ended up having to get the ball far down in La Plazuela, where we were not supposed to go. Most of the plazuelas or plazas have a fountain in the center, and of course it was a lot of fun for my cousins and me to go and sit by the fountain and play with the water.*

This is yet another recipe from my grandmother Mamá Jesusita, who always managed to have these enjitomatadas *ready for any of her grandchildren who decided to drop in to visit. The term "enjitomatada" or "enmolada" means that the tortillas, although dipped and served with a chile sauce, have no filling like an enchilada does. They are usually served as a side dish or as a light first course with cream and cheese on top.*

Enjitomatadas *go very well with* Milanesas *(page 76).*

2 LARGE TOMATOES, SEEDED AND
  QUARTERED

1/2 MEDIUM ONION

2 SMALL CLOVES GARLIC

2 SERRANO CHILES

1 TEASPOON VEGETABLE OIL

1/4 CUP CANNED TOMATO SAUCE

2 PACKETS (1 TABLESPOON EACH)
  INSTANT CHICKEN BOUILLON

OIL FOR FRYING

12 CORN TORTILLAS

1/2 CUP CRUMBLED *QUESO FRESCO* OR
  FETA CHEESE

1/2 CUP MEXICAN CREAM OR CRÈME
  FRAÎCHE (PAGE 148)

In a blender, process the tomatoes, onion, garlic, and chiles with about 1/2 cup water until well blended. In a small saucepan, heat the oil over medium heat and sauté the tomato mixture for a few minutes before adding the canned tomato sauce and chicken bouillon. Simmer the sauce for 5 to 8 minutes, or until it thickens. If necessary, adjust the liquid and quantity of canned tomato sauce for a more robust tomato flavor. Keep warm.

In a frying pan, heat the oil almost to the point of smoking. Quickly dip each tortilla in the hot oil, drain, and place on paper towels to absorb excess oil. Cover with paper towels to keep warm, until all the tortillas are done.

Dip each fried tortilla into the tomato sauce, fold in half, and place on a serving platter or divide them among individual plates, topped with cheese and cream.

FRIED TORTILLAS WITH MOLE POBLANO

Enmoladas   *4 servings*

MOLE POBLANO, *THE KING OF MEXICAN CUISINE! Legend has it that it was created by the nuns in the convent of Santa Rosa, in the city of Puebla. When the bishop announced the visit of Count Paredes y Marqués de la Laguna, the viceroy of colonial Mexico, Sor Andrea de la Asunción, the nun in charge of preparing a dish to impress him, quite unprepared for such a dignitary, raided the cupboards, selecting various spices, dry chiles, some almonds and peanuts, a few tortillas, tomatillos, and the final touch, a piece of bitter chocolate. It must have been a big responsibility to create a dish worthy of their guest.*

Mole poblano joins the Spanish and Mexican cuisines. The combination of sesame seeds and almonds brought by the Spaniards, but of Arabic origin, mixed to perfection with Mexican chiles, spices, and chocolate makes a delectable sauce, worth trying. Traditionally, mole poblano *is served with either chicken or turkey, and garnished with toasted sesame seeds.*

Enmoladas, as opposed to enchiladas, are not filled with chicken. They are another way of enjoying the delicious mole and a good way to use the leftover sauce. Serve hot as a first course or to accompany grilled meats.

Outside of Mexico, mole poblano *is available in jars in major supermarkets and specialty stores. Good brands to look for are La Costeña and Doña Maria. Once prepared, mole sauce freezes very well.*

1 1/2 TO 2 CUPS *MOLE POBLANO* (PAGE 61)

1/2 CUP CHICKEN BROTH

OIL FOR FRYING

8 CORN TORTILLAS

1/4 CUP FINELY CHOPPED ONION

1/2 CUP MEXICAN CREAM OR CRÈME FRAÎCHE (PAGE 148)

1/2 CUP CRUMBLED *QUESO FRESCO* OR FETA CHEESE

REFRIED BEANS (PAGE 168; OPTIONAL)

In a heavy saucepan, heat the *mole poblano* over medium heat. Cover and keep warm. If the mole is too thick, add some chicken broth. Because of all the thickening agents used, mole thickens very quickly, so keep the broth on hand while preparing the enmoladas.

In a shallow frying pan, heat the oil over medium-to-high heat. Using a slotted spatula, quickly fry the tortillas for about 2 seconds each. The tortillas should be very soft. Drain the tortillas on paper towels to remove excess oil. Keep warm until they are all fried. Immerse each tortilla in the hot mole, just to coat it with the sauce. Place two *enmoladas* on each plate, add more mole sauce, sprinkle with the onion, and top with the cream and cheese. Serve at once.

GUAJILLO CHILE ENCHILADAS

Enchiladas de Chile Guajillo   *4 to 6 servings*

DRIED GUAJILLO CHILES can be found in major supermarkets, usually in cellophane bags. They are very similar in shape and color to New Mexico chiles grown in the Rio Grande Valley.
  Serve these enchiladas with scrambled eggs on the side for a very Mexican brunch.

4 TO 6 DRY *GUAJILLO* OR NEW MEXICO CHILES

½ CUP CHICKEN BROTH, HOT

2 LARGE TOMATOES, SEEDED AND CHOPPED

¼ CUP CHOPPED ONION

2 LARGE CLOVES GARLIC

1 TABLESPOON VEGETABLE OIL, PLUS ADDITIONAL OIL FOR FRYING

SALT AND PEPPER

8 TO 12 CORN TORTILLAS

½ CUP CRUMBLED *QUESO FRESCO* OR FETA CHEESE

½ CUP MEXICAN CREAM OR CRÈME FRAÎCHE (PAGE 148)

Wipe the chiles clean with a damp paper towel. Break off the stems and shake out the seeds. In a small bowl, soak the chiles in the broth for about 10 minutes, or until soft. In a blender, mix the chiles and the soaking liquid with the chopped tomato, onion, and garlic until well blended.

In a small saucepan, heat the oil over medium heat and fry the chile mixture, stirring. Bring the chile sauce to a boil, add salt and pepper to taste, and simmer for 10 to 12 minutes, or until the sauce has thickened. Remove from the heat and keep warm.

Heat the oil in a small frying pan, almost to the point of smoking. Quickly fry the tortillas for about 2 seconds each. Drain each tortilla on paper towels to remove the excess oil. Immerse each tortilla in the hot salsa, just enough to coat it. Place two enchiladas on each plate, add more salsa, sprinkle with cheese, and top with the cream.

HOMEMADE CORN TORTILLAS

Tortillas de Maiz Hechas en Casa　　　　　*Yield 15 to 20, depending on size and thickness*

NO MATTER HOW GOOD *store-bought tortillas may be, homemade ones are always the best. Granted, they are a bit time consuming, however, they are certainly an option when important guests are coming for dinner and you want to impress them with a magnificent Mexican meal.*

2 CUPS MASECA OR MASA HARINA
　　CORN FLOUR

¹/₂ TEASPOON SALT

1¹/₄ CUPS WARM WATER

A TORTILLA PRESS OR AN
　　ELECTRIC TORTILLA MAKER

Place the corn flour and salt in a food processor with a metal blade. With the motor running, pour the warm water through the feed tube in a steady stream. Let the motor run until the dough forms a ball, scraping the sides to keep dough together. If dough feels dry, add 1 to 2 tablespoons of water; the *masa* should feel fluffy and light. Divide the masa into twelve to fifteen small balls and place in a bowl covered with a damp cloth to keep them moist at all times. Unused *masa* can be stored in the refrigerator for several days. If a food processor is not available, use your hands to mix the corn flour with salt, adding the warm water slowly until well mixed and the *masa* feels fluffy and light.

If you are using a tortilla press, cut two pieces of plastic wrap and lightly sprinkle them with water, shaking off the excess. Line the base of the press with one sheet of the dampened plastic wrap. Place a ball of *masa* in the center, cover with the other sheet of plastic, and lower the top of the press, pushing the handle down. Lift the handle and gently smooth out entire tortilla surface on both sides, to facilitate the peeling off of the plastic. Carefully peel away the top plastic and place your left hand under the tortilla. Flip the tortilla onto your right hand, so the plastic underneath it is now on top, and gently peel away the remaining plastic.

Slide the tortilla from your hand onto a very hot griddle or *comal*, and cook until the top begins to puff. Turn the tortilla and let it cook for about 2 minutes longer. Be careful not to overcook the tortillas, or they will harden. Remove each tortilla from the griddle and wrap in a cloth napkin to keep warm.

If you are using an electric tortilla maker, follow the manufacturer's instructions for either flour or corn tortillas.

Corn tortillas keep very well in the refrigerator, wrapped in a cloth and inside a plastic bag, and can be reheated in a dry frying pan or *comal*.

QUICK POBLANO ENCHILADAS

Enchiladas Rápidas de Mole   *4 servings*

IN THIS RECIPE, THE POBLANO CHILES do not have to be roasted, but only wiped clean, stemmed, and seeded, cutting down the preparation time considerably. This poblano sauce can also be used for pasta.

These quick enchiladas may be served as a first course, instead of soup or to accompany breaded chicken breasts (page 58) or Milanesas (page 76).

2 LARGE POBLANO CHILES, STEMMED AND SEEDED (PAGE 111)

½ CUP MILK

1 TEASPOON BUTTER

½ SMALL ONION, SLICED INTO RINGS

1 CUP MEXICAN CREAM OR CRÈME FRAÎCHE (PAGE 148)

SALT

VEGETABLE OIL FOR FRYING

8 CORN TORTILLAS

½ LB (250 G) FARMERS CHEESE, THINLY SLICED

In a blender, purée the chiles with the milk. In a small saucepan, melt the butter over medium heat and sauté the onion until translucent. Add the chile mixture and fry it for 2 to 3 minutes. Mix in ½ cup of the Mexican cream and simmer gently for about 2 minutes. Remove from heat and keep warm.

In a frying pan, heat the oil and lightly fry the tortillas on both slides. Transfer to paper towels to remove excess oil. Dip each tortilla into the sauce, place two slices of cheese in the middle, and fold in half. Add more sauce on top, and garnish the enchiladas with a swirl of cream.

Divide the enchiladas among four plates and serve at once.

MOLE POBLANO
ENCHILADAS

Enchiladas de Mole Poblano   *4 servings*

THIS IS THE PERFECT USE for leftover mole poblano *sauce. While assembling the enchiladas, they can be kept warm on an ovenproof serving platter or baking dish, in a very low oven, until ready to be served. Also, keep in mind that mole thickens very quickly. It is best to keep some extra chicken broth on hand to thin the sauce while preparing the enchiladas.*

1 WHOLE CHICKEN BREAST

1 STALK CELERY WITH LEAVES

$^1/_2$ MEDIUM ONION, CUT IN HALF

2 CUPS *MOLE POBLANO* (PAGE 61)

1 CUP CHICKEN BROTH

VEGETABLE OIL FOR FRYING

12 CORN TORTILLAS

$^1/_2$ CUP MEXICAN CREAM OR CRÈME
FRAÎCHE (PAGE 148)

$^1/_2$ CUP CRUMBLED *QUESO FRESCO* OR
FETA CHEESE

In salted boiling water, cook the chicken breast with the celery and a one of the onion halves for about 10 to 12 minutes. Drain the chicken breast and cool, reserving the broth. Discard the celery and onion. When cool enough to handle, shred the chicken with your fingers and set aside. Thinly slice the remaining onion.

In a heavy saucepan, gently heat the mole, covered to avoid splattering. Add $^1/_2$ cup of chicken broth to lighten the sauce.

In a shallow frying pan, heat the oil over medium-to-high heat and quickly fry the tortillas. Drain the excess oil on paper towels. Keep warm.

Immerse a tortilla in the hot mole, to coat it with the sauce. Place the tortilla on a plate, add 2 tablespoons of the shredded chicken in the middle, and fold in half. Repeat the process with all the tortillas, placing three enchiladas on each plate. Spoon more hot mole sauce over the enchiladas and top with the slices of onion, cream, and cheese. Serve at once with a bowl of hot *Frijoles de la Olla* (page 164).

PENEQUES IN TOMATILLO SAUCE

Peneques en Salsa Verde   *4 servings*

PENEQUES *ARE SMALL CORN TORTILLAS, a bit thicker than a regular tortilla, folded in half and sealed all around. In Mexico, they are sold by* marchantas *(street vendors), in markets, and sometimes outside the big grocery stores. If you are looking for better quality tortillas for a particular dish, these women usually carry a basket with small tortillas and* peneques *made with the best* masa *available. They are sold by the dozen and are a bit more expensive than the ones sold in stores.*

Peneques are stuffed with cheese and fried, and may be served in either tomatillo or tomato sauce. These make a tasty merienda *(light supper), a relatively fast meal if the salsa is prepared in advance. Where* peneques *are not available, here is an easy version you might like to try.*

12 TOMATILLOS, HUSKS REMOVED AND WASHED

4 TO 6 SERRANO CHILES, STEMMED AND CHOPPED

½ CUP ONION, CHOPPED

½ CUP FRESH CILANTRO LEAVES, WASHED

1 TEASPOON VEGETABLE OIL

8 CORN TORTILLAS

½ LB (250 G) MANCHEGO OR MONTEREY JACK CHEESE, SLICED

OIL FOR FRYING

½ CUP MEXICAN CREAM OR CRÈME FRAÎCHE (PAGE 148)

SALT

In a small saucepan, cover the tomatillos and chiles with water. Bring the water to a boil and simmer for about 5 to 7 minutes, or until they change in color to a lighter green. With a slotted spoon, transfer the tomatillos and chiles to a blender with ¼ cup of the hot cooking liquid, the onion and cilantro, and process until the mixture is well blended.

In a small saucepan, heat the oil over medium heat, add the tomatillo mixture, and add salt to taste. Bring the sauce to a boil and simmer for 4 to 5 minutes, or until the sauce thickens. Remove from the heat and keep warm.

On a dry frying pan or *comal*, quickly warm each tortilla until it is pliant and can be folded easily without breaking. Place a slice of cheese on one half and fold the other half over it.

In a frying pan, heat the oil almost to the point of smoking and quickly fry each *peneque*, until the cheese starts to melt. Drain on paper towels to remove excess oil, and keep warm. Place on a serving platter or individual plates, cover with the hot salsa, and garnish with the cream.

NAYARIT-STYLE
PRAWN TACOS

Tacos de Camarón Estilo Nayarit   *2 servings or 8 tacos*

FOR *MANY YEARS OUR BEST FRIENDS* and neighbors in Mexico City were a family of Lebanese descent from the port of Veracruz. They were no different from other people living on the coast, in that they favored seafood over beef. Eventually, for health reasons, Susana Banduni, the daughter, moved to Tepic, in the Pacific coastal state of Nayarit, land of the Huichol Indians, and of wonderful seafood. This recipe was one of her favorites and it became a highlight of my visits.

These delicious tacos are different from the ones we serve in Mexico City in that they are filled with prawns instead of chicken or beef, and are served with shredded cabbage instead of lettuce. This variation of the regular taco, in my opinion, is a true gastronomic success!

32 PRAWNS (HEADS REMOVED)

1 LIME, HALVED

SALT

8 CORN TORTILLAS

OIL FOR FRYING

2 GARLIC CLOVES

1 CUP *SALSA VERDE CON AGUACATE*
    (PAGE 157)

1 SMALL CABBAGE, FINELY SHREDDED

OLIVE OIL FOR DRESSING

PEPPER

In salted boiling water, cook the prawns for about 2 minutes, or until red and firm. Drain and cool. Carefully peel the prawns, removing the tail, and rub each with lime. Season with salt and set aside.

In a dry frying pan or *comal*, warm each tortilla until soft, place two or three prawns on it, and roll the tortilla as tightly as you can. If necessary, use a toothpick to hold each tortilla in place. Heat the oil in frying pan and sauté the garlic cloves until browned. Remove the garlic from the oil and fry each taco until crisp. Drain on paper towels to remove the excess oil, and keep warm.

Serve the prawn tacos topped with the avocado salsa and the cabbage, dressed with olive oil and lime juice, and seasoned with salt and pepper. Pour the remaining salsa into a small bowl or *salsera* so people can add more salsa to their tacos if they so desire.

CACTUS PAD, POBLANO CHILE, AND CHORIZO QUESADILLAS

Quesadillas de Nopales con Poblano y Chorizo

2 servings or 8 quesadillas

QUESADILLAS ARE THE FAVORITE SNACK in Mexico. They are very versatile, easy to make and light enough to be served at any time of the day. Quesadillas are usually accompanied with salsa or guacamole.

6 CACTUS PADS (PAGE 171), CHOPPED INTO BITE BITE-SIZE PIECES

1 TEASPOON VEGETABLE OIL

2 POBLANO CHILES, ROASTED, PEELED, AND SEEDED (PAGE 111)

1/2 SMALL ONION, SLICED INTO RINGS

1/2 LB (250 G) CHORIZO SAUSAGE

1/2 CUP CRUMBLED *QUESO FRESCO* OR FETA CHEESE

8 CORN TORTILLAS

1/2 CUP SOUR CREAM

2 TABLESPOONS 2% MILK

Heat a dry pan and slowly cook the cactus over a very low heat for about 8 to 10 minutes, stirring, or until the natural sap of the pads has evaporated completely. In a frying pan, heat the oil over medium heat and fry the chile strips and onion until the vegetables are barely cooked. Add the pads and continue frying the vegetables for another 2 minutes. In a separate pan with very little oil, fry the chorizo until crumbly and add to the vegetables. Stir in half of the cheese, and remove from the heat. Keep the mixture warm.

Reheat the dry frying pan and heat the tortillas until soft. Combine the sour cream with the milk. Fill each tortilla with 1 to 2 tablespoons of the vegetable mixture, fold the tortilla in half, and serve at once, topped with the sour cream mixture and more cheese if desired.

MUSHROOM
QUESADILLAS

Quesadillas de Hongos   *2 servings or 6 to 8 quesadillas*

SOME RESTAURANTS IN MEXICO *serve small quesadillas—*quesadillitas*—as appetizers. The filling varies, depending on the region. The one thing in common is that they are always served either with guacamole or a spicy salsa.*

6 TO 8 HOMEMADE CORN TORTILLAS,
   UNCOOKED (PAGE 130)

2 TABLESPOONS VEGETABLE OIL, PLUS
   ADDITIONAL OIL FOR DEEP-FRYING

½ CUP CHOPPED ONION

2 TO 3 CLOVES GARLIC, CHOPPED

2 TO 3 SERRANO CHILES, MINCED

4 CUPS SLICED MUSHROOMS

½ CUP SOUR CREAM OR MEXICAN
   CREAM

½ CUP CHOPPED FRESH CILANTRO

In a medium-size saucepan, heat 2 tablespoons of oil over medium heat, add the onion and garlic, and sauté until the onion is translucent. Stir in the chiles and mushrooms and fry for 2 to 3 minutes, or until the mushrooms are barely cooked. Remove from the heat, add the sour cream, and stir in the chopped fresh cilantro. Set aside and keep warm.

Heat the oil in a deep frying pan. Spoon 1 to 2 tablespoons of the vegetables into half a tortilla, fold over the remaining half to form the quesadilla, and press the edges together. Fry each quesadilla in the hot oil, turning it once, until golden brown. Drain on paper towels to remove excess oil. Serve at once.

QUESADILLAS WITH POTATO AND CHORIZO

Quesadillas de Papa con Chorizo   *2 servings or 6 to 8 quesadillas*

QUESADILLAS, EITHER FOR A SNACK or to accompany a soup, are always served with a good salsa or at least with canned jalapeño or chipotle chiles. The quesadilla is broken open, and the salsa or chiles placed in the middle.

2 LARGE RED POTATOES, PEELED AND QUARTERED

1 TEASPOON VEGETABLE OIL, PLUS ADDITIONAL OIL FOR DEEP-FRYING

½ LB (250 G) CHORIZO SAUSAGE

SALT AND PEPPER

6 TO 8 HOMEMADE CORN TORTILLAS (PAGE 130)

In salted boiling water, cook the potatoes for about 8 to 10 minutes, or until soft. Remove from the heat, drain, and mash. Set aside and keep warm.

In a frying pan, heat 1 teaspoon of oil over medium heat. Add the chorizo and quickly sauté until crumbly. Stir in the mashed potatoes and mix well. Season the mixture with salt and pepper, and keep warm.

Heat oil in a deep frying pan. Spoon 1 to 2 tablespoons of the potato mixture onto half of an uncooked tortilla, fold over the remaining half to form the quesadilla, and press the edges together. Fry each quesadilla in the hot oil until golden brown. Drain on paper towels. Serve at once with the salsa of your choice.

SHREDDED BEEF FLAUTAS WITH AVOCADO SAUCE

Flautas con Salsa de Aguacate   *4 servings*

THE WORD FLAUTA, *meaning "flute," refers to a thin, rolled taco. They are usually longer than the average taco, although flautas can also be made with regular small tortillas. The beautiful color of the avocado sauce makes this tempting dish most attractive.*

Avocados grew in Mexico, Africa, and Polynesia long before they were planted in Florida. Records show that although this magnificent pear-shaped fruit has been grown commercially since the 1900s, English North America did not totally accept the fruit until the 1950s. When I came to Canada in 1976, avocados were hard to find. They come in a variety of sizes, ranging from very small, such as the criollo variety, to large such as the Haas avocado. Some have a leathery, rough peel and others a very smooth one, depending on where they are grown. Big exporters of Mexican avocados are in the states of Puebla, Querétaro, and Michoacán.

In addition to containing monounsaturated fat, the "good" fat that helps to lower the cholesterol, avocados are also rich in vitamin B6, and contain about 60% more potassium than bananas. Potassium is an important nutrient essential for all our body cells, and is also a good source of folate, which helps in the formation of hemoglobin.

1 LB (500 G) FLANK STEAK

2 MEDIUM-RIPE AVOCADOS, PEELED AND PITTED

1 TO 2 SERRANO CHILES, CHOPPED

1 TABLESPOON LIME JUICE

SALT AND WHITE PEPPER

12 CORN TORTILLAS

VEGETABLE OIL FOR FRYING

¾ CUP CRUMBLED *QUESO FRESCO* OR FETA CHEESE

Chop the flank steak into chunks of about 2 inches. In salted boiling water, cook the meat about 15 minutes, or until you can easily shred it. Drain and cool, reserving ¾ to 1 cup of the broth. Shred the chunks of meat with your fingers and set aside.

In a blender, process the avocados with the chiles, lime juice, and of the reserved broth until completely puréed. The avocado sauce should be smooth and not very thick. Season with salt and pepper and keep at room temperature.

In a dry pan or *comal*, warm each tortilla to soften it, and fill it with about 1 to 2 tablespoons of the shredded steak, and roll tightly to form a thin taco.

In a frying pan, heat the oil over medium heat and fry the flautas in batches of 3 or 4, depending on the size of your pan. Flautas should be golden brown and crisp. Drain on paper towels to remove the excess oil and keep warm.

Divide the *flautas* among four plates and serve at once with the avocado sauce on top. Garnish with a generous amount of cheese.

STEAK AND CHEESE SOFT TACOS

Tacos de Bistec con Queso   *2 servings or 6 tacos*

TACOS ARE THE MEXICAN SNACK *par excellence.* Taquerías *are found all over Mexico City, near government offices, hospitals, movie theaters, schools—wherever there is a heavy traffic of people. On street corners you see vendors with big baskets covered with a cloth to keep the popular* tacos de canasta *(basket tacos) warm. Among the locals, this profitable business is called "the underground economy," meaning that vendors are in business but do not pay rent or taxes.*

Well-established taquerías *like El Farolito, among many others, are worth a visit. The variety of tacos and salsas they offer is amazing, always made with small and almost paper-thin fresh tortillas, which by Mexican standards are no longer fresh after one day. However, they are never wasted. Thrifty cooks usually will cut old tortillas into quarters, fry them until crisp, and serve them as* totopos, *the Mexican name for "nachos," to accompany refried beans, when these are served as a side dish.*

For these soft tacos, be sure to get plain roulades and not the cured or marinated ones. These tacos go very well with the Salsa de Pasilla con Tomate Verde.

---

1 LB (500 G) BEEF ROULADES OR THIN
   SIRLOIN STRIPS

SALT AND PEPPER

1 TEASPOON MAGGI SAUCE

1 TEASPOON WORCESTERSHIRE SAUCE

1 TEASPOON VEGETABLE OIL

6 SMALL CORN OR FLOUR TORTILLAS

1/2 LB (250 G) MANCHEGO OR
   MONTEREY JACK CHEESE

JUICE OF 1 LIME

1 CUP *SALSA DE PASILLA CON TOMATE VERDE*
   (PAGE 152)

With a very sharp knife, cut the beef into bite-size pieces. Sprinkle with salt and pepper, add the Maggi and Worcestershire sauces, and mix well.

In a nonstick frying pan, heat the oil over medium heat and sauté the meat for about 2 minutes, or until barely cooked. Remove from the heat and keep warm.

In a dry frying pan over medium heat, quickly warm a tortilla, and place 1 or 2 slices of cheese on top, until it melts. Transfer the tortilla to a serving plate, add 2 or 3 tablespoons of the meat, sprinkle with lime juice, and fold in half. Repeat with the other tortillas. Serve at once with the salsa. Keep in mind that tortillas become soggy very quickly.

SWISS ENCHILADAS

Enchiladas Suizas   *4 servings*

THE NAME FOR THESE ENCHILADAS *deserves an explanation. It is not going to be brief, but I think you will find it interesting.*

Enchiladas are usually made with a chile-based sauce. These enchiladas, however, have a cream-based sauce, and the chile is just a flavoring. I don't think there is any other restaurant in Mexico that serves baked enchiladas with a cream-based sauce, except the Sanborn's Restaurants. And here is where the story begins.

La Casa de los Azulejos (The House of Tiles), located in the Centro Histórico *(Historic Center) of Mexico City, was where the first Sanborn's Restaurant opened for business in 1919. This beautiful building was originally the home of the counts of the Orizaba Valley, descendants of Hernán Cortés, the Spanish conquistador. It is a magnificent example of the Spanish colonial architecture. This unique building and the Casa del Marqués de Ramos in Lima, Perú, are considered by experts to be the only such buildings outside Spain, masterly preserved for almost five hundred years.*

With the fall of the Aztec empire on August 13, 1521, a chapter in history of more than two hundred years of one of the most extraordinary cultures of America came to an end. Cortés began organizing the political, economic and religious life of La Nueva España or New Spain, and one of the very first things he did was to provide his best men with land where they could build homes and start a family. Cortés gave them a few years either to bring a wife from Spain, or to marry an Indian. Thus commenced the amazing conversion of the New World to Catholicism.

The history of the palace is divided into three stages. The first started around 1530, at the onset of the colony, when construction began on a modest house built for the first count of Orizaba. In the course of several decades, the house was passed on to the different heirs, who made additions to the house to accommodate their family necessities. This first period ended in approximately 1828 with the death of the seventh count, who decorated the already majestic house with the blue tiles known as Talavera of the Queen. This is how the name the "House of Tiles" came about.

During the second period, perhaps the one with most changes, the Orizaba heirs struggled to keep the house by mortgaging the property several times. During this period, there were many wealthy people among the Mexican aristocracy who wanted to buy this magnificent property, situated across from the imposing Church and Convent of San Francisco and on the same street where other splendid mansions had been built.

Rafael Martinez de la Torre, a well-known businessman and a good friend of the family, bought the property and lived in the house for only ten years, during which he organized literary gatherings with the most prestigious poets and writers of that time. He died and the property was sold to the Iturbe family, who only lived in the house very briefly. In fact, they were living in Paris when they decided to rent the house to two Americans in the restaurant business, the Sanborn brothers, Walter and Frank. The government was severely criticized for allowing the Iturbe family to rent such a property to foreigners. The deal went through with the condition that the building would be properly maintained and the architecture preserved.

The third stage of the House of Tiles began in 1919, when the Sanborn Brothers converted the house into a restaurant, introducing sandwiches and the so-called "American" coffee, among other things to Mexico.

These entrepreneurs not only maintained and preserved the colonial style of the building but, coached by prestigious architects, added their own touch. One of the most important changes is the glass vault ceiling that covered the beautiful courtyard and permitted the painting of murals by such famous muralists as Diego Rivera and Jose Clemente Orozco.

It is quite an experience to visit this restaurant to admire the building and to try the famous Enchiladas Suizas. If you ever happen to be in the area, this is a must-visit. The second floor of the house was later opened for business and, from the balconies, you can admire the beautiful French architecture of the Palace of Fine Arts on one side, and on the other, the magnificent building of the old Post Office. If you don't look down to the millions of cars on the streets, you will feel transported to another era.

In the meantime, until you are able to pay a visit to Mexico City and to La Casa de los Azulejos, here is a sensational recipe that my good friends Polo and Nancy Aguado shared with me and that will certainly tempt your tastebuds.

1 LARGE CHICKEN BREAST

½ CELERY STALK WITH LEAVES

¼ SMALL ONION

2 TABLESPOONS CORNSTARCH

2 CUPS WHIPPING CREAM

½ CUP CHOPPED BLACK OR GREEN OLIVES

3 GREEN ONIONS, CHOPPED

¼ CUP CHOPPED SERRANO CHILES, SEEDED

SALT AND PEPPER

VEGETABLE OIL FOR FRYING

12 CORN TORTILLAS

1 CUP SHREDDED MANCHEGO OR FARMER CHEESE

In salted boiling water, cook the chicken breast with the celery and onion for about 10 to 12 minutes. Drain the chicken breast and cool, reserving the chicken broth for future use. Discard the celery and onion. When cool enough to handle, shred it with your fingers and set aside.

In a small bowl, dissolve the cornstarch in ¼ cup of the whipping cream. In a saucepan, mix the dissolved cornstarch with the remaining whipping cream and heat over medium heat, stirring, until the cream starts to boil. Add the olives, onions, chiles, and salt and pepper to taste. Preheat the oven to 350°F.

Remove the sauce from the heat and keep it warm. Mix about ½ cup of this cream sauce with the shredded chicken. Set the chicken and the rest of the cream sauce aside.

In a frying pan, heat the oil over medium-to-high heat almost to the point of smoking. Using a spatula, quickly dip each tortilla in the hot oil and transfer to paper towels to drain. Keep them warm until you have finished frying all the tortillas.

Dip a tortilla into the cream sauce, add 2 tablespoons of the chicken, and roll up. Place the enchilada in a baking dish. Repeat this process with the rest of the tortillas. Spoon the remaining sauce over the enchiladas and cover with the cheese. Bake the enchiladas for about 8 to 10 minutes, or until the cheese is melted and they are heated through. Serve at once.

TACOS FILLED WITH SHREDDED PORK IN ACHIOTE SAUCE

Tacos de Cochinita Pibil   *4 servings*

THE BEST ACHIOTE (ANNATTO) comes from the Yucatan Peninsula, where it is very popular and the main seasoning in the famous cochinita pibil, *a traditional Yucatan dish. You can tell if the condiment is fresh because of the aroma it exudes even through the package. If it is old, the condiment will not have any flavor.*

Outside of Mexico, achiote is sold at specialty stores. Unused achiote will keep for at least two months covered with plastic wrap in a dry place without losing its flavor.

3 CLOVES GARLIC

¼ TEASPOON PEPPERCORNS

¼ TEASPOON GROUND CUMIN

¼ TEASPOON OREGANO, PLUS AN EXTRA DASH

¼ TEASPOON CINNAMON

1 CUP FRESH ORANGE JUICE

¾ CUP CIDER VINEGAR

1 (3.56 OZ/110 G) PACKAGE ACHIOTE

1 LB (500 G) PORK LOIN

½ MEDIUM YELLOW ONION, HALVED

1 LARGE RED ONION, SLICED

VEGETABLE OIL FOR FRYING

12 CORN TORTILLAS

JUICE OF ½ LIME

2 TO 4 SERRANO CHILES, SEEDED AND MINCED

In a *molcajete* or mortar and a pestle, crush 1 clove of the garlic and the peppercorns. Add the cumin, oregano, and cinnamon and mix well.

In a small bowl, combine the orange juice with ¼ cup of the vinegar, and mix in ½ of the achiote. Crush until the achiote is completely dissolved. Stir in the garlic mixture and mix well. Set aside.

Cut the pork loin into 2-inch chunks and cook in salted boiling water with one of the pieces of yellow onion. Lower the heat and simmer for about 15 minutes, or until the meat is tender. Drain and cool, reserving ½ cup of the broth. When cool enough to handle, shred it with your fingers and set aside.

In a blender, process the remaining quarter of yellow onion and the remaining 2 cloves of garlic with ½ cup of the meat broth until puréed. In a saucepan, heat about 1 tablespoon of oil over medium heat, add the onion mixture, and fry for 2 minutes. Add the shredded meat, the achiote mixture, and about ½ cup of pork broth. Sprinkle with salt to taste. Bring to a boil, lower the heat, and simmer for 8 to 10 minutes, or until the sauce thickens. Keep warm.

In a small saucepan, heat the remaining ½ cup vinegar, add the red onion and cook, covered, for about 4 to 5 minutes. Drain the red onions and set aside.

Meanwhile, heat the oil in a frying pan, almost to the point of smoking and quickly fry each tortilla, draining it on paper towels to remove excess oil. Fill a tortilla with about 2 to 3 tablespoons of the *cochinita pibil*, fold the tortilla in half, and place on a serving platter. Keep warm until all the tortillas have been filled.

Arrange slices of the red onion on top of the tacos and add more oregano. On a separate plate, squeeze the lime juice on the chiles, and serve these at the table for everyone to add as much or as little as they want to their tacos.

SALSAS

EVEN THOUGH THE TERM "SALSA" can be used to describe any kind of sauce, in Mexico, salsas always contain chiles and are served as a condiment, rather than as a dip. These can be prepared from virtually any chile or a combination of chiles, fresh or dried, usually mixed with tomatoes and/or tomatillos. The variety of salsas is endless and the different combinations provide you with something to enhance most every dish.

No Mexican meal is complete without salsa on the table. They are the indispensable accompaniment to *antojitos* and countless other dishes. Salsas are usually served freshly made because raw salsas, for example, are not good keepers. Normally, salsas are not prepared in batches and frozen because the quality and flavor is lost. If there are any leftovers, they may be finished off the following day.

There are a variety of bottled salsas that I recommend when a fresh salsa is not available. Good brands to look for outside of Mexico are La Costeña, La Valentina, Herdez and Bufalo.

Keep in mind that a simple dish is always enhanced by a good salsa.

HOMEMADE MAYONNAISE

Mayonesa Hecha en Casa *Yields 1½ cups*

THIS VERSATILE RECIPE HAS BEEN IN MY FAMILY since my children were little. To this day, my daughter uses it on top of pasta, vegetables, and rice. In my opinion, recipes that call for mayonnaise, and there a few in the appetizers section, are much more flavorful with homemade mayonnaise, if for no other reason, than because real eggs are used. Of course, commercial mayonnaise may be used.

Because it contains raw eggs, keep homemade mayonnaise refrigerated at all times. It keeps for up to one week.

2 EGGS

1 TABLESPOON CIDER VINEGAR

1 TABLESPOON MUSTARD

1 TEASPOON SALT

1 CUP VEGETABLE OIL

Break the eggs into a blender, and add the vinegar, mustard, and salt. Run the motor on high until the mixture emulsifies, about 2 to 3 minutes. Without stopping the motor, add the oil in a thin stream and let the mayonnaise blend until it thickens, another 2 minutes. If necessary, stop the motor and scrape down the sides with a rubber spatula before running the motor again.

CRÈME FRAÎCHE

Crema Espesa   *Yields 1 cup cream*

THE PERFECT TOPPING FOR ANTOJITOS, crème fraîche is an adequate substitute for the Mexican cream that is normally available in Mexican markets and often in specialty stores outside of Mexico. It is a thick, runny cream, lightly sour, and spreads freely over any sauce or the inside of a chicken or beef taco. Besides being used in most of the antojitos, it is very commonly served on top of beans.

1 CUP WHIPPING CREAM

2 TABLESPOONS BUTTERMILK

DASH OF SALT

In a glass or nonmetal bowl, combine the cream with the buttermilk, add the salt, and whisk until well combined. Cover the bowl with plastic wrap and let it stand in a warm place for 24 hours. A turned-off pilot gas oven works well, since it is usually warm with the heat from the pilot elements above.

Crème fraîche keeps very well for up to one week in the refrigerator, in a lidded container. Beat the cream with a wooden spoon before serving. If it becomes too thick, thin it with a bit of 2% milk.

GUACAMOLE

Yields about 1 to 1$\frac{1}{2}$ cups

THIS SECTION WOULD NOT BE COMPLETE *without my mother's guacamole. Her secret was, as she used to say,"a little olive oil and fiery serrano chiles." The hottest serranos are usually the smallest ones.*

Her molcajete *(stone mortar and pestle), from which she always served guacamole, stood out in the middle of the big table full of all the different taco fillings during any sort of birthday celebration or Sunday family gathering.*

2 LARGE RIPE AVOCADOS, PEELED

1 TEASPOON FRESH LIME JUICE

1 LARGE RIPE TOMATO, CHOPPED

2 TABLESPOONS MINCED ONION

2 TO 4 SERRANO CHILES, FINELY CHOPPED

1 TEASPOON OLIVE OIL

$\frac{1}{4}$ CUP CHOPPED FRESH CILANTRO

SALT

Reserving the pit, mash the avocados with a fork and sprinkle with the lime juice. Add the tomato, onion, and chiles to the mashed avocados and mix well. Stir in the olive oil and cilantro. Season the guacamole with salt to taste and serve at once at room temperature with the pit in the middle, covered with the guacamole, to prevent darkening.

CASCABEL CHILE SALSA

Salsa de Chile Cascabel   *Yields 1 to 1½ cups*

WHEN FRESH, THIS CHILE IS KNOWN AS manzano, *because of its apple shape and yellowish color, the dry version, called* cascabel *is dark red and very hot.* Cascabel *means "rattle," and the seeds make the sound of a rattle against the hollow chile. It is more commonly used dried than fresh.*

Serve in a salsera. *This flavorful salsa is a wonderful accompaniment to beef, pork, and fish tacos.*

6 DRY *CASCABEL* CHILES

¼ CUP VEGETABLE OIL

1 CUP CHICKEN BROTH

½ MEDIUM ONION

1 LARGE TOMATO, ROASTED AND PEELED

2 LARGE CLOVES GARLIC

¼ TEASPOON GROUND CUMIN

2 BAY LEAVES

SALT AND PEPPER

Wipe the chiles with a damp paper towel. In a frying pan, heat the oil almost to the point of smoking and quickly fry the chiles on all sides. Transfer to paper towels to remove excess oil. In a small bowl soak the chiles in the chicken broth for 15 to 20 minutes, or until soft.

Roast the tomato in a dry frying pan until the peel is charred. When cool enough to handle, peel and remove the seeds. Remove and discard the stem and seeds from the chiles, and transfer with the soaking liquid to a blender. Add the onion, tomato, garlic, cumin, bay leaves, and salt and pepper to taste. Blend to a soft paste, adding more chicken broth if necessary. The salsa should be slightly thick.

CHILE DE ARBOL AND GUAJILLO SALSA

Salsa de Chile de Árbol y Guajillo　　　　　　　　　*Yields 1½ to 2 cups*

CHILES DE ÁRBOL *ARE USUALLY* quite hot. *Adjust the piquancy by reducing or increasing the number of chiles used.*

Add crumbled queso fresco *or feta cheese on top, if this salsa is to be served as a dip with corn chips. It is the ideal salsa for barbequed pork or chicken.*

8 TOMATILLOS, HUSKED AND WASHED

10 DRY *CHILES DE ÁRBOL*

2 DRY *GUAJILLO* OR NEW MEXICO CHILES

½ CUP CHICKEN BROTH, WARM

1 LARGE TOMATO

1 LARGE CLOVE GARLIC

1 TEASPOON SALT

In a small saucepan, cover the tomatillos with water and boil for about 4 to 6 minutes, or until they change to a lighter green color. Drain and set aside. Stem the chiles and shake out the seeds. Wash them under running water and soak in the chicken broth for 15 minutes, or until soft.

Meanwhile, in a dry pan, roast tomato until peel is charred. When cool enough to handle, peel and seed the tomato.

In a blender, combine the chiles with the chicken broth, tomatillos, tomato, garlic and salt, and purée. Adjust the liquid to make a slightly thick salsa. Transfer the salsa to a serving bowl or *salsera*, and serve at room temperature.

PASILLA CHILE AND TOMATILLO SALSA

Salsa de Pasilla con Tomate Verde   *Yields 1 cup*

PASILLA CHILES ARE AVAILABLE AT SPECIALTY GROCERY stores, usually in small cellophane bags. They are used in moles or fried and coarsely chopped over tortilla and other soups. Serve this salsa with scrambled eggs or to accompany fried chicken, pork chops, or fish.

1 TO 2 DRY PASILLA CHILE(S)

½ CUP CHICKEN BROTH

1 TABLESPOON VEGETABLE OIL

¼ CUP CHOPPED ONION

2 CLOVES GARLIC, CHOPPED

6 TOMATILLOS, HUSKED, WASHED, AND
  CHOPPED

SALT

Under running water, wash the chile(s) and pat dry with a paper towel. With a small kitchen knife, cut them open and remove the seeds and stem. In a small bowl, soak the chiles in the chicken broth for 10 to 15 minutes, or until soft. Drain the chiles and chop finely.

In a small saucepan, heat the oil over medium heat and sauté the onion, garlic, and tomatillos, until the onion is translucent. Add the pasilla chiles and the reserved chicken broth. Simmer for 3 to 4 minutes, or until the sauce thickens. Adjust the liquid, if necessary, and season with salt to taste.

DRUNKEN SALSA

Salsa Borracha   *Yields 1 to 1^1/$_2$ cups*

THIS IS ONE OF THE MOST POPULAR *salsas in Mexico. Almost all* taquerías *serve* salsa borracha *because it goes so well with the popular* tacos al pastor *(tacos of thinly sliced marinated pork).*

Traditionally, this salsa was made with pulque, *a fermented alcoholic beverage extracted from the maguey cactus (agave), thus its name. Because* pulque *is not readily available anymore, beer or white wine is used instead.*

3 DRY PASILLA CHILES

^{3}/$_4$ CUP FRESH ORANGE JUICE

2 CLOVES GARLIC, CHOPPED

2 TABLESPOONS CHOPPED ONION

^{1}/$_4$ CUP DARK BEER OR WHITE WINE

SALT

^{1}/$_2$ CUP CRUMBLED *QUESO FRESCO* OR FETA CHEESE

Stem the chiles, shake out the seeds, and wash under running water. In a small bowl, soak the chiles in the orange juice for about 10 to 15 minutes, or until completely softened. Transfer the chiles and the soaking liquid to a blender. Add the garlic and onion and process until well blended.

Pour the chile mixture into a *salsera* or a ceramic bowl, add the beer, and season with salt. Serve the *salsa borracha* topped with a generous amount of *queso fresco*.

PICO DE GALLO

Pico de Gallo   *Yields 1 1/2 to 2 cups*

EVERY REGION IN MEXICO seems to have a different version of this salsa. *The literal translation of* pico de gallo *is "cock's beak." This version seems to be the most popular one. It is easy and fast to make, since most of the ingredients are usually on hand.*

1/2 CUP FINELY CHOPPED ONION

2 LARGE RIPE TOMATOES, PEELED, SEEDED AND CHOPPED

3 TO 4 SERRANO CHILES, FINELY CHOPPED

1/4 CUP CHOPPED FRESH CILANTRO

JUICE OF 1/2 LIME

1 TABLESPOON OLIVE OIL

SALT

In a glass bowl, combine the onion with the tomatoes, chiles, and cilantro. Add the lime juice and oil. Season the salsa with salt and mix well. Let the salsa stand, at room temperature, for at least 1 hour before serving.

Serve with tacos, quesadillas, and grilled meats, or as a dip with *totopos*, those delicious, fried, small pieces of corn tortilla made with stale corn tortillas.

RED SALSA WITH FRIED ANCHO CHILE

Salsa Roja con Chile Ancho Frito   *Yields about 1 to 1¼ cups*

THE AROMA OF ANCHO CHILES reminds me so much of kitchens in Mexico, a warm place where families gather around the table to exchange recipes and to talk about the latest family events, while helping in the preparation of the food. Somehow, chopping, peeling and stirring become less of a chore in such a friendly atmosphere.

This salsa with its distinct combination of chiles, one dry and sweet, and the other fresh and spicy hot, result in a fabulous salsa, ideal for grilled meats. When buying the dry chiles, make sure that they are soft to the touch and not crumbly, otherwise they will not be very flavorful.

1 DRY ANCHO CHILE

1 TEASPOON VEGETABLE OIL

1 LARGE CLOVE GARLIC

3 TABLESPOONS CHOPPED ONION

2 LARGE PLUM TOMATOES

2 TO 3 SERRANO CHILES, STEMMED

3 TABLESPOONS CANNED TOMATO SAUCE

SALT

Wipe the ancho chile clean, stem, and cut open to remove the seeds. In a small saucepan, heat the oil over medium heat, and fry the chile for about 2 minutes, or until barely crisp. Drain on paper towels to remove excess oil, reserving the oiled pan.

In a blender or food processor, purée the garlic, onion, tomatoes, serrano chiles, and the fried ancho chile with ½ cup water.

Reheat the same saucepan where the ancho chile was fried, over medium heat, and pour in the puréed ingredients. Add the tomato sauce, season with salt, and simmer for 5 to 8 minutes, or until the salsa has thickened slightly.

Serve at room temperature.

GREEN SALSA

Salsa Verde   *Yields 1½ cups*

VERSATILE CILANTRO, *also commonly known as Chinese parsley, is widely used in Asian, Caribbean, and Latin American cooking. It is used not only in salsas, but also in salad dressings, chutneys, and other sauces. It is the natural herb to combine with tomatillos and serrano chiles.*

To keep cilantro fresh in your refrigerator, trim the stems a bit, put the bunch in a glass with water, and cover the leaves with a plastic bag. It usually keeps for about a week or longer if you change the water every two days. Before cooking cilantro, separate the sprigs you are going to use, gently wash them in cold water, and dry on paper towels. Both the leaves and stems can be used.

This salsa is used in the popular Enchiladas Verdes, *fried tortillas that are dipped in the salsa, stuffed with shredded chicken breast, and garnished with Mexican cream and cheese. It is also used in the filling of* Tamales Verdes *(page 104).*

12 TOMATILLOS, HUSKED AND WASHED

4 TO 6 SERRANO CHILES

¼ CUP CHOPPED ONION

½ CUP CHOPPED FRESH CILANTRO

1 TEASPOON VEGETABLE OIL

SALT

In a medium-size saucepan, boil the tomatillos and chiles in enough water to cover them, for about 6 to 8 minutes, or until they change color to a lighter green. Drain the tomatillos and chiles and transfer them to a blender, reserving 1 cup of the boiling liquid. Add the onion, cilantro, and the reserved liquid, and process until well blended.

In a small saucepan, heat the oil over medium heat, stir in the tomatillo mixture, and bring the salsa to a boil. Lower the heat and simmer for 6 to 8 minutes, or until the salsa thickens. Season with salt to taste.

GREEN SALSA WITH AVOCADO

Salsa Verde con Aguacate

Yields about 1 to 1½ cups

THE AVOCADO GIVES A CREAMY consistency to an ordinary tomatillo salsa. Sprinkle a few drops of lime juice on the remaining half of the avocado with the pit, cover with plastic wrap and refrigerate for future use.

This salsa goes extremely well with pork chops, fish, or quesadillas, and it is a natural for Tacos de Camarón Estilo Nayarit *(page 134). Leftovers can be kept in the refrigerator for up to twenty-four hours without losing its beautiful color.*

8 MEDIUM TOMATILLOS, HUSKED, STEMMED, AND WASHED

3 TABLESPOONS CHOPPED ONION

1 LARGE CLOVE GARLIC

4 SERRANO CHILES, STEMMED

½ MEDIUM AVOCADO, PEELED

A FEW DROPS OF LIME JUICE

SALT

In a blender or food processor, combine the tomatillos, onion, garlic, chiles, avocado, lime juice, ¼ cup water, and salt to taste and purée until smooth. Add a bit of liquid if the salsa is too thick. Transfer the salsa a serving bowl or *salsera*, and serve.

TOMATO SALSA WITH CHILES DE ARBOL

Salsa Roja de Chile de Árbol

Yields about 1 cup

A GOOD SALSA AT THE TABLE can make the difference between a tasty meal and an ordinary one. Salsas have the power of transforming dishes. That is probably the reason why in the United States they seem to sell better than ketchup.

This is a smooth and hot salsa that goes very well on top of eggs, any style.

1 LARGE TOMATO

2 TO 3 DRIED *CHILES DE ÁRBOL*

1 TEASPOON VEGETABLE OIL

2 CLOVES GARLIC

¼ CUP CHOPPED ONION

2 TABLESPOONS CANNED TOMATO SAUCE

SALT AND PEPPER

CHOPPED FRESH CILANTRO FOR
  GARNISH

In a dry pan, roast the tomato until the peel is charred. When cool enough to handle, peel and remove the seeds. In a blender or food processor, purée the tomato and the chiles with ¼ cup water.

In a small saucepan, heat the oil over medium heat and sauté the garlic and onion until the onion is translucent. Stir in the tomato mixture; add the canned tomato sauce, and salt and pepper to taste. Bring the salsa to a boil, and simmer for 6 to 8 minutes, or until thick.

Serve at room temperature, garnished with chopped fresh cilantro.

PICKLED
JALAPEÑO CHILES

Chiles en Vinagre   *12 to 20 chiles*

THESE CHILES ARE QUITE HANDY. I keep them in a nice clear glass jar, and they are attractive enough to go directly from the refrigerator to the table. Red and green chiles may be combined, for a more colorful and enticing look. They also make a sensational present at Christmastime.

Although they can be served immediately, it is better to let the vegetables marinate for a couple of days in the refrigerator. Chiles en Vinagre *can be kept refrigerated for up to two months, if they last that long. They usually do not.*

12 JALAPEÑO OR 20 SERRANO CHILES

¼ CUP OLIVE OR VEGETABLE OIL

¾ CUP CIDER VINEGAR

1 LARGE ONION, SLICED INTO RINGS

4 LARGE CLOVES GARLIC, COARSELY
   CHOPPED

1 LARGE RAW CARROT, PEELED AND
   THINLY SLICED

1 MEDIUM RED PEPPER, SEEDED, CORED,
   AND SLICED

6 CAULIFLOWER FLORETS

1 BAY LEAF

¼ TEASPOON DRIED OREGANO

¼ TEASPOON DRIED THYME

6 TO 8 WHOLE PEPPERCORNS

SALT

8 MUSHROOM CAPS, SLICED

Wash the chiles under running water and make two cuts forming a cross on the tip of the chiles, so that the oil and vinegar will penetrate them while they are cooking.

In a deep saucepan, combine the oil and the vinegar. Add the onion, garlic, carrots, and red pepper. Bring the vegetables to a boil and simmer for about 5 to 8 minutes, or until the carrots are barely cooked. Add the chiles, cauliflower, herbs, and salt to taste. Continue simmering for another 8 to 10 minutes, or until the chiles have changed in color to a lighter green. Add the mushrooms about 5 minutes before the chiles are ready. The vegetables and the chiles should be crisp. Keep in mind that, because of the size difference, jalapeño chiles will take a bit longer to cook than serranos.

Let the pickled chiles cool and transfer them to a glass jar with a tight lid. Keep refrigerated.

BEANS
FRIJOLES

WHEN THE SPANIARDS ARRIVED IN TENOCHTITLÁN, later to be called New Spain, markets full of vendors from other regions already were displaying an amazing variety of goods to sell or trade and beans were no exception.

Paintings exhibited at the National Museum of History, in Chapultepec Castle, depict vendors displaying more than twenty different bean varieties native to Mexico. Among them, to name just a few, are black, brown, pinto, white, red, *canario*, *cacahuate*, *porraliño*, *piru*, *negro mecentral*, *alubia grande*, *blanco*, *flor de mayo*, *amarillo*, *tórrido*, *moro*, *garbancillo*, *ojo de cabra*, *mantequilla*, *pinto americano*, and *oyocote negro*. Of all these, the most common in central Mexico are black beans, pinto, *flor de mayo*, *alubia*, and *canario*.

Corn, beans, and squash are the three basic food elements in the New World. This is the reason why historians sometimes called them "the trinity of the Indians in the American continent." Beans have always been, and continue to be, the main staple of Mexican food. Today, beans are served more as a side dish than as a separate course, but very rarely are absent from any meal. My father, for example, would never end his main meal without a bowl of *Frijoles de la Olla* (page 164).

Cooked beans are blended into soup, used as a sauce on top of flautas, refried to accompany various antojitos, as a spread in tostadas, or in *tortas* (the Mexican sandwich). They can be served topped with cream or chopped chile and cilantro or with chicharrón, the fried pork rind Mexicans love to eat. The list is endless.

Beans are rich in protein, contain fiber, and are very inexpensive. A common phrase in Mexico when people complain about the high cost of living, is: *"Ya no alcanza ni para frijoles,"* which is very loosely translated, "One can't even afford to buy beans."

BEANS WITH BACON
AND BEER

Frijoles Borrachos   *4 to 6 servings*

LITERALLY MEANING "DRUNKEN BEANS," this recipe, like many others in Mexican cooking, calls on beer to add its singular flavor to the beans. And since Mexican beer is especially good, it is no wonder that it is frequently used in pork and chicken dishes as well. Black or pinto beans are equally good in this dish. Served with rice it can be a whole meal in itself.

¹/₂ TEASPOON VEGETABLE OIL

4 SLICES BACON, CHOPPED

¹/₄ CUP CHOPPED ONION

1 MEDIUM TOMATO, CHOPPED

2 TO 3 SERRANO CHILES, MINCED

2 CUPS COOKED BEANS (PAGE 164)

¹/₂ (12 OZ/355 mL) CAN LIGHT BEER

¹/₂ CUP CHOPPED FRESH CILANTRO

In a saucepan, heat the oil over medium heat, add the bacon, onion, tomato, and chiles, and sauté for 3 to 4 minutes, or until the onion is translucent and the bacon is cooked. Add the beans with their *caldo* (cooking liquid). Bring to a boil, lower the heat, and simmer for about 8 to 10 minutes to thicken the sauce. Add the beer and continue simmering for a few minutes more, to allow the flavors to blend.

Serve hot, garnished with cilantro, with warm Homemade Corn Tortillas (page 130).

BEANS IN THE POT

Frijoles de la Olla   *About 6 cups of beans*

IN A MEXICAN HOUSEHOLD, *there is always a freshly cooked pot full of beans. And if there is a baby in the family, a cup of the cooking liquid, called* caldo de frijol, *is reserved for the baby before the beans are fried and the liquid is thickened. My three-year-old grandson Sebastian had a taste of the caldo, and has loved black beans ever since, just like his daddy.*

This recipe goes a long way. You might like to freeze half and use the rest, for soup, to accompany another dish, or for refried beans.

It has been a while since we stopped using lard in our cooking; however, if you are really interested in having a delicious pot of beans for that special meal, use lard instead of oil.

2 CUPS BLACK OR PINTO BEANS

1 MEDIUM ONION, QUARTERED

2 TEASPOONS LARD, OR 1 TABLESPOON VEGETABLE OIL

2 SPRIGS EPAZOTE OR CILANTRO

1 TEASPOON COARSE SALT

CILANTRO TO GARNISH (OPTIONAL)

SERRANO CHILES TO GARNISH (OPTIONAL)

Pick over the beans and rinse them thoroughly. In a large pot, cover the beans with boiling water and soak for several hours or overnight. Before cooking the beans, discard the soaking liquid and add about 6 cups of water, one piece of the onion, 1 teaspoon of the lard, the epazote, and the salt. Bring the beans to a boil and simmer for 1 to 1½ hours, or until they are very soft. (If a pressure cooker is used, reduce the water to 4 cups and simmer 35 to 45 minutes.) Discard the cooked onion. Chop the remaining onion.

In a separate saucepan, heat the remaining lard over medium heat. Add 3 heaping tablespoons of drained beans and the chopped onion, and mash the beans while they cook with the onion. Add the remaining cooked beans with their liquid and the epazote, and bring to a boil. Add salt if necessary. Lower the heat and simmer the beans for 15 to 20 minutes more, or until the liquid is thickened slightly. Discard the epazote sprigs.

Serve hot, with chopped fresh cilantro and serrano chiles if desired.

BEAN SAUCE

Salsa de Frijol

Yields 1½ to 2 cups of sauce

THIS SAUCE, SPOONED OVER *stuffed poblano chiles, scrambled eggs, or tacos is quite flavorful and attractive. Serve this sauce hot and top with good* queso fresco, *where available, or mild feta cheese.*

1½ CUPS OF COOKED BLACK OR PINTO BEANS (PAGE 164)

1 TABLESPOON VEGETABLE OIL

2 TABLESPOONS MINCED ONION

In a blender, purée the beans with their *caldo* (cooking liquid) until puréed. The bean mixture should be runny.

In a frying pan, heat the oil over medium heat and sauté the onion until translucent. Add the bean mixture and continue cooking, stirring with a wooden spoon, for about 5 to 8 minutes, or until the beans are fried but still a bit runny.

SPANISH-STYLE BEANS

Frijoles a la Española   *4 to 6 servings*

ONE OF THE CHILES that the Spaniards took back to Spain was the sweet pimiento, or paprika, widely used now in Hungarian cooking, as well as in Spanish dishes.

Good Spanish or Mexican chorizo, which are flavored with different spices is essential for this recipe. Black or pinto beans may be used for this dish.

Almost a meal in itself, these beans can be served as a separate dish with good French bread or corn tortillas.

2 LARGE TOMATOES, ROASTED AND PEELED

2 TABLESPOONS CHOPPED ONION

1 TEASPOON VEGETABLE OIL

2 CHORIZO SAUSAGES (ABOUT ½ LB)

1 TABLESPOON PAPRIKA

2 CUPS COOKED BEANS (PAGE 164)

Roast the tomatoes in a dry pan until the peel is charred. When cool enough to handle, peel and remove the seeds. In a blender or food processor, blend the tomatoes and onion until puréed.

In a small saucepan, heat the oil over medium heat and sauté the chorizo until crumbled. Stir in the tomato mixture and the paprika, and cook for 4 to 5 minutes, or until the sauce has thickened slightly. Add the cooked beans, bring to a boil, and simmer for another 5 to 8 minutes, for all flavors to blend.

PINTO BEANS WITH ROASTED RED PEPPERS

Frijoles con Chiles Morrones   *4 servings*

THESE BEANS ENHANCE any meal. They team up beautifully with beef stews and grilled meats.

1 TEASPOON VEGETABLE OIL

1 SMALL ONION, CHOPPED

2 CLOVES GARLIC, CHOPPED

1 LARGE RIPE TOMATO, SEEDED AND
    CHOPPED

2 CUPS COOKED PINTO BEANS (PAGE 164)

2 LARGE CANNED ROASTED RED BELL
    PEPPERS, SLICED

SALT AND PEPPER

3 TO 4 SLICES TOASTED BREAD, CUBED

In a saucepan, heat the oil over medium heat and fry the onion, garlic, and tomato until the onion is translucent. Add about $1/4$ cup of drained beans, mash them to a paste, and cook the mixture, stirring continuously for 2 or 3 minutes, before adding the peppers and the rest of the beans with their liquid. Season with salt and pepper and simmer for 3 to 5 minutes, or until slightly thickened.

Serve hot, topped with the toasted bread.

REFRIED BEANS
WITH TOTOPOS

Frijoles Refritos con Totopos   *3 to 4 servings*

BEFORE SPANISH CUISINE ARRIVED *in the New World, it was already a product of several different influences. Cooking oil, for example, was introduced in Spain by the Arabs. After the conquest of Mexico, stews and vegetables changed with the addition of the oil brought by the Spaniards. This new ingredient served to prepare all kinds of* caldillos *such as the* Caldillo de Jitomate *(tomato sauce, page 29), the base of many soups and other dishes, by mashing tomato and garlic in a* molcajete *(a stone mortar and pestle), in some cases adding the native chiles, and then frying the mixture in oil, creating new and more refined meals.*

Although beans had been eaten plain, cooked only with the aromatic epazote, after the addition of cooking oil, they were fried with chorizo, mashed and spread on tostadas, and topped with cheese that the Europeans also brought to America along with other dairy products.

Generally, canned "refried" beans are not fried, but only mashed to a thick paste. The term refrito *(refried) however, means that beans have indeed been fried and then refried to attain the desired look and consistency. This added step is really the secret to a good side dish of refried beans.*

VEGETABLE OIL FOR FRYING

2 DAY-OLD CORN TORTILLAS, QUARTERED

¼ CUP FINELY CHOPPED ONION

1 CUP COOKED BLACK OR PINTO BEANS
(PAGE 164)

¼ CUP SHREDDED CHIHUAHUA OR
MONTEREY CHEESE

In a heavy frying pan, heat the oil over medium heat and fry the tortilla until golden brown and crisp. Place the fried tortillas on paper towels to absorb excess oil.

In the same frying pan, sauté the onion until translucent, add the beans, and mash them to a soft paste. Add the oil and keep stirring the beans, adding more oil a bit at a time, so the beans do not stick to the pan. Continue stirring until the beans are thick enough to spread on bread. The beans are ready when the color becomes darker and they no longer stick to the pan.

On a serving dish, mound the refried beans into a loaf, stick the *totopos* into the top, and garnish with the shredded cheese. Serve at once.

BAKED EGGS ON
REFRIED BEANS

Huevos al Horno con Frijoles Refritos   *2 to 4 servings*

THIS IS A SOPHISTICATED WAY *to serve fried eggs. In Mexico, eggs appear not only at breakfast or brunch but for a* merienda, *which is usually served to children in the early evening, or around 10:00 P.M. for adults. Café au lait or hot chocolate and* bizcochos *(sweet rolls) complement the* merienda.

▼▼▼▼▼▼▼▼▼▼▼▼▼▼▼▼▼▼▼▼▼▼▼▼▼

2 CUPS COOKED BLACK OR PINTO BEANS
(PAGE 164)

OIL FOR FRYING

4 EGGS

SALT AND PEPPER

1 TABLESPOON CHOPPED FRESH
CILANTRO

2 PICKLED JALAPEÑO CHILES, SLICED
INTO STRIPS (PAGE 159)

In a blender, purée the beans with some of their liquid, until smooth. In a frying pan, heat the oil over low heat and fry the puréed beans, stirring, for 6 to 8 minutes, or until they are no longer runny and you can form a soft ball. Preheat the oven to 350°F.

In an 8-inch (20-cm) baking dish, place a layer of beans, and form four indentations deep enough for the eggs. Break the eggs into the wells, sprinkle with salt and pepper, and garnish with the cilantro and chiles. Bake the eggs for about 8 to 10 minutes, or until they are barely cooked. Adjust the baking time depending on whether you want a runny or a hard egg yolk.

Serve with warm tortillas and more marinated jalapeño chiles.

SALADS, CREPES, AND VEGETARIAN CASSEROLES

ABOUT *NOPALES* (CACTUS PADS)

When the Indians from the northwestern coastal region of Aztlán, from which the Aztec name is derived, began their trek inland (the Aztec exodus), they were looking for the "promise land" that their Gods had said would be recognizable by way of an eagle perched on a *nopal* (a type of cactus) devouring a serpent.

Thus, the humble *nopal*, though only a perch, became part of the official emblem of modern Mexico. To my knowledge, no other country in the world incorporates its most characteristic, versatile and downright delicious food staple in the official seal. While corn, chile and beans are certainly mainstays of the Mexican diet, this is also the case in many other Latin American countries. Cactus pads, however, are unique to the highlands of Mexico, and a true delicacy.

Now, it seems that the old Aztec gods were not just of an epicurean bent. They were also looking after their children. The cactus leaf, it turned out, is nothing short of a miracle plant, as nutritionists and scientists have since discovered astounding characteristics in the unpretentious vegetable.

Extensively and imaginatively used in prehispanic and contemporary Mexican cuisine (there are now more than 150 different ways of cooking cactus). In Mexico alone, about 110 different species of cactus can be found. The maguey cactus produces *pulque*, the oldest fermented liquor in the Americas. In addition, the *tuna* (cactus pear) is one of the most refreshing, sweet, and juicy fruits you will ever taste, considering the very dry soil where it grows.

At this point, you are probably wondering if tequila and *mezcal* come from the maguey as well. I must clarify that these are obtained from different cacti. Tequila, from the *Agave tequilana* (blue) is grown according to law only in the states of Jalisco, Michoacán, and Nayarit. It is fermented as well as distilled; whereas pulque is only fermented. *Mezcal* is distilled but not fermented, and does not have to meet the rigid standards that govern the production of tequila. The agave that produces *mezcal* is grown mainly in the state of Oaxaca.

In the following pages, you will find a few simple ways to make your acquaintance with this humble yet magical desert plant. In this book, I have included recipes for a tasty soup, various salads, casseroles, quesadilla fillings, and also what is today a very popular cooler in Mexico City's trendy restaurants.

There is, however, a little preparation to be done before enjoying cactus. With a sharp knife, slice off any thorns or black nodes all around the edges and the sides of each pad, until it is completely clean. Chop the nopales according to the way you are going to serve them, and cook, very slowly and at low temperature, in a dry saucepan, for about six to eight minutes, or until the natural sap has completely evaporated and they look cooked. Now prepare the nopales according to the recipe of your choice.

In Mexican markets, it is very common to find an old vendor sitting beside a pile of cactus pads. Knowing a little bit about this preparation myself, it is an absolute delight to watch how fast and efficiently the removal of the thorns is done by such a person! There is certainly a lot of practice involved in this. It is almost as common to catch a tourist trying to get a picture of the vendor performing this everyday chore.

BABY POTATOES WITH POBLANO CHILES

Papitas Criollas con Rajas   *4 to 6 servings*

POTATOES ORIGINATED IN SOUTH AMERICA. *There is no other place in the whole world where you can find so many varieties in color as Perú: yellow, purple, white, brown, and black, and in so many different sizes and shapes: small, big, round, and oval.*

Potatoes were not cultivated in Mexico until after the Spaniards arrived. Soon after the conquest, however, they became an important part of soups and stews. In Mexico there are about six hundred varieties of potatoes, cultivated in different states of the Mexican Republic, like Puebla, Guanajuato, Michoacán, and the valley that surrounds Mexico City.

Even though potatoes arrived in Europe around 1534, it was not until the nineteenth century that the English and Irish discovered the vast nutrients in the potato and from then on it became an integral part of the diet of the Anglo-Saxon and Nordic people.

4 TO 5 POBLANO CHILES, ROASTED,
   PEELED, AND SEEDED (PAGE 111)

1 TABLESPOON VEGETABLE OIL

1 SMALL CLOVE GARLIC, MINCED

½ MEDIUM ONION, SLICED

1 FRESH TOMATO, CHOPPED

¼ CUP CANNED TOMATO SAUCE

1 LB (500 G) RED BABY POTATOES,
   BOILED AND PEELED

SALT AND PEPPER

1 CUP SOUR CREAM

¼ CUP 2% MILK

¾ CUP CRUMBLED *QUESO FRESCO* OR
   FETA CHEESE

Cut the chiles into ½ inch wide strips. In a saucepan, heat the oil and sauté the garlic, onion, and poblano chile strips for 2 minutes. Stir in the tomato, tomato sauce, and potatoes, and season with salt and pepper. Simmer for 2 to 3 minutes, or until the vegetables are cooked and the potatoes are heated through. Mix the sour cream with the milk. Just before serving, top with the sour cream mixture and the cheese.

BAKED CHAYOTE SQUASH

Chayotes al Horno   *4 servings*

THE SUBTLE FLAVOR OF THE CHAYOTE SQUASH makes it easy to combine with just about anything. There are two types of chayotes in Mexico; only the peel is different: One has a smooth peel and seems to be available outside Mexico, almost year-round in major supermarkets. The other one has a darker green, prickly peel and, for some reason, is not available as often. Both are quite common and are used interchangeably.

For a light lunch, add blanched, chopped almonds to the cooked chayotes, salt and pepper them, and serve them on their own or as a side dish to an omelet with a savory filling.

4 CHAYOTE SQUASH

SALT AND PEPPER

½ CUP SOUR CREAM

¼ CUP MILK

½ CUP GRATED CHIHUAHUA OR
  MONTEREY JACK CHEESE

Peel the chayotes with a potato peeler. Cut in half lengthwise, and remove the pits. Cook in boiling salted water for about 15 minutes, or until tender. Drain and discard the water. Preheat the oven to 350°F.

When cool enough to handle, slice the chayotes lengthwise or into cubes. Mix the sour cream with the milk. Place chayotes in an 8-inch square baking dish, sprinkle with salt and pepper, add the sour cream mixture, and cover with the cheese.

Bake the chayotes for 5 to 8 minutes, or until the cheese melts and the casserole is heated through. Serve hot as an accompaniment to any beef, pork or chicken dish.

WARM CACTUS PAD SALAD

Ensalada Caliente de Nopales   *2 servings*

IT IS MORE COMMON TO SERVE CACTUS PADS in cold salads; however, in this recipe, they are cooked and then lightly fried. This salad goes well with any meat or chicken dish, or can be served on its own as a first course.

1 TABLESPOON VEGETABLE OIL

½ SMALL ONION, SLICED

2 CLOVES GARLIC, CHOPPED

6 MEDIUM CACTUS PADS, COOKED (PAGE 171)

¼ CUP CHOPPED FRESH CILANTRO

SALT

2 TABLESPOONS CRUMBLED *QUESO FRESCO* OR FETA CHEESE

Heat the oil in a frying pan and sauté the onion and garlic until the onion is translucent. Add the cactus pads, the cilantro, and salt to taste. Continue frying for 2 or 3 minutes, or until they start to brown on the edges.

Serve this salad warm, garnished with the cheese.

JICAMA, RED ONION, AND ORANGE SALAD

Ensalada de Jícama y Cebolla Morada   *4 to 6 servings*

THE GROCERY STORES THAT CARRY SUCH FRESH PRODUCE *as cilantro and chiles usually carry jicamas as well. This juicy and refreshing vegetable is eaten in Mexico with lots of lime juice, salt, and piquín chile, the fiery and diminutive chile that can make you cough and sneeze, but gives fruit and vegetables alike the incomparable pungent sensation characteristic of spicy hot chiles. Where pequín chile is not available, ground cayenne pepper may be used instead.*

This colorful salad is ideal for a hot summer afternoon. It may be served as a first course, or between a fish course and a meat course to cleanse your palate.

1 MEDIUM JICAMA, PEELED

1 LARGE ORANGE, PEELED

JUICE OF 1 LIME

SALT

1 SERRANO CHILE, MINCED

½ CUP CHOPPED FRESH CILANTRO

½ MEDIUM RED ONION, THINLY SLICED
    INTO RINGS

DASH OF PIQUÍN CHILE

Slice the jicama into ¼-inch rounds and then into thin strips. Slice the orange into wedges. In a bowl, combine the jicama, lime juice, and salt, then add the orange, serrano chile, cilantro, and half of the onion. Let the salad sit for an hour.

Just before serving, toss the salad well so that the lime juice coats all the ingredients. Sprinkle the piquín chile on top of the salad and garnish with the remaining onion.

SPICY CARROT SALAD

Ensalada Fría de Zanahoria con Picante 4 to 6 servings

MEXICANS ARE VERY FOND OF CONDIMENTS, and Maggi sauce is a favorite. The combination of Maggi sauce and Worcestershire sauce with lime juice and piquín chile turns an otherwise ordinary carrot salad into an interesting and tasty one. It is very good with fried chicken, sandwiches, and fish. It is definitely a summer salad.

4 CARROTS, PEELED AND COARSELY
   GRATED

2 TABLESPOONS MAGGI SAUCE

2 TABLESPOONS WORCESTERSHIRE SAUCE

½ CUP LIME JUICE

DASH OF PIQUÍN CHILE OR CAYENNE
   PEPPER

Mix the shredded carrots with the Maggi and Worcestershire sauces, the lime juice, and the piquín chile until well combined. Serve the salad at room temperature.

SARDINE, TOMATO, AND FETA CHEESE SALAD

Ensalada de Sardinas   *4 servings*

SARDINES ARE AN EXCELLENT *source of protein and are high in calcium and iron. Some of the Spanish and Portuguese canned sardines come prepared in a tasty thick tomato sauce, or in olive oil. In Canada, these come in tomato sauce, with hot Tabasco peppers, or in mustard sauce. Any of these would be quite good for this highly nutritious and easy salad. If possible, prepare it a few hours in advance to let the juices of the tomatoes and the sardines marinate the rest of the ingredients.*

Serve as a first course with French bread or as a main dish with rice.

2 (3 OZ/90 G) CANS SARDINES IN TOMATO SAUCE

2 LARGE RIPE TOMATOES, SLICED

SALT AND PEPPER

¾ CUP CRUMBLED *QUESO FRESCO* OR FETA CHEESE

1 TABLESPOON EXTRA-VIRGIN OLIVE OIL

1 LARGE RIPE AVOCADO, PEELED AND SLICED

Cut the sardines in half. On a round serving platter, arrange the slices of tomatoes, and sprinkle with salt and pepper to taste. Top each tomato slice with a piece of sardine, cover with the crumbled cheese, and drizzle with the olive oil.

Just before serving, garnish the salad with the avocado.

CACTUS PADS IN CHEESE AND MUSHROOM SAUCE

Nopales en Salsa de Queso

4 servings

ALL CUISINES HAVE CHANGED to accommodate our busy lives. Contrary and Mexican cuisine is no exception. Here is an easy way to prepare a tasty and nutritious dish that can be equally suited for a light merienda *or a substantial dinner.*

1 (4 OZ/125 G) PACKAGE CREAM CHEESE

1 (10 FL OZ/284 ML) CAN CREAM OF MUSHROOM SOUP

1 (10 FL OZ/284 ML) CAN MUSHROOMS, DRAINED AND CHOPPED

6 TO 8 SMALL COOKED CACTUS PADS (PAGE 171), CHOPPED

½ CUP CRUMBLED CORNFLAKES

2 TABLESPOONS BUTTER

Preheat the oven to 350°F. With a fork, cream the cheese until soft, add the soup and mushrooms, and mix well. In an 8-inch square pan, cover the cactus with the cream cheese mixture and garnish with the cornflakes. Dot with butter and bake for about 8 to 10 minutes, or until heated through.

CHAYOTE SQUASH AND EGGPLANT CASSEROLE

Ensalada de Chayote y Berenjena   *4 servings*

CHAYOTE SQUASH MIXED WITH EGGPLANT and mushrooms makes a splendid and versatile vegetable dish that goes as well with an omelet as with grilled chicken or fish.

3 TABLESPOONS EXTRA-VIRGIN OLIVE OIL

2 CLOVES GARLIC, CHOPPED

1 SMALL ONION, SLICED INTO RINGS

2 CHAYOTE SQUASH, PEELED, COOKED, AND CUBED

1 MEDIUM EGGPLANT, CUBED

1 FRESH RED BELL PEPPER, SLICED

1 CUP SLICED MUSHROOMS

1/4 CUP CHOPPED FRESH FLAT-LEAF PARSLEY

SALT AND PEPPER

1/2 CUP SHREDDED MOZZARELLA CHEESE

Preheat the oven to 350°F. In a large, nonstick frying pan, heat the olive oil over medium heat and sauté the garlic and onion. Add the chayotes, eggplant, red pepper, and mushrooms, and sauté until cooked but still firm. Stir in the parsley and season with salt and pepper.

Transfer the vegetables to a 8 x 12-inch baking dish, cover with the cheese, and bake for about 6 to 8 minutes, or until the cheese is melted and the casserole is heated through.

BASIC CREPES

Crepas Basicas   *Yields 15 to 18 crepes*

FEW PEOPLE IN ENGLISH-SPEAKING NORTH AMERICA *associate the very French crepes with Mexican cuisine. In 1861, Mexico was invaded by the army of Napoleon III and in the famous 5 de Mayo Battle (1862) in Puebla, the Mexican army defeated the French.*

Unfortunately our joy did not last long. Austrian Emperor Maximilian of Habsburg and his wife Carlota were imposed upon the people of Mexico by Napoleon III. Their empire lasted only from 1864–67, but during this short period, the influence of French cuisine, then popular in Austria, was very strong, leaving a legacy of cream, mustard, and cheese sauces and crepes became part of the everyday menus.

At the beginning of the century and well into the 1930s, during la época Porfiriana *(the thirty years when President Porfirio Díaz was in power), the Mexican aristocracy fully embraced French cuisine. Carmelita Díaz, the president's wife, hired a French chef, and the president, who was born in Oaxaca, had to talk to their old cook on the side in order to get some Mexican antojitos and mole from Oaxaca once in a while.*

2 EGGS

¾ CUP MILK

1½ CUPS FLOUR

1 TEASPOON VEGETABLE OIL

½ TEASPOON SALT

BUTTER OR MARGARINE

In a small bowl, beat the eggs with a whisk. Beating with each addition, add the milk, the flour, and ½ cup water, until well mixed and lumpfree. Stir in the oil and the salt. The batter must be light to obtain paper-thin crepes.

Heat a nonstick frying pan over medium heat. For the first crepe, lightly grease the pan with butter. Pour one tablespoon of batter into the hot pan and quickly slide the batter toward the sides to form a round, thin crepe. Turn once and transfer the crepe to a plate. Repeat the same procedure with the rest of the batter. At the end, you might have to add a little more water to thin the batter.

Crepes can be made ahead of time and kept refrigerated for two to three days.

CREPES FILLED WITH CUITLACOCHE

Crepas Rellenas de Cuitlacoche   *4 servings*

THE FRENCH INVASION HAD A STRONG INFLUENCE on everyday life. Food did not escape this influence, creating a new and enriched cuisine, especially in the capital city. Many years passed before people went back to serving the very Mexican cuitlacoche, among other traditional delicacies.

Even though this corn fungus, also spelled huitlacoche, had been around since the days of the Aztecs, it was considered a delicacy only after it was served as a crepe filling to the Shah of Iran and his wife, Farah Dibba, during a visit to Mexico City in the '70s. When the menu was published in the newspaper, the president's wife, Doña Esther as she was often called, was highly criticized for offering our distinguished guests something considered more appropriate for peasants than for such dignitaries. As it turned out, the state dinner was quite a success and Doña Esther was ultimately commended for the superb use of native ingredients throughout the menu.

As is often the case, people began to cook cuitlacoche more and more. Chefs in fancy restaurants devised new ways of serving it and now it is widely considered a delicacy of the highest order. Cuitlacoche is sautéed with chopped onion, garlic, cilantro or epazote, and serrano and/or poblano chile, and served accompanied by warm tortillas or as a quesadilla filling. Its flavor is similar to that of wild mushrooms.

Cuitlacoche is also available in cans at Hispanic markets. It usually comes prepared, meaning that it has been cooked and seasoned. Serve these crepes as a first course with fresh lettuce leaves sprinkled with lime juice, on the side.

1 (13 OZ / 380 G) CAN PREPARED
   CUITLACOCHE

2 TABLESPOONS BUTTER

1 TEASPOON FLOUR

1 CUP 2% MILK

SALT AND PEPPER

12 CREPES (PAGE 181)

½ CUP GRATED MANCHEGO OR
   MONTEREY JACK CHEESE

In a small saucepan, heat the *cuitlacoche* and keep warm. In a separate saucepan, melt the butter, stir in the flour, and add the milk. Bring to a boil, season with salt and pepper, and simmer for 3 to 5 minutes, or until the sauce starts to thicken. Remove from the heat. Preheat the oven to 350°F.

Fill each crepe with 2 tablespoons of the prepared *cuitlacoche*, then roll up and place in an 8 x 12-inch rectangular baking dish.

Pour the white sauce over the crepes and top with a generous amount of cheese. Bake for about 8 minutes, or until the cheese melts and the crepes are heated through. Keep in mind that milk and cheese sauces tend to dry out very quickly, so be careful not to overbake the crepes.

CREPES FILLED WITH POBLANO AND PINE NUTS

Crepas de Rajas con Piñones   *4 servings*

IN THIS PARTICULAR RECIPE, *pine nuts are combined with the poblano chiles and the end result is truly magnificent. There are about eighty varieties of edible pine nuts. The trees grow all over the world, including in Europe, Asia, Africa, and North America. The cream-color variety,* pignoli, *is found in Italy, Spain and North Africa and has a slightly sweet taste. Its delicate flavor makes it a very suitable ingredient for pestos, pilafs, salads, and pasta dishes.*

Another variety, piñón *(Indian nut), grows in Mexico and the American Southwest, but rarely appears in markets outside this region. Similar in quality and shape to the Italian* pignoli, piñones *are of a light pink color, have a rich, sweet taste, and are consequently an ideal ingredient in the sweet milk candies so popular in Mexico, especially in the states of Puebla, Zacatecas, and Querétaro.*

4 MEDIUM POBLANO CHILES, ROASTED, PEELED, AND SEEDED (PAGE 111)

1 TABLESPOON VEGETABLE OIL

⅓ CUP CHOPPED ONION

1 LARGE CLOVE GARLIC, CHOPPED

1 MEDIUM TOMATO, SEEDED AND CHOPPED

¼ CUP PINE NUTS

1 (4 OZ/125 G) PACKAGE CREAM CHEESE, SOFTENED

SALT

1 TABLESPOON BUTTER

1 TEASPOON FLOUR

1 CUP 2% MILK

PEPPER

12 TO 14 CREPES (PAGE 181), WARMED

Slice the chiles into 1-inch pieces. In a medium-size frying pan, heat the oil over medium heat and, stirring with a wooden spoon, sauté the onion, garlic, and chile until the onion is translucent and the other vegetables are cooked. Stir in the chopped tomato and the pine nuts. Add the cream cheese in small pieces and season with salt. Continue sautéing the vegetables with the cheese for about 3 minutes longer, or until the cheese melts and is completely blended with the rest of the ingredients. Preheat the oven to 350°F.

Meanwhile, prepare a white sauce: Melt the butter in a small saucepan, stir in the flour, add the milk, and continue stirring until the flour is completely dissolved. Bring the sauce to a boil and simmer until slightly thickened. Add salt and pepper to taste, and keep the sauce warm.

Fill each crepe with 2 or 3 tablespoons of the chile mixture, roll, and place in an 8 x 12-inch rectangular baking dish. Cover with the white sauce and bake for about 5 to 7 minutes, or until the crepes are heated through. Be careful not to overbake, as white sauce tends to dry out very fast.

VEGETABLE-FILLED CREPES

Crepas de Verdura al Horno   *4 servings*

FOR MANY YEARS ONE OF THE FINEST RESTAURANTS in Mexico City, The Ambassadeurs, situated on the Paseo de la Reforma, a beautiful avenue designed with the Champs-Élysées in mind, was a common gathering place for the most important businessmen of the time. The owner, Don Dalmau Costa, a well-known entrepreneur and a sharp businessman, coordinated an exchange of chefs between France and Mexico, resulting in one of the most successful culinary experiences ever, helping to place our cuisine among the most sophisticated in the world. The Ambassadeurs has changed hands several times, and, from what I understand, it has not been the same since.

Another famous French restaurant was Normandie, also on the Paseo de la Reforma, right in the heart of the Colonia Juárez, where French architecture is at its best, making it easy for good restaurants to choose large and stately buildings for their business. The Normandie, located on a second floor, offered wonderful food and a magnificent view of the Paseo de la Reforma to its clientele.

Enjoy these crepes as a light supper dish or as a first course for dinner.

2 MEDIUM CARROTS, PEELED

2 ZUCCHINI

1 LARGE RED POTATO, PEELED

2 LEEKS, WASHED AND SLICED (WHITE PART ONLY)

¼ CUP BUTTER, CUT IN SMALL PIECES PLUS 2 TABLESPOONS BUTTER

SALT AND PEPPER

12 CREPES (PAGE 181)

¾ CUP MEXICAN CREAM OR CRÈME FRAÎCHE (PAGE 148)

½ CUP CRUMBLED *QUESO FRESCO* OR FETA CHEESE

Preheat the oven to 350°F. Julienne the carrots, zucchini and potato, or slice them into thin strips. Combine the vegetables with the leeks, and sauté in butter until the vegetables are cooked but still crisp. Season with salt and pepper and add about 4 tablespoons of the Mexican cream. Spoon the vegetables onto each crepe and roll up tightly. Transfer the crepes to an 8 x 12-inch baking dish. Sprinkle with the crumbled butter and cover with the remaining cream and the cheese.

Bake the crepes for 6 to 8 minutes, or until heated through. Be careful not to overbake them, or the cream will be dry.

TORTILLA AND PASILLA CHILE CASSEROLE

Corona de Tortillas y Chile Pasilla　　　　　　　　　*6 to 8 servings*

THIS CASSEROLE IS QUITE POPULAR. *It is an attractive buffet dish, or a complete meal. It has the nutrients of the corn, the sweet flavor of the pasilla chile and the enticing spiciness of the chorizo.*

The filling and also part of the assembly of the casserole can be prepared ahead of time, leaving only the frying of the tortilla strips and the chile to the very last minute. I always use a ring mold because it looks more attractive, however, a rectangular baking dish may be used as well.

OIL FOR FRYING

8 TO 10 CORN TORTILLAS, SLICED INTO STRIPS

1 DRIED PASILLA CHILE, STEMMED AND SEEDED

¼ CUP CHOPPED ONION

2 LARGE TOMATOES

½ CUP CANNED TOMATO SAUCE

SALT AND PEPPER

½ CUP *QUESO FRESCO* OR CRUMBLED FETA CHEESE

FILLING:

1 TEASPOON OIL

¼ CUP CHOPPED ONION

½ LB (250 G) CHORIZO SAUSAGE

1 LARGE TOMATO, SEEDED AND CHOPPED

2 TABLESPOONS CANNED TOMATO SAUCE

½ CUP MEXICAN CREAM OR CRÈME FRAÎCHE (PAGE 148)

In a saucepan, heat the oil over medium heat and fry the tortilla strips in batches, until crisp. Transfer the tortillas to paper towels to remove excess oil, and set aside. In the same saucepan, lightly fry the pasilla chile and remove from heat. Add the onion to the same pan and sauté until translucent. Preheat the oven to 350°F and lightly grease a 10-inch ring mold.

Roast the tomatoes in a dry pan until charred. When cool enough to handle, peel and seed the tomatoes. In a blender or food processor, purée the tomatoes with just enough liquid to let the motor run. Add the puréed tomatoes and canned tomato sauce to the onion and cook for 5 to 8 minutes, or until thickened. Stir in the tortilla strips, pasilla chile, salt and pepper, and about ½ cup water. Simmer the tomato mixture until almost all the liquid has evaporated. Remove the chile, reserve for later use, and add the cheese.

TO MAKE THE FILLING: In a small frying pan, heat the oil and sauté the onion, stir in the chorizo, and fry until the chorizo is crumbled. Add the chopped tomato and the tomato sauce. Simmer, covered, for 5 to 8 minutes, or until the vegetables are cooked and the flavors have blended.

TO ASSEMBLE: Transfer half of the tortilla mixture to the prepared pan, cover with the filling, and top with the remaining tortilla mixture. Bake for 10 to 12 minutes, or until heated through and slightly browned around the edges. Invert onto a platter, top with the cream, and garnish with the pasilla chile, crumbled.

CUITLACOCHE AND ZUCCHINI BLOSSOM CASSEROLE

Pastel de Cuitlacoche y Flor de Calabaza   *8 to 10 servings*

FROM THE FABULOUS RECIPE COLLECTION *of my favorite sister-in-law, Raquel Cuervo de Duclaud, this magnificent vegetable casserole is quite an experience. Granted, the recipe is a bit labor intensive, however it is worth every minute. The fillings can be made a day ahead of time and kept refrigerated until assembling the dish, which can be done a couple of hours before dinner time.*

I served this fantastic dish in a gorgeous ceramic dish to members of the Mexican Circle Association in Victoria, Canada and it was a big hit. Enjoy this succulent casserole as a main dish served with lettuce leaves on the side.

CUITLACHOCHE FILLING:

VEGETABLE OIL FOR FRYING

$^1\!/_2$ MEDIUM WHITE ONION, CHOPPED

3 SERRANO CHILES, MINCED

$1^1\!/_2$ CUPS CANNED CUITLACOCHE

1 SPRIG EPAZOTE, CHOPPED OR $^1\!/_4$ CUP CHOPPED FRESH CILANTRO

SALT

ZUCCHINI BLOSSOM FILLING:

VEGETABLE OIL FOR FRYING

$^1\!/_2$ MEDIUM WHITE ONION, CHOPPED

1 LARGE POBLANO CHILE, ROASTED, PEELED, SEEDED AND SLICED (PAGE 111)

1 CUP FRESH CORN KERNELS

$1^1\!/_2$ CUPS CANNED ZUCCHINI BLOSSOMS, DRAINED

1 SPRIG EPAZOTE OR $^1\!/_4$ CUP CHOPPED FRESH CILANTRO

SALT

FOR THE *CUITLACOCHE* FILLING: In a small saucepan, heat the oil over medium heat and sauté the onion and chiles until the onion is translucent. Stir in the *cuitlacoche*, *epazote*, and salt to taste and simmer for a few minutes for flavors to blend. Set aside.

FOR THE ZUCCHINI BLOSSOM FILLING: In a separate saucepan, heat the oil over medium heat and sauté the onion and chiles until the onion is translucent and the chile is cooked. Stir in the corn kernels, the zucchini blossoms and the epazote, add salt to taste, and set aside. Preheat the oven to 350°F.

ASSEMBLY:

VEGETABLE OIL FOR FRYING

10 TO 12 CORN TORTILLAS

1/2 CUP CANNED TOMATO SAUCE

1 CUP MEXICAN CREAM OR CRÈME
   FRAÎCHE (PAGE 148)

1/2 LB (250 G) OAXACAN *QUESILLO*
   OR 3/4 CUP SHREDDED MONTEREY
   JACK CHEESE

TO ASSEMBLE: In a frying pan, heat the oil almost to the point of smoking and lightly fry the tortillas, one at a time. Drain each tortilla on paper towels to remove excess oil. Slice each tortilla into three strips and use some to cover the bottom of a round 11-inch baking dish.

Cover the tortillas with some of the zucchini mixture, top with cream and cheese, and cover with more tortilla strips. Layer on the *cuitlacoche* mixture, top with more cream and cheese, and cover with tortilla strips. Continue layering the fillings, and top with a final layer of tortillas, the remainder of the cream combined with the tomato sauce, and a generous amount of cheese.

Bake the casserole for about 20 minutes, or until heated through. Be careful not to overbake, or the tortillas will toughen and the casserole will be hard to cut.

VEGETABLE CASSEROLE

Cacerola de Verduras   *4 to 6 servings*

CACTI HAVE BEEN CULTIVATED in *Mexico for centuries. The cardona cactus can be easily identified by the red prickly pears that grow between its pads. These are commonly served in soups, cold salads, and drinks, and are a good source of fiber and other nutrients.*

The addition of the cactus pads to this otherwise plain vegetarian casserole gives it a tasty and distinctive flavor. The sour cream and the cheese may be omitted if desired.

8 MEDIUM SIZE CACTUS PADS, COOKED (PAGE 171)

2 EGGS, LIGHTLY BEATEN

3 POBLANO CHILES, ROASTED, PEELED, AND SEEDED (PAGE 111)

2 LARGE RED POTATOES, PEELED

2 MEDIUM ZUCCHINI

2 MEDIUM CARROTS, PEELED

½ LB (250 G) GREEN BEANS

1 TABLESPOON BUTTER

1 CUP MEXICAN CREAM OR CRÈME FRAÎCHE (PAGE 148)

½ CUP GRATED MONTEREY JACK CHEESE

Mix the cooked *nopales* with the eggs and set aside. Julienne the potatoes, zucchini, carrots and green beans. In salted boiling water, cook the vegetables for about 4 to 5 minutes or until cooked but still crisp. Preheat the oven to 350°F and grease an 8 x 12-inch baking dish.

Layer the vegetables, including the nopales mixed with the egg and chiles in the prepared pan. Cover with the cream and top with a generous amount of cheese.

Bake for about 8 to 10 minutes, or until heated through, the egg is cooked, and the cheese is melted. Serve hot.

SPINACH AND POTATO CASSEROLE

Budín de Espinaca   *6 to 8 servings*

THERE IS ALWAYS A TIME WHEN, the more you think, the less you can come up with a different way of serving vegetables. This budín *is easy to make. The potatoes and spinach may be cooked the day before and the casserole assembled just minutes before your guests arrive. It is an additional bonus that spinach is a good source of iron. This goes very well with meat loaf and roasts. Serve hot as a side dish.*

2 TABLESPOONS FINE DRY BREAD CRUMBS

3 LARGE RED POTATOES, PEELED AND
    BOILED

½ CUP GRATED EDAM CHEESE

¼ CUP BUTTER

SALT AND PEPPER

1 EGG YOLK

1 TABLESPOON VEGETABLE OIL

½ MEDIUM ONION, CHOPPED

2 BUNCHES FRESH SPINACH, COOKED,
    DRAINED AND CHOPPED

2 RIPE TOMATOES, SEEDED AND
    CHOPPED

1 TABLESPOON CANNED TOMATO SAUCE

2 SERRANO CHILES, FINELY CHOPPED

Preheat the oven to 350°F. Grease a 9-inch round baking dish and coat with the bread crumbs. Mash the potatoes and combine with the cheese, butter, salt and pepper, and egg yolk. Cover the bottom of the pan with this mixture and set aside.

In a small saucepan, heat the oil over medium heat and sauté the onion until soft. Add the drained spinach, tomatoes, tomato sauce, and serrano chiles. Season the vegetables with salt and pepper and simmer for 5 minutes.

Cover the mashed potatoes with the spinach mixture and bake for about 6 to 8 minutes, or until heated through.

ZUCCHINI BLOSSOM, POBLANO CHILE, AND CORN CASSEROLE

Budín de Flor de Calabaza y Elote   *4 to 6 servings*

THIS IS A VERY NUTRITIOUS VEGETARIAN DISH *that may be served on its own or as a buffet dish. Keep in mind that if you use fresh zucchini blossoms, the pistil should be removed as it sometimes has a bitter taste. You will notice that if you use the canned ones, they do come with the pistil, but in this case it does not have to be removed.*

Serve cut into wedges, as a side dish, to accompany breaded chicken breasts or as a first course.

1 TABLESPOON VEGETABLE OIL

$\frac{1}{2}$ CUP CHOPPED ONION

2 POBLANO CHILES, ROASTED, PEELED, AND SEEDED (PAGE 111)

1 CUP FRESH OR FROZEN CORN KERNELS

1 SMALL ZUCCHINI, CUBED

$1\frac{1}{2}$ CUPS CHOPPED ZUCCHINI BLOSSOMS OR 1 (7 OZ/200 G) CAN, DRAINED

SALT

6 CORN TORTILLAS

$\frac{1}{2}$ CUP SOUR CREAM

$\frac{1}{4}$ CUP 2% MILK

$\frac{3}{4}$ CUP CRUMBLED *QUESO FRESCO* OR FETA CHEESE

Preheat the oven to 350°F.

In a small saucepan, heat the oil over medium heat and sauté the onion and chile for a few minutes, or until cooked. Add the corn and the zucchini, and continue cooking, stirring, for about 5 to 8 minutes. Add the zucchini blossoms. Season the vegetables with salt to taste, and bring to a boil. Lower the heat and simmer, covered, for 5 minutes more.

Meanwhile, in a frying pan, heat the oil almost to the point of smoking, and lightly fry tortillas. Transfer each tortilla to paper towels to remove excess oil.

Combine the sour cream and milk. In a 9-inch round pan, place one tortilla, cover it with some of the vegetables, and top with some of the sour cream mixture and cheese. Continue layering all the ingredients in the same order, ending with sour cream and cheese. Bake the casserole for about 8 to 10 minutes, or until it is heated through and the cheese is melted.

BEVERAGES

BEBIDAS

MEXICO BOASTS AN ARRAY OF COLORFUL and refreshing *aguas frescas*. These are mostly fruit blended with water and sweetened with either sugar or *piloncillo* (unrefined brown sugar). There are also *aguas frescas* made from such vegetables as cucumbers, beets, or a variety of vegetable juices blended with orange or lime juice.

Vendors on street corners are ready to squeeze fresh orange juice for you on demand; it is usually served in a tall glass. Other customers may order an *horchata* with ice, a most refreshing rice and milk beverage served with powdered cinnamon on top.

When I was growing up in Mexico City, my mother used to shop at the Mercado de Medellín. When there was no school, I got to go with her, and before she began her shopping we would both head for the *aguas frescas* stand. I always had a hard time deciding what I wanted—the colors were so vivid and they all looked so refreshing. More often than not, I ordered carrot juice with lots of lime juice. What a treat!

Every market in Mexico has a stand selling *aguas frescas* and, with the amazing variety of fruit that Mexico has been blessed to have all year round, it is indeed very difficult to ignore the sensuous scent of tropical fruits.

BEET AND
ORANGE JUICE COOLER

Agua Fresca de Betabel y Jugo de Naranja   *Yields about 4 cups*

BEETS HAVE BEEN CULTIVATED *since prehistoric times, originally in the Mediterranean. They are one of the healthiest vegetables available. The amount of fiber they provide is about four times the same amount shredded cabbage, and a beet contains as much potassium as a banana. As for our daily requirement of folic acid, a serving of beets provides 25 percent. They are also an excellent source of vitamin C, iron, and magnesium.*

When you are making a beet salad, do not throw away the boiling liquid. It contains some of the nutritious elements mentioned above and you will enjoy this sweet, delicious, and invigorating cooler. Serve it cold, preferably in a clear glass pitcher.

1 LARGE BEET, PEELED AND CHOPPED

½ CUP FRESH ORANGE JUICE

JUICE OF ½ LIME

SUGAR

Boil the chopped beet in 2 cups water for about 20 to 25 minutes, or until soft. Let cool and drain the beet liquid into a pitcher. Reserve the beets for another use.

Add the orange juice, lime juice, and sugar to taste. Add 2 more cups water and refrigerate until ready to serve.

CACTUS JUICE

Jugo de Nopales

Yields about 6 cups of juice

A FEW YEARS AGO, TRENDY RESTAURANTS in Mexico City started serving this juice for breakfast as a novelty, in addition to the customary orange, grapefruit, or carrot juice, and with great success. Besides being a tasty and refreshing juice, the newly discovered medicinal properties of the cactus were too good to ignore.

The cactus leaves, or cactus pads, are at their best when they are very fresh. You can usually determine freshness by the deep, bright green color. If the color is a bit dull, they are better to use in salads, rather than for juice.

2 LARGE CACTUS PADS, COOKED
(PAGE 171)

1 CUP FRESH ORANGE JUICE

SUGAR

In a blender, process cactus pads with 2 cups water until puréed. Strain into a pitcher and add 2 more cups water, the orange juice, and sugar to taste.

This beverage is equally good made with raw cactus pads. Wash the pads and remove the thorns, then chop and process in a blender. Add the rest of the ingredients as above. Refrigerate for approximately 2 hours, and serve very cold.

CACTUS PEAR COOLER

Agua de Tuna   *Yields about 4 cups*

WHO COULD EVER IMAGINE *that this juicy and refreshing fruit comes from a cactus.* Tunas *(cactus pears) are the size of a small apple, are oval in shape, and have a thick peel that is quite easy to remove. The flesh is full of edible seeds, but for cosmetic reasons, are strained in this cooler.*

Tunas *are eaten raw, caramelized, or served in syrup. In Central Mexico, mainly in the states of Aguas Calientes and Zacatecas,* tunas *are made into a hard, sweet paste called* queso de tuna *(cactus pear cheese), a real favorite of people with a sweet tooth. My father was one of them, and I have discovered lately that his brothers and sisters were the same and that they would only eat the* queso de tuna *that came from Zacatecas.*

Outside Mexico, tunas *usually turn up during the summer in local supermarkets. Make sure that they are of a bright color and very firm to the touch. Serve the* agua de tuna *in a clear glass pitcher to show off its strikingly crimson color.*

8 RED OR GREEN CACTUS PEARS

SUGAR

Slice open the cactus pears and remove the peel. Chop the fruit and transfer to a blender or food processor. Add 2 cups water and process until well blended. Strain the juice into a pitcher, and add 2 more cups water and sugar to taste.

Refrigerate the cooler and serve cold with ice cubes if desired.

CUCUMBER COOLER
WITH TEQUILA

Agua de Pepino con Piquete   *Yields about 6 cups*

IN MEXICO, LIMES ARE SMALLER than the ones you see in the rest of North America, and they have a particular *flavor that imparts a delicious tang to fruit, vegetables, soups, fish, meat, salsas or dips, coolers, you name it. Mexicans add limes, and in great quantities, to much that they eat, a quality of the cuisine that I did not fully apprehend until I moved away.*

In Canada, it took me a while to learn that limones *were not limes, but lemons. And even then I still confuse the terms. They should not be substituted for one another in cooking; limes bring up the flavor of any dish in a different way than lemons do. They work wonders with fish; mangoes acquire a delightful tartness, and cucumbers and jicama go hand in hand with limes.*

The addition of the tequila transforms an ordinary cooler into a nice treat.

2 LARGE CUCUMBERS, PEELED

JUICE OF 3 LIMES

SUGAR

2 TABLESPOONS TEQUILA

ICE CUBES

Seed and chop the cucumbers. In a blender, combine the cucumbers, lime juice, and sugar with 1 cup water, and process until completely blended.

Transfer the cucumber cooler to a glass pitcher, stir in the tequila and add about 4 more cups cold water. Adjust the quantities of lime juice and water to suit your taste.
Refrigerate the cooler until ready to serve.

Add the ice cubes before serving.

FRESH FRUIT AND VEGETABLE JUICE

Jugo de Frutas y Vegetales   *2 servings*

FOR A VARIETY OF FRUIT JUICES, a visit to the Juices Colima in Mexico City is a must. This is an establishment that has been in business since I was a child. The original Colima opened in Polanco, a very plush area in the city, where I used to take my daughter Mariana for a treat. She had not been to Mexico for about five years, and when she went back to visit her grandfather, one of the first things she wanted was a fruit juice from Colima.

The colorful array of all the different fruits available is quite spectacular and she was so delighted that she took several photos of the pineapples, mameyes *(oval-shaped fruit with brown leathery skin),* cherimoyas *(white-fleshed fruit with big shiny seeds and dark green skin), the aromatic* guayabas *(guavas, a small yellowish tropical fruit with lots of seeds and yellow skin), red or green* tunas *(cactus pears), pears,* zapotes *(sapodillas, a round fruit with black flesh and green soft skin, or with light brown flesh and darker brown skin),* limas *(limes), the list is endless. Combinations of fruits and vegetables, like lime and carrot juice, my favorite, are also available.*

Similar establishments have now emerged in different parts of the big city. Los Colorines in Pedregal de San Angel, in the southern part of the city, is extremely popular since it happens to be adjacent to the popular taquería, *El Farolito. Imagine enjoying tacos with one of these magnificent fruit juices! This is a must-visit for me every time I am in Mexico City.*

This creation is from my friend Nora Corral of Lagos de Moreno in Jalisco. She is very good at mixing fresh vegetables with fruits and very often comes up with the most amazing and refreshing beverages.

If pineapple from Hawaii is used, increase to three slices. Mexican pineapples are almost double the size.

JUICE OF 5 ORANGES

JUICE OF 1 LIME

2 SLICES FRESH PINEAPPLE

1 CELERY STALK

1 SMALL CACTUS PAD, PEELED
(PAGE 171)

1 TABLESPOON CHOPPED PARSLEY

Combine all the ingredients in a blender and process until well mixed. Refrigerate before serving.

CAFÉ AU LAIT

Café con Leche   *2 servings*

IT WAS QUITE SURPRISING to me that drinking café au lait became a trend in Canada in the last few years. I grew up having café con leche with supper every single evening. Living in the British side of Canada for many years now, I have switched to English tea, and when I visit my family in Mexico, they tease me that I am not Mexican anymore, because I do not drink coffee or café au lait with supper.

When I was a child, my parents used to take me to a restaurant downtown called La Super Leche (The Super Milk), where the waiters were constantly going around to every table, with a large pitcher of milk in one hand and coffee in the other, pouring both in tall glasses similar to the ones used for ice-cream floats—that big! It was, as I remember, a busy place at the time of the merienda. Patrons leaving a movie or theater were ready for a nice light supper before going home, and nothing was better than good café con leche with the traditional bizcochos (sweet rolls) from the main bakeries in town.

Unfortunately, this restaurant did not survive the earthquake that devastated Mexico City in 1985. Today, people wanting to savor a traditional café con leche with a bisquet, (similar to a tea biscuit but made with lard), go to the Chinese cafés that are all over town. The custom of drinking milk with coffee is still prevalent in most of the country, for breakfast and for supper as well.

1½ CUPS 2% MILK

1 CUP FRESHLY BREWED
   MEXICAN COFFEE

SUGAR

In a saucepan, heat the milk over low heat until bubbles form and it is about to boil. Turn off the heat immediately and pour the milk into mugs, about ¾ full. Add the coffee to the brim and serve at once, with sugar to taste.

COFFEE FROM
A CLAY POT

Café de Olla   *2 servings*

IN MEXICO, CAFÉ DE OLLA is usually served in the traditional posadas that take place every day from December 16 to the twenty-third. Posadas are a daily reenactment of Mary and Joseph's journey to Bethlehem: A procession is formed, led by two people carrying small figurines of Mary and Joseph. The pilgrims go from house to house, carrying lit candles and singing, seeking posada (shelter) because Mary is about to give birth. When a posada is finally found, the owner, singing back, invites them in, and Mary and Joseph are placed in the nacimiento (manger). Then everybody kneels at the manger to pray and sing.

Posadas are one of the many beautiful traditions brought to Mexico by the Spaniards who celebrated the first Christmas in Mexico in 1538. Each day, the ceremony is followed by a feast where a clay piñata full of candies, seasonal fruit, and small presents wrapped in colored tissue paper, is hit with a stick by the joyful children until the clay bowl that holds the candies and fruit is broken and all the goodies fall to the floor. Needless to say, whoever breaks the piñata first gets the best bundle to take home. For the adults, hot café de olla and buñuelos are the perfect treat for a cold December evening.

Nowadays, the clay olla has been replaced by layers and layers of glued newspaper to prevent someone being hit in the head by a piece of clay. In December, you can find the most amazing and colorful piñatas in every market in Mexico. They are made by hand, usually by the vendors' families who get together to make these elaborate pieces of art in the shape of elephants, giraffes, ducks, donkeys, and sail boats, to name just a few. Piñatas have also become part of children's birthday parties, year-round.

2 (3-INCH) CINNAMON STICKS

2 TABLESPOONS DEMERARA OR BROWN
    SUGAR

4 WHOLE CLOVES

2 TABLESPOONS COARSELY GROUND
    MEXICAN VERACRUZ COFFEE

Pour 2¼ cups water into a pot, preferably a clay pitcher, and bring to a boil. Add the cinnamon sticks, cloves, and sugar, and let the mixture boil for about 15 minutes. Stir in the coffee, bring it to a boil, and quickly remove it from the heat. Cover the pitcher with a thick cloth or tea cozy.

Let the coffee steep for 5 minutes. Strain into *barro* (clay) mugs and serve hot with one cinnamon stick in each mug.

COFFEE WITH A STING

Café con Piquete   *2 servings*

MEXICANS, LIKE ITALIANS, LOVE COFFEE—*the stronger the better. A gathering of friends or family extends into the evening, and it is not uncommon, near the end, that one of the guests decides to have a second or third cup of coffee, this time with a "sting," before continuing with the chatting.*

   It is certainly a delightful way to finish a Mexican dinner!

4 TABLESPOONS COFFEE LIQUEUR

2 TABLESPOONS GOOD TEQUILA

2 CUPS STRONG COFFEE

½ CUP WHIPPED CREAM (OPTIONAL)

Pour 2 tablespoons of the coffee liqueur and 1 tablespoon of the tequila into each mug. Fill the mugs with the coffee and top with a dollop of whipped cream, if desired.

EASY RICE COOLER

Horchata Fácil   *Yields 6 cups*

THIS IS ANOTHER VERY POPULAR COOLER *from the hottest parts of Mexico, such as the Yucatán Peninsula, Chiapas and Tabasco. Sunday meals in Mexican households mean family gatherings. Usually all the married children and their own families visit the grandparents, and it is the grandmother who generally cooks the whole meal.*

It is easy to forget that a great part of Mexico still enjoys the privilege of having a servant who helps with the elaborate cooking. In the old days, those servants stayed with the family for years and years, eventually becoming part of the family. I remember with great fondness my nanny Francisca who left us when I was already in my teens, and only because she had to tend to her sick and elderly mother. Needless to say, her departure was certainly a sad event in my young life.

These servants were and still are an integral part of families. Their help in running a household was certainly a blessing, making things easier for the head of the family to hold the Sunday meals.

Things in Mexico, like everywhere else, have changed in this respect and, fortunately, it is now harder and harder to get people to work in households. I say fortunately, because these wonderful people are now going to school, and starting to work in offices, as nurses in the hospitals, working in factories, making a better life for themselves. Needless to say, this situation has not deterred families from getting together to enjoy a family dinner.

Try this cooler on a hot summer afternoon.

2 CUPS LONG-GRAIN WHITE RICE

2 (FOUR-INCH) CINNAMON STICKS

2 CUPS COLD 2% MILK

SUGAR

In a large bowl, soak the rice in 3 cups of warm water for 5 to 6 hours, or overnight. Crumble the cinnamon sticks and toast them lightly on a *comal* or in a dry pan.

Drain the rice and grind it, in batches, in a blender with the cinnamon and the milk. Strain the rice mixture into a pitcher and dilute by adding 4 cups cold water. Add sugar to taste.

Refrigerate and serve very cold.

MEXICAN EGGNOG

Rompope Casero   *Yields 3 to 3½ cups*

THIS DELICIOUS BEVERAGE, Mexico's very own version of eggnog was created by the nuns in the Convent of Santa Clara in Puebla. In fact, one of the most popular rompopes *is called* Rompope Santa Clara.

There are innumerable convents all over Mexico, all of them housed in beautiful colonial buildings. The nuns who populated those convents are responsible for countless recipes of elaborate dishes, desserts, sweet rolls, cakes and cookies.

3¼ CUPS 2% MILK

1½ CUPS SUGAR

1 TABLESPOON CORNSTARCH

6 EGG YOLKS

2 TABLESPOONS VANILLA EXTRACT

1 CUP DARK RUM

Combine 3 cups of the milk and the sugar in a heavy saucepan. Bring to a boil and simmer for about 15 to 20 minutes, or until reduced to 2½ cups. Dissolve the cornstarch in the remaining ¼ cup milk. Stir the cornstarch mixture into the reduced milk until completely dissolved. Continue simmering 3 to 4 minutes longer, or until slightly thickened. Cool the milk mixture completely.

With an electric mixer, beat the egg yolks until they become lemon colored, add the vanilla, and mix well. Stir the egg yolks into the milk mixture and heat, taking care not to let it boil. Add the rum, and mix well. Chill before serving.

HOT CHOCOLATE AND CORN DRINK

Champurrado   *Yields 4 to 5 cups*

CHAMPURRADO *OR CHOCOLATE* ATOLE, *is a unique combination of corn and chocolate, two ingredients Mexico gave to the world, and surprisingly enough they combine very well.* Atole *is a corn-based drink widely enjoyed by Mexicans. It is prepared by diluting corn flour in boiling water and boiling it until it thickens to the consistency of a milkshake, then flavoring it with fresh fruit. The most popular atoles are flavored with fresh strawberries, guavas, pineapple, or pecans.*

Champurrado *is usually sweetened with* piloncillo *(unrefined brown sugar). If Mexican chocolate is used, reduce the sugar to* ½ *cup, since the chocolate is already sweetened and spiced with cinnamon, which add an aromatic flavor and a special texture to the* champurrado. *Good brands of Mexican chocolate are Carlos V, Abuelita, and Morelia Presidencial.* Atole *and* champurrado *are traditionally served with tamales.*

½ CUP MASA HARINA

1 CUP BROWN SUGAR

3 CUPS 2% MILK

1 (3.16 OZ/90 G) TABLET MEXICAN
   CHOCOLATE, CHOPPED OR 3 (1 OZ)
   SQUARES UNSWEETENED CHOCOLATE
   PLUS 1 TEASPOON GROUND
   CINNAMON

In a large saucepan, combine the Masa Harina with 3 cups water. Stir over low heat until the mixture thickens. Remove from the heat and stir in sugar to taste. Add the milk and the chocolate, stirring until the chocolate is completely dissolved.

Serve the *champurrado* steaming hot.

HOT CHOCOLATE FOR TAMALES AND CHURROS

Chocolate Caliente   *Yields 4 cups*

"THE DRINK OF THE GODS" is what the Aztecs called the sensuous and, to most of us, addictive substance known as chocolate. It was, however, the Olmec and the Maya peoples who first cultivated the cacao tree, and not the Aztecs as is commonly believed. Linguists and historians have been able to reconstruct the ancient Olmec vocabulary, and have found that the word cacao *was part of the vocabulary of the Olmec people, one of the earliest Mesoamerican civilizations, who occupied the tropical forests south of Veracruz on the Gulf of Mexico.*

Several centuries after the demise of the Olmecs, the Maya established themselves in the Yucatan Peninsula and the states of Chiapas, Guatemala and Belize. Historians have also found that the Maya wrote their books on folding screens of bark paper, and many of the drawings depict the cacao tree. The Maya called the cacao tree cacahuáquchtl. *Carved images of cacao pods, symbol of life and fertility, were also found in the magnificent Mayan temples.*

After the mysterious fall of the Mayan empire, the gifted and supremely civilized Toltecs, later followed by the Aztecs, settled in former Mayan territory. Quetzalcóatl, the Toltec king, left the capital and fled south to the Yucatan Peninsula, promising to return in a preordained year to reclaim his kingdom. The legend of his exile became part of Aztec mythology, and astrologers predicted that in 1519 a white-faced king would return to release his people.

It is well known that Moctezuma had extravagant taste and had his servants prepare him the most exquisite meals. For the Aztecs, chocolate was believed to be a source of spiritual wisdom, and tremendous energy. The divine drink was given to warriors to fortify them before going to war and Moctezuma used to drink chocolate in a gold cup before visiting his many wives. Cacao beans were also used as currency.

The story goes that in 1502, when Christopher Columbus arrived, he was greeted by the Aztecs who offered him a sackful of cocoa beans and explained that a very special drink, xocolatl, *was made with these beans.*

Seventeen years later when Hernán Cortés arrived in the New World, the emperor Moctezuma believed Cortés to be a reincarnation of Quetzalcóatl, the exiled Toltec god-king whose return had been predicted for that year, making it easier for the Spaniards to gain access to the great Tenochtitlán, the Aztec capital.

It was not until Cortés took the cacao plants to Spain that sugar was added to chocolate and became the drink that we enjoy today. From Spain, the passion for chocolate spread to Holland, where the industrious Dutch found a way to extract some of the fat from it to make cocoa powder.

Try this chocolate with tamales or churros for a nice, warm Mexican-style merienda *(light supper). Unsweetened cocoa powder can be used instead, although you need to add perhaps twice as much as the package says, plus a bit of flour to get the right flavor and richness.*

Ibarra is my preferred brand; Abuelita and Morelia Presidencial will also work. A molinillo *is a very handy utensil to make the chocolate frothy. Mexican chocolate and* molinillos *can be found in any Mexican market.*

4 CUPS MILK

1 TABLET (3.16 OZ/90 G) MEXICAN
   CHOCOLATE, CHOPPED

Heat the milk, preferably in a clay pitcher or a saucepan, and add the chocolate, stirring until melted. Bring the milk to a boil, stirring constantly, lower the heat, and continue simmering for just a few minutes longer, so that the chocolate thickens. Serve steaming hot.

LIME-SPIKED BEER

Chelada   *2 servings*

IN 1544, ALFONSO HERRERA established Latin America's first brewery in Mexico City. For many years, beer was a cottage industry, but by 1890, the beer industry started growing, first in the northern states of Mexico and then in the state of Veracruz, where the beverage was made using spring water from the Pico de Orizaba volcano.

With the support from President Porfirio Díaz, French and German entrepreneurs introduced European technology that eventually made Mexican beer famous. By 1904, it was considered among the best in the world. The industry continued growing and peaked in 1945, when production doubled and it began to be exported to other parts of the world. Mexico is now the third-largest beer exporter in the world, after Holland and Germany. Today, Corona, Sol, Dos Equis, and Pacífico are the most popular brands.

2 (12 OZ/355 ML) BOTTLES LIGHT BEER, SUCH AS DOS EQUIS SPECIAL LAGER

CRUSHED ICE

A FEW DROPS OF FRESH LIME JUICE

DASH OF SALT

Serve the beer in cold glasses with ice crusted on the rim and add lime juice and salt. Enjoy!

SPICY LIME-SPIKED BEER

Michelada   *2 servings*

2 (12 oz/355 mL) bottles Pacífico
   Clara beer

A few drops Maggi sauce

A few drops fresh lime juice

Dash of chile powder

Dash of salt

Serve the beer in tall, ice-cold glasses. Add the rest of the ingredients according to taste.

WHITE RUSSIAN

Ruso Blanco   *1 serving*

⅓ CUP COFFEE LIQUEUR, SUCH AS
    KAHLÚA OR TÍA MARÍA

⅔ CUP 2% MILK, COLD

Mix the liqueur with the milk and serve in a cold glass. Double the quantities if you plan to enjoy a *Ruso Blanco* with a friend.

VAMPIRE

Vampiro   *1 serving*

SQUIRT OR OTHER SPARKLING GRAPE-
    FRUIT BEVERAGE

STORE-BOUGHT SANGRITA

JUICE OF 1 LIME

SALT

Mix the ingredients together in a cold glass according to your taste.

PRUNE AND RUM PUNCH

Ponche de Ciruela Pasa   *Yields 6 cups*

THIS PUNCH CAN BE SERVED HOT OR COLD. Garnish with thin slices of lime or orange, if desired. For a more sophisticated punch, substitute brandy for the rum. Enjoy this comforting punch on a cold evening by the fire.

12 PRUNES, PITTED

1 (3-INCH) CINNAMON STICK

JUICE OF 2 ORANGES, PLUS THE PEEL
   FROM ½ ORANGE

¼ CUP RUM

JUICE OF 1 LIME

SUGAR

Boil the prunes in 4 cups water with the cinnamon stick and orange peel for about 10 minutes, or until the prunes are soft. Remove the peel. Add the orange juice and the rest of the ingredients. Bring the mixture to a boil and simmer for 4 or 5 minutes longer, just to blend flavors. Do not overcook the prunes, as they should remain whole.

SPICED TOMATO JUICE CHASER

Sangrita   *Yields about 6 cups*

There are many versions of the popular SANGRITA, *a chaser for a straight shot of tequila. It is common in Mexico City to serve premium tequila accompanied with* sangrita, *a favorite of my family back in Mexico. There always seems to be a batch of this sophisticated* sangrita *in the fridge.*

This is my sister-in-law Beatriz's version, and I must say it is quite good. She serves sangrita *in a clear glass pitcher and it looks extremely appealing. It keeps very well, refrigerated, for up to two days.*

2 GREEN ONIONS OR ¼ CUP OF MINCED
WHITE ONION

¾ CUP FINELY CHOPPED FRESH
CILANTRO LEAVES

3 TO 4 SERRANO CHILES, FINELY
CHOPPED

4 CUPS V-8 OR TOMATO JUICE

JUICE OF 2 LIMES

JUICE OF 2 ORANGES

1 TEASPOON WORCESTERSHIRE SAUCE

1 TEASPOON TABASCO SAUCE

1 TEASPOON MAGGI SAUCE

SALT AND PEPPER

In a bowl, mix the onion, cilantro, and chiles with the V-8, lime and orange juices. Add the Worcestershire, Tabasco, and Maggi sauces, and salt and pepper to taste.

Transfer the *sangrita* to a glass pitcher and refrigerate, covered, overnight or for several hours before serving.

TEQUILA COCKTAILS

WHEN THE SPANIARDS arrived in Tenochtitlán, later called la Nueva España (New Spain), they discovered that the native Indians drank a sweet and aromatic juice from one of the agave plants, and that juice when fermented produced a wonderful state of being.

The Spaniards brought with them their knowledge of the distillation process learned from the Moors, giving birth to one of the most wonderful beverages: Tequila.

Agave tequilana Weber is the scientific name of the cactus that produces tequila. This agave plant grows in a semi-dry climate in clay-like soil with a high basalt and iron content, conditions that are found mainly in the State of Jalisco, around the city of Guadalajara where the township of Tequila is located.

Tequila is aged in white oak casks. Once this process is finished, tequila is ready to be bottled. The name "Tequila" is protected and recognized as a native beverage. This recognition establishes that the name can only be used by the factories and distilleries in the protection zone that exclusively use the cactus Agave tequilana Weber.

Until the world discovered margaritas, standard brands of tequila sold in the United States and Canada at almost the same prices of similar quality whisky, rum or vodka. When demand exceeded the supply, the price of tequilas suitable for mixing, for example, Sauza Gold or Silver, quickly jumped to one and a half times. Really fine tequilas suitable for sipping, for example Herradura Reposado, Jimador, Don Julio, Mayorazgo, now sell for two and a half to three times the price of good quality whisky. Any tequila worth buying will have on its label: 100% de Agave.

Keep in mind that the information given for the following beverages is only a guideline; you might like to adjust the quantities according to your taste.

MOCAMBO

Mocambo   *2 servings*

A VASO TEQUILERO, *used specially for tequila, is a small, tall glass with capacity of about $3^{1}/2$ tablespoons. A shot is thus about $3^{1}/2$ tablespoons of straight tequila.*

▼▼▼▼▼▼▼▼▼▼▼▼▼▼▼▼▼▼▼▼▼▼▼▼▼▼▼

2 SHOTS (ABOUT $3^{1}/2$ TABLESPOONS
   EACH) TEQUILA

2 TABLESPOONS LIME JUICE

1 TABLESPOON SUGAR

Combine the tequila with the lime juice and sugar, stirring well. Divide into two tequila glasses and serve.

TEQUILA POP

La Paloma   *2 servings*

TEQUILA POP OR LA PALOMA, *as it is called in the Guadalajara area, is a very popular drink among young people. It is very refreshing and not too strong.*

▼▼▼▼▼▼▼▼▼▼▼▼▼▼▼▼▼▼▼▼▼▼▼▼▼▼▼

JUICE OF $^{1}/2$ LIME

2 SHOTS (ABOUT $3^{1}/2$ TABLESPOONS
   EACH) TEQUILA

$1^{1}/2$ CUPS SQUIRT OR OTHER SPARKLING
   GRAPEFRUIT DRINK

DASH OF SALT

4 ICE CUBES

In a cocktail shaker, combine the lime juice with the tequila, Squirt, salt, and ice cubes, and shake vigorously to mix well. Divide the drink between two glasses and serve at once.

FLOWER OF AZHAR

Flor de Azhar   *2 servings*

▼▼▼▼▼▼▼▼▼▼▼▼▼▼▼▼▼▼▼▼▼▼▼▼▼▼

2 SHOTS (ABOUT 3$\frac{1}{2}$ TABLESPOONS
   EACH) TEQUILA

$\frac{1}{2}$ CUP WHITE DRY VERMOUTH

1 CUP FRESH ORANGE JUICE

Combine all the ingredients and divide between two glasses. Serve cold.

MEXICAN FLAG

Bandera   *2 servings*

IF YOU ARE FAMILIAR WITH THE COLORS OF THE MEXICAN FLAG, you have already guessed why this beverage is called Bandera *(flag). In this particular recipe, the lime juice is also served in a separate* vaso tequilero *(tequila glass). This way, you serve the three glasses in the order displaying the colors of the flag: lime juice, tequila, and* sangrita.

▼▼▼▼▼▼▼▼▼▼▼▼▼▼▼▼▼▼▼▼▼▼▼▼▼▼

1 SHOT (ABOUT 3$\frac{1}{2}$ TABLESPOONS)
   FRESH LIME JUICE, IN 2 GLASSES

2 SHOTS (ABOUT 3$\frac{1}{2}$ TABLESPOONS
   EACH) TEQUILA

2 SHOTS (ABOUT 3$\frac{1}{2}$ TABLESPOONS
   EACH) *SANGRITA* (PAGE 210)

WHITE WINE SANGRIA

Sangria de Vino Blanco   *6 to 8 servings*

In Spain, particularly in Andalucía, where summers can be quite hot, white wine sangria is very popular and very often served with the added flavor of a liqueur, like Cointreau, for a sweet sangria, or cognac for a dry sangria. In Mexico, red sangria is more popular, however, white sangria is occasionally served.
You might like to try these options and experiment.

1 (750-ML) BOTTLE DRY WHITE WINE, CHILLED

2 CUPS GINGER ALE, CHILLED

JUICE OF 2 LIMES

2 (3-INCH) CINNAMON STICKS

1 APPLE, PEELED AND CHOPPED

1 ORANGE, PEELED AND SLICED INTO WEDGES

1 DOZEN ICE CUBES

In a punch bowl, combine the wine, ginger ale, lime juice, and cinnamon sticks, with the apple and orange. Refrigerate for about an hour, to allow the flavors to blend.

Just before serving, add the ice cubes and serve in chilled wine glasses.

BREADS AND DESSERTS
PANES Y POSTRES

THE SPANIARDS WHO ARRIVED IN TENOCHTITLÁN, now Mexico City, were not numerous, however, once they became the dominant class they modified many of the existent institutions. Christian churches and convents were built where the *teocallis* (ancient temples) had stood. In those convents, friars taught the natives other ways to cultivate the land, new methods to preserve food, and different procedures to prepare it.

Around the seventeenth century, the convents emerged and with them, elaborate and elegant cakes and desserts were created, to impress the viceroy and his people. These were rich and mostly liqueur-based.

Sugarcane, an important product brought from the Old World, soon became an essential element in preparing the desserts for which the nuns became famous. Brown sugar in the form of a hard cone called a *piloncillo* or *panocha* was favored more by the common people. *Capirotada*, a dessert traditionally served during Easter, a very sweet bread pudding with a thick syrup, garnished with raisins, almonds, and shredded cheese, is still made with *piloncillo*.

Many of these cakes, puddings, and other desserts are still served, perhaps with the amount of sugar reduced, since in the last few years we have considerably cut down our sugar intake. I have altered some of these recipes to this effect and they are still delicious.

MEXICAN CORN BREAD

Pan de Maiz   *Yields 20 to 22 slices*

IN A COUNTRY WHERE THERE ARE ABOUT FIVE HUNDRED *different kinds of* bizcochos *(sweet rolls) baked daily, breads such as coffee cake or banana bread are baked only for special occasions. All these bizcochos have various names, so it is easy to order exactly the ones you want. There are* conchas, cemitas, gendarmes, cuernos, hojaldras, limas, cocoles, novias, monjas, chilindrinas, trenzas, corbatas, cubiletes, *and many, many more. Bakeries also sell cakes, gelatins, fruit pies, and so on.*

On Sundays after the evening mass, and as the time of the merienda *approaches, it is a tradition to visit the bakeries to buy enough* bizcochos *for supper as well as breakfast. A very light supper usually consists of an assortment of fresh fruit, hot chocolate, and a variety of delicious* bizcochos.

You will find this corn bread a bit different than the ones you are used to. The difference is in using corn flour instead of corn meal, so the texture is smoother, without the grainy consistency that corn meal provides. Corn flour is commonly found in the same grocery aisle as other types of flour.

This corn bread is equally good for teatime, with a little bit of butter, or to accompany meats.

1 CUP ALL-PURPOSE FLOUR

1 CUP CORN FLOUR

2 TEASPOONS BAKING POWDER

$\frac{1}{2}$ CUP SUGAR

$\frac{1}{2}$ TEASPOON SALT

1 EGG

1 CUP MILK

$\frac{1}{4}$ CUP BUTTER, MELTED

Preheat the oven to 400°F. Grease an $8\frac{1}{2}$ x $4\frac{1}{2}$-inch loaf pan and dust with flour, shaking off the excess.

Sift the dry ingredients into a bowl. Add the egg and the milk, and beat for 2 minutes at medium speed with an electric mixer. Stir in the butter and continue beating until well mixed. Pour the mixture into the prepared pan.

Bake the corn bread for about 35 to 40 minutes, or until the top springs back when lightly touched.

BREAD FOR
THE DAY OF THE KINGS

Rosca de Reyes   *6 to 8 servings*

THE TRADITION OF LOS TRES REYES MAGOS, *or The Three Kings, came from Spain and holds that the Three Kings, the Magi from the East, set out for Spain each year on January 5, the eve of the Epiphany, to pay homage to the infant Christ. Legend has it that the Kings brought gifts not only for the holy Infant, but also for every child.*

On the evening of January 5, just before children go to bed, every member of the family puts out a pair of shoes with the absolute confidence that the Kings, Melchor, Gaspar, and Baltazar, will come and fill the shoes with gifts and treats. In most families, parents leave three different dishes of food for the Kings and fill their shoes with straw for the camels. The excitement starts that evening and culminates the following morning when the children wake up to open the gifts left by the Three Kings.

The traditional celebration of King's Day is a merienda *(light supper), at which Rosca de Reyes and hot chocolate are served. The* roscón, *as the ring is called in Spain, is a yeast bread with a tiny doll, representing the Christ Child, baked inside the* rosca, *and topped with candied fruit and sugar. Anyone lucky enough to discover the doll in his or her slice will enjoy good luck all through the year and is obligated to throw a party on February 2 (Candlemas) for all the friends who attended the* merienda.

The Dia de la Candelaria, *is still part of the holiday season and is usually celebrated with fireworks, to the delight of all the children.*

The tradition of the Three Kings in Mexico, as many other traditions, is intimately linked with Spain. There are slight variations in terms of the food left for the tired Kings that evening, having to do more with the different customs of each region in Mexico than with any other reason.

2 TABLESPOONS ACTIVE DRY YEAST

¼ CUP WARM WATER

DASH OF SUGAR, PLUS EXTRA FOR
  SPRINKLING

2⅓ CUPS FLOUR

9 EGG YOLKS

1 (14 OZ / 300 ML) CAN CONDENSED
  MILK

½ LB (250 G) BUTTER

1 WHOLE EGG, BEATEN

1 CUP CANDIED FRUIT, SUCH AS
  ORANGE, PINEAPPLE, FIGS, AND
  CITRON, SLICED INTO STRIPS

1 TINY HEATPROOF DOLL (OPTIONAL)

In a bowl, dissolve the yeast in the warm water. Add a dash of sugar and flour, and let the mixture stand for about 10 minutes. With a spoon, gradually mix in half of the flour, and beat for about 1 minute. Continue adding the rest of the flour, stirring. Add the egg yolks, 1 cup of the condensed milk and the butter, and mix well. When the dough begins to leave the sides of the bowl, turn it out onto a lightly floured board. The dough will be a bit sticky. Knead the dough, folding it toward you and then pressing it away from you with the heel of your hand. Knead the dough thoroughly for 10 minutes. Continue kneading until the dough becomes smooth and elastic.

Return the dough to a generously greased bowl and let it stand, covered, in a warm place for about an hour, or until doubled in volume. Knead the dough again and shape into a *rosca* (ring). Carefully transfer the ring to a greased baking sheet and let it rise for 45 minutes to an hour. Preheat the oven to 450°F.

Brush the *rosca* with the beaten egg and decorate it with the candied fruit. Sprinkle it with more sugar and bake for about 10 minutes. Remove the *rosca* from the oven and carefully insert the tiny doll into the dough. Lower the heat to 400°F and continue baking for another 20 to 25 minutes, or until a toothpick inserted comes out clean.

EGG YOLK BUÑUELOS

Buñuelos de Yema   *About 12 to 18 buñuelos*

Traditionally served around Christmas, buñuelos are round, paper-thin fritters about the size of a corn tortilla. They are usually served with a syrup made from piloncillo, *the hard cone of unrefined brown sugar that is very popular in Mexican desserts.*

As in other recipes, different states have their own version of buñuelos. In Veracruz, for instance, they are round with a hole in the middle, just like a doughnut. Regionally, the dough remains more or less the same, only the shape changes. In this recipe, buñuelos are cut into thin strips and sweetened with confectioners' sugar rather than syrup.

8 EGG YOLKS

¼ CUP ORANGE JUICE

¼ CUP SHERRY

2 CUPS ALL-PURPOSE FLOUR

1 TEASPOON LARD OR SHORTENING

OIL FOR DEEP-FRYING

CONFECTIONERS' SUGAR

Beat the egg yolks for 4 to 6 minutes, or until frothy and pale yellow. Add the orange juice, little by little, ⅓ cup water, and the sherry. Stir in the flour to form a soft paste, and then stir in the lard. Knead just until the ingredients are combined.

Form small balls of dough and roll out to make paper-thin about 2 x 1-inch strips. In a large frying pan, heat the oil, about ¼ inch deep, over medium heat, almost to the point of smoking, and quickly fry the buñuelos, one at a time. Transfer to paper towels to drain excess oil.

While still warm, place the buñuelos on a serving platter and sprinkle with the confectioners' sugar.

FANCY CHURROS

Churros Elegantes   *Yields about 24 churros*

IN MEXICO CITY, THE MOST FAMOUS CHURRERÍAS *were located in the old downtown. These were always full of people going to the movies and heading home after savoring a delicious, thick, hot chocolate with hot and crisp churros, the Mexican version of doughnuts, the only things on the menu and their specialty. Today you may also find* churrerías *in other parts of the big city.*

I understand that in Los Angeles, with so many Mexicans living there, churros are now very popular, and that you can find a few vendors around the city selling them hot out of the pan.

These churrerías *were usually small, with just enough space to accommodate a few tables for those who wanted to have their chocolate and churros right there and then. Others would buy enough to nibble on their way back to work or home. I still remember my parents taking us, as a big treat, to have churros and hot chocolate on a cool evening after the theater.*

Churros have to be eaten fresh and hot. Usually there was a man in charge of frying them on the spot, while at the same time putting the ones that were ready in a cone made of absorbent paper and handing the cone to a customer.

A canvas pastry bag is needed for the dough and can be found in specialty stores that sell cake-decorating supplies.

½ CUP MILK

1 TABLESPOON SUGAR

½ CUP BUTTER

1 CUP ALL-PURPOSE FLOUR

4 EGGS

VEGETABLE OIL FOR DEEP-FRYING

1 CUP GRANULATED SUGAR

2 TEASPOONS GROUND CINNAMON

CANVAS PASTRY BAG WITH A ½-INCH
   STEEL STAR TIP

In a heavy saucepan, combine the milk with ½ cup water, the sugar, and butter. Bring the mixture to a boil. Stir in the flour all at once and, with a wooden spoon, beat the mixture vigorously until smooth. Transfer to a mixing bowl. With an electric mixer, beat in the eggs, one at a time, beating well after each addition. Transfer the dough to the pastry bag fitted with the star tip.

In a large, cast-iron frying pan, heat the oil almost to the point of smoking and pipe about 5 inches of dough into the hot oil, cutting the end close to the tip with kitchen scissors. Fry the churros for about 3 to 4 minutes, turning them frequently until browned. With tongs, transfer the churro to paper towels to drain. Repeat this procedure until the dough is finished. While still warm, toss the churros with the cinnamon sugar. Serve warm with a good cup of steaming hot Mexican chocolate (page 204).

CHEESE CARAMEL FLAN

Queso Napolitano   *8 to 10 servings*

SOME RESTAURANTS IN MEXICO *feature a dessert called* Queso Napolitano, *a deceiving name that suggests a wedge of Italian cheese rather than a caramel flan made with cream cheese.*

The addition of the cream cheese to the traditional caramel flan, originally a Spanish dessert, gives it a different texture that is quite noticeable when you slice it. The purists are not in favor of this addition; however, it makes for an interesting variation worth trying.

¾ CUP SUGAR

4 EGGS

1 (4 OZ / 125 G) PACKAGE CREAM
  CHEESE

1 (14 OZ / 300 ML) CAN CONDENSED
  MILK

1⅓ CUPS 2% MILK

1 TEASPOON VANILLA EXTRACT

In a custard mold, or any deep baking pan, about 7-inches in diameter with a tight-fitting lid, heat the sugar until it melts and turns golden brown. Carefully remove the pan from the heat and quickly tilt to coat the mold, covering the bottom and all sides of the pan as high as possible. Cool and set aside. Preheat the oven to 350°F.

In a blender or food processor, blend the eggs and cream cheese until smooth. Stir in the condensed milk, the 2% milk, and the vanilla extract, and mix until thoroughly combined. Making sure that the caramel has set completely, pour the mixture into the mold and cover tightly with the lid.

Place the mold into a larger pan and add water to come halfway up the sides of the pan. Bake the flan for 1 to 1½ hours, or until a knife inserted comes out clean. Remove from the pan and cool for about 1 hour, then refrigerate at least 4 hours before serving.

To unmold the flan, run a knife around the sides and invert onto a serving platter, scraping as much of the caramel as possible onto the flan.

PECAN CARAMEL FLAN

Flan de Nuez   *6 to 8 servings*

THIS IS YET ANOTHER VERSION OF THE TRADITIONAL *caramel flan, the Spanish version of the French crème caramel. Caramel flan, in different versions, is very popular all through Latin America. In South America, for instance, a very flavorful caramel flan is made with squash laced with cinnamon, ginger, and nutmeg.*

Pecans are grown in the temperate climate of northern and central Mexico, particularly in the state of Nuevo León where the trees grow in abundance. This is reason enough to use these nuts in many desserts and candies like the famous palanquetas de nuez *(brittle).*

1¼ CUPS SUGAR

4 EGGS

½ CUP FINELY GROUND PECANS

1 CUP WHIPPING CREAM

1 CUP 2% MILK

In a custard mold or any deep baking pan, about 7-inches in diameter and with a tight-fitting lid, heat ¾ cup of the sugar, stirring occasionally, until melted and a deep amber color, about 5 minutes. Quickly turn the mold to coat it with the liquid caramel, covering the bottom and all the sides of the pan as high as possible. Cool until the caramel hardens. Set aside.

Preheat the oven to 350°F. In a mixing bowl, beat the eggs until well mixed and stir in the pecans. In a small saucepan, heat the cream and the milk with the remaining ½ cup of sugar, over medium heat, until hot and the sugar is dissolved. Remove from the heat and gradually whisk into the egg mixture. Mix all the ingredients well. Pour the mixture into the caramel mold and cover tightly with the lid.

Place the mold into a larger pan and add water to come halfway up the sides of the pan. Bake the flan for about 1½ hours, or until set. Cool and refrigerate. If a pressure cooker is used, place the mold inside the cooker and fill with water three quarters up the sides of the mold, and reduce the baking time to about 35 to 40 minutes. Cool the mold and refrigerate overnight before serving.

Just before serving, use a spatula to loosen all the sides of the mold and invert the flan onto a round platter. Scrape out the remaining caramel and add to the custard. The flan should be served cold or at room temperature.

GUANAJUATO-STYLE CORN FLAN

Flan de Elote Estilo Guanajuato   *6 to 8 servings*

NO OTHER INGREDIENT CAN MATCH *the delicate aroma and flavor of vanilla from Mexican soil, specifically from Papantla in the state of Veracruz. The Olmecs cultivated the beans for centuries before the Totonacas used them to pay their taxes to the great Tlatoani, Moctezuma, and they called it* xanal *or* xanat *(black flower). The word* vanilla *was born after the Spaniards discovered the* vaina *(pod) in the black flower.*
The use of the aromatic vanilla in combination with corn places this dessert in a class of its own.

¾ CUP GRANULATED SUGAR

4 EGGS

2 CUPS FRESH CORN KERNELS

1½ CUP 2% MILK

1 (14 OZ / 300 ML) CAN CONDENSED
MILK

1 TABLESPOON VANILLA EXTRACT

In a custard mold or any deep baking pan, about 7-inches in diameter with a tight-fitting cover, heat the sugar until melted and of a deep amber color. Remove from heat and quickly tilt the mold, to coat it, covering the bottom and all sides of the pan as high as possible. Let cool until the caramel hardens to the point that you can turn the mold upside down and the caramel does not drip. Set aside.

In a mixing bowl, beat the eggs just enough to mix and set aside. In a blender, process the corn with the 2% milk until well blended. Pour the corn mixture into the beaten eggs, add the condensed milk and vanilla extract, and mix well. Pour the mixture into the caramelized mold and cover tightly with the lid.

Please refer to Pecan Caramel Flan (page 223) for baking, unmolding, and serving procedures.

COFFEE LIQUEUR MOUSSE

Mousse de Licor de Café   *4 to 6 servings*

NOT MANY OF US HAVE SEEN COFFEE TREES *with their shiny green leaves and beautiful clusters of white, sweet aromatic flowers. It is hard to believe that this bushy tree with red coffee berries will eventually become a cup of coffee. Native to Ethiopia,* Coffea arabica *was known as early as the first century, but it was not until the fifteenth century that coffee, as it is known today, spread out into Arabia and then Egypt.*

In all probability, coffee was first introduced to Europe by way of the port of Venice, a most important trading center at that time. Today, more than 50 percent of the world supply comes from the New World. Central America, Mexico, Venezuela, Colombia, and Brazil are now the main suppliers.

For years and years, I used to bring coffee from Veracruz especially for my husband, who was the coffee drinker in the family. To this date, the restaurant La Parroquia in the port of Veracruz is famous for its coffee, served piping hot at any time of the day or year.

---

1 CUP WHIPPING CREAM

½ TABLESPOON INSTANT COFFEE

¼ CUP COFFEE LIQUEUR, SUCH AS KAHLÚA OR TÍA MARÍA

4 TEASPOONS SUGAR

1 EGG WHITE

DARK CHOCOLATE SHAVINGS FOR GARNISH

In a chilled bowl, beat the cream until soft peaks form, stir in the coffee, and continue beating until stiff. Add the liqueur and 2 teaspoons of the sugar. Continue beating until the mixture is very stiff.

In a separate bowl, beat the egg white to soft peaks, add the remaining sugar, and beat until stiff. Fold the egg white into the mixture, cover, and chill.

To serve, mound the coffee mousse in dessert glasses and decorate with chocolate shavings.

CREPES WITH CAJETA AND COFFEE LIQUEUR

Crepas de Cajeta con Licor de Café   *6 servings*

IF, FOR SOME REASON, THERE IS NO HOMEMADE DESSERT at the end of the main meal, I can assure you that there is an open jar of cajeta stored in the refrigerator. One spoonful of this marvelously sweet caramel spread on a piece of bolillo or French bread is enough to take the craving away.

My mother and I used to spend Easter at a dairy farm, owned by my mother's aunt and her huge family, while my father stayed behind unable to abandon his medical practice. The farm was located right in the heart of the city of Querétaro, in the plateau region, northwest of Mexico City, at that time still a small town. To spend the Semana Santa (Holy Week) at the farm was quite an adventure in more ways than one. Meals were heavy and long. Warm fresh milk, queso fresco, and beans were part of each meal. Freshly made tortillas with a few slices of avocado (Querétaro is also famous for its avocados) to accompany a good plate of red rice was the everyday sopa seca (dry soup).

One of the obligatory trips in Querérato was to Celaya, in the state of Guanajuato, home of wonderful candies, made with milk and pecans or pine nuts, in all sorts of beautiful shapes and colors, and of course, cajeta. At that time, this rich, thick and sweet dessert, made with goat's milk, was sold in small cajetes (wooden boxes), thus the name. Later on, cajeta was produced in larger quantities and is now sold in supermarkets throughout the country. The oldest brand is Coronado (1932) and it usually comes in 23.3 oz/660 G plastic containers or glass jars. Outside of Mexico, cajeta can be bought at Hispanic markets.

As long as we brought back a few boxes of cajeta and a reasonably good quantity of dulces de leche (milk candies), my father was quite content to stay home and tend to his patients.

½ CUP BUTTER

1 CUP CAJETA

½ CUP WHIPPING CREAM

¾ CUP ORANGE JUICE

¼ CUP COFFEE LIQUEUR, SUCH AS
    KAHLÚA

12 CREPES (PAGE 181)

½ CUP CHOPPED PECANS

Melt the butter in a large, nonstick skillet. With a wooden spoon, stir in the cajeta until smooth. Add the cream and stir until the mixture is well blended and has thickened slightly. Pour in the orange juice and coffee liqueur, and simmer the cajeta mixture until it is thick enough to lightly coat the spoon, usually 2 to 4 minutes. Reduce the heat.

Dip each crepe into the hot cajeta sauce, fold in half, and then fold again. Quickly transfer the crepes to a warm dessert plate, allowing two crepes per serving. Pour the remaining hot sauce over the crepes, garnish with the pecans, and serve at once.

CREPES FILLED WITH
MANGO IN BRANDY SAUCE

Crepas de Mango en Almíbar con Brandy   *4 servings*

FRESH MANGOES ARE A MOST DELECTABLE and scrumptious fruit when ripe. When they are in season, elaborate or complex desserts are not needed. In Mexico, the season starts in May and lasts until mid or late July. It is a delightful sight, at this time of the year to see the street vendors selling mangoes in all their glory. Other vendors sell them peeled, sliced and sprinkled with a very popular combination of lime juice and piquín chile powder, also used with jicamas, cucumbers, and corn on the cob.

For this recipe, canned mangoes in syrup may be used instead of fresh mangoes. If this is the case, warm up the mangoes with the syrup, add the butter and the brandy, and omit the sugar. Simmer for two or three minutes for flavors to blend. The crepes can be prepared in advance and kept refrigerated until ready to be used in this elegant and splendid dessert.

4 TO 5 FRESH RIPE MANGOES

¼ CUP BUTTER

½ CUP SUGAR

1 CUP BRANDY

12 CREPES (PAGE 181)

Peel the mangoes and cut them into long slices, about 2 inches wide. In a medium-size saucepan, melt the butter, then add the mango slices and the sugar. Simmer until the sugar is completely dissolved. Add the brandy and continue simmering for about 4 to 6 minutes, or until the sauce has a syrupy consistency. Preheat the oven to 350°F.

With a slotted spoon, fill each crepe with a spoonful of the mango mixture, roll up, and place the crepes in an 8-inch square baking dish. Top with the remaining syrup and add more brandy if desired. Bake the crepes for 4 to 5 minutes and serve at once.

MANGO PUDDING

Dulce de Mango   *4 to 6 servings*

THE BEST MANGOES FOR THIS SIMPLE DESSERT *are the champagne or Manila mangoes. However, if these are not available, other varieties like haden or petacón mangoes may be used. Make sure that the mangoes are ripe, but at the same time firm. The best time to buy them, outside of Mexico, is late June, July, and August.*

The recipe calls for evaporated milk, which gives it a thicker consistency. For a lighter dessert, 2% milk works well too.

3 MEDIUM-SIZE MANGOES

1 (12 OZ/385 ML) CAN EVAPORATED MILK

JUICE OF ½ LIME

2 TABLESPOONS RUM

SUGAR

Peel the mangoes, working from stem to tip to avoid wasting flesh. Chop the mangoes and purée in a blender or food processor with the milk, lime juice, rum, and sugar to taste.

Transfer to parfait glasses and refrigerate before serving.

MANGO MOUSSE WITH WHITE WINE

Mousse de Mango con Vino Blanco   *6 to 8 servings*

Originally from the Far East, mangoes are now cultivated in the warmer parts of Mexico. They vary in flavor, size, and color. The Manila or champagne mango, my favorite, is a rather longish fruit with a uniform yellow peel. It is customarily eaten with a mango fork, a three-pronged device whose middle prong is long enough to enter the pit and hold it. The ataulfo mango is very similar to the Champagne variety in shape and flavor, but has a slightly more reddish peel.

The petacón variety is a very fleshy, rounder mango whose peel can be yellow with patches of red. The best way to eat this variety is by cutting a slice as close as you can get to the pit, on both sides, and eating the flesh with a spoon. This way, you only have to peel it around the pit, without wasting any flesh at all.

Any variety of mangoes will be good for this splendid dessert. Canned mangoes may be used as well, reducing the amount of sugar by about half, since these usually come in syrup. Drain the mango slices well and discard the syrup.

3 CUPS CHOPPED MANGO

⅔ CUP SUGAR

1½ CUPS LIGHT CREAM

⅔ CUP LIME JUICE

1 CUP SOUR CREAM

⅓ CUP DRY WHITE WINE

2 ENVELOPES (1 TABLESPOON EACH)
   UNFLAVORED GELATIN

LIME PEEL TO GARNISH

In a blender or food processor, mix the mango with the sugar until puréed. In a mixing bowl, combine the cream with the lime juice and sour cream.

In a small saucepan, heat the wine over low heat, sprinkle the gelatin over it and stir until the gelatin is completely dissolved, about 3 to 4 minutes, or until clear. Stir the gelatin mixture into the cream mixture and add the mango purée. Mix well and pour into parfait glasses. Chill until firm.

Before serving, garnish each glass with lime peel.

MERINGUE WITH CARAMEL AND COFFEE LIQUEUR

Merengue Caramelizado   *6 to 8 servings*

Meringue and ice cream is a common combination when you have to come up with a dessert on short notice. In Mexico, one can count on bakeries selling small freshly baked meringues.

In this recipe, the meringue is baked in a ring mold and covered with a caramel sauce laced with coffee liqueur. The result is magnificent.

1¾ CUPS GRANULATED SUGAR

6 EGG WHITES

PINCH OF SALT

¼ TEASPOON CREAM OF TARTAR

¼ CUP COFFEE LIQUEUR, SUCH AS KAHLÚA

VANILLA OR CHOCOLATE ICE CREAM

In a dry, heavy saucepan, cook 1 cup of the sugar over medium heat until it begins to melt. Continue cooking, stirring with a wooden spoon, until it is completely melted and deep gold. Pour the caramel into a 1½-quart ring mold. Tilt and rotate the mold to coat the bottom and the sides. Let the caramel set.

Preheat the oven to 350°F. With an electric mixer, beat the egg whites with the salt until foamy. Add the cream of tartar, and continue beating until the egg whites hold stiff peaks. Beat in the remaining sugar, little by little, until the meringue looks glossy.

Spoon the meringue into the ring mold, tapping it sharply on a hard surface to expel any air bubbles and to smooth the top. Place the ring mold in a large baking dish or on a rimmed baking sheet, pour about 1 inch of water around it, and bake for about 1 hour. The meringue will rise and then deflate. Turn the oven off and let the meringue stand for 15 minutes. Transfer the mold to a rack and cool completely.

Invert the mold onto a deep, round serving plate, letting the caramel drip to cover the meringue. Put the mold in a skillet of simmering water and heat the hardened caramel, stirring occasionally until it has melted. Stir in the coffee liqueur and drizzle over the meringue. Serve with ice cream.

OLD-FASHIONED
ALMOND CREAM

Dulce Antiguo   *6 to 8 servings*

ONE OF THE MOST IMPORTANT LEGACIES *of the French occupation was probably the* bolillo *or French bread, as it is also called. Bolillos did not replace the Spanish* telera *bread but came to complement it. Bakeries, usually in the hands of Spaniards, bake both every day. Usually the* telera *is used for* tortas *(sandwiches) and the* bolillo *to accompany food or, in this unique recipe, to give the creamy texture and to act as a thickening agent.*

Here one can clearly see how cuisines, like languages, evolve in accordance with different influences. First the corn tortilla came from the native Indians, then came the Spanish telera, *and next the French* bolillo, *followed by the well-known baguette so popular around the world now*

The result is a sort of a bread pudding beautifully blended with almonds, another example of our Spanish roots with a distinct Moorish heritage, and the aromatic vanilla, native to Indian soil.

1 (3 OZ/90 G) BOLILLO OR CRUSTY
 FRENCH ROLL

1 TABLESPOON CORNSTARCH

½ CUP 2% MILK

1 (14 OZ/300 ML) CAN CONDENSED
 MILK

3 EGGS, SEPARATED

¼ CUP SHERRY

½ TEASPOON VANILLA EXTRACT

¼ TEASPOON ALMOND EXTRACT

PINCH OF CREAM OF TARTAR

1 TABLESPOON CONFECTIONERS' SUGAR

¾ CUP CHOPPED ALMONDS

In a blender, purée the *bolillo* with 2 cups water until well blended. Transfer to a saucepan, heat over medium heat, and bring to a soft boil. Dissolve the cornstarch in ¼ cup of the milk in a saucepan. Stir in the condensed milk and simmer for 5 to 7 minutes, or until thickened to a creamy consistency. Remove from heat and cool. Stir in the egg yolks beaten with the remaining ¼ cup of milk, sherry, vanilla extract, and almond extract. Mix well and transfer to parfait glasses.

Beat the egg whites with the cream of tartar until soft peaks form. Add the sugar and continue beating until glossy and stiff. Top the parfait glasses with this meringue and garnish with the almonds. Chill before serving.

WHIPPED ORANGE AND CREAM CHEESE GELATIN

Gelatina Batida de Naranja con Queso Crema   *6 to 8 servings*

GELATINS IN MEXICO are the everyday dessert. Bakeries sell them in a variety of colors, with layers of different flavors, beautifully garnished with fresh fruit in contrasting colors. They are the perfect present for a convalescing friend or as an additional dessert to bring when invited for dinner. Gelatins are so light that they go with almost everything and they are certainly a nice way to finish off a spicy meal.

1 (3 OZ/90 G) PACKAGE ORANGE OR PEACH GELATIN POWDER

1 CUP FRESH ORANGE JUICE

1 CUP 2% MILK

1 (4 OZ/125 G) PACKAGE CREAM CHEESE

1 TABLESPOON GRATED ORANGE RIND

In a small saucepan, heat the orange juice and, just before it boils, sprinkle with the gelatin, stirring until dissolved. Remove the saucepan from the heat and let the gelatin cool. Refrigerate until set.

Transfer the gelatin to a blender or food processor, add the cream cheese in small chunks and the milk, and process until the mixture is thoroughly blended. Transfer to individual molds and refrigerate until set.

Just before serving, unmold and garnish with the orange rind. Parfait or any other individual dessert glasses may be used instead of the molds.

GLOSSARY

DRY CHILES

ANCHO:

The ancho (wide) chile is the dry form of the poblano chile. It is a deep reddish-brown color, about 5 inches x 2 to 2½ inches wide. It is most commonly used in sauces and moles or stuffed with cheese or beans and served in tomato sauce.

CASCABEL:

This is a fairly small, round chile, almost the size of the Scotch Bonnet, but dark red, with a nutty flavor. The seeds make a rattling noise when shaken, thus its name: *cascabel*, meaning rattle. It is used mainly in salsas.

CHIPOTLE:

Chipotles, the dry form of jalapeño chiles, are about 2 inches long, with a wrinkled skin and a smoky flavor. They are often marinated in vinegar, tomato, and various herbs. Whether dry-packed or canned, chipotles are always quite hot.

DE ÁRBOL:

This dry chile is very thin and about 2 inches long. It is deep red in color, and can be very hot. It is used extensively in salsas.

GUAJILLO:

A rather long chile, about 4 to 5 inches, dark red, with a very smooth skin, similar to the New Mexico chile grown in the Rio Grande Valley. Guajillo, called *puya* when fresh, is grown in Central and Northern Mexico and is mainly used in sauces for enchiladas or in salsas in combination with other chiles.

MULATO:

Grown in Central Mexico, the mulatto chile is about the size of the ancho chile but a bit narrower. It is widely used in moles and salsas.

PASILLA:

Also known as *chile negro*, this is the dry *chilaca*, which is a variety of the poblano chile but much hotter. The pasilla chile is about 4 to 5 inches long, thin, and almost black. It is grown in the Central Mexican Valley.

PIQUÍN:

One of the smallest chiles, the piquín chile is the size of a small marble. It is also one of the hottest chiles in the market, if not the hottest. Usually used ground, and sprinkled on corn on the cob, jicama, mangoes, and cucumber.

Fresh Chiles

Banana:

A yellow pepper, about 2 inches long. Similar in shape to the jalapeno, but larger. It is always used fresh and is ideal for stews.

Güero or Largo:

Very similar in shape and color to the banana pepper, but hotter and different in flavor. It is widely used pickled, for dishes like dry cod, fresh fish, and chicken stews with heavy tomato sauces. An excellent substitute when this chile is not available is the Italian peperoncini, usually found in glass jars in the same section of the grocery store where the olives and the roasted peppers are located.

Jalapeño:

This chile is probably the most widely known in the rest of North America. In Mexico, however, the jalapeño is not used as much in salsas as it is pickled or in *escabeche*.

Habanero:

The habanero chile is a round, yellow, and sometimes light orange chile, very common in the Yucatán Peninsula. It is almost the size of the scotch bonnet. It is always used fresh and is very hot with a unique, floral flavor.

Poblano:

Poblanos are of a fairly large size and dark green in color. They are used for stuffing or in strips with cheese and cream. Sometimes incorrectly labeled *pasilla*, poblanos are mainly grown in the state of Puebla, thus their name.

Serrano:

A small green chile, about 2 inches long and thinner than a jalapeño, the serrano chile is probably the chile that we use the most, especially in central Mexico. It is always used fresh, either chopped or ground in salsas or stews, or simply minced on top of beans, soups, or other dishes.

Herbs:

Cilantro:

Also called Chinese parsley and coriander, cilantro is the Spanish name for the leaves of the coriander plant. It is the most widely used herb in Mexican cookery. Although the leaves are similar to flat-leaf parsley, the aroma and pungent flavor is quite different.

Epazote:

This is another widely used herb in Mexican cooking. Epazote provides black beans, mushrooms, zucchini blossoms, and *cuitlacoche*, with a wonderful flavor. It grows wild in some areas and its botanical name is *Chenopodium ambrosioides*. Available fresh in fine greengrocers or farmers' markets, epazote is one of the most important staples to achieve authentic Mexican flavors.

Yerbas de Olor:

This usually refers to a combination of bay, sage, thyme, and marjoram leaves. It is very common in family recipes to find the term *yerbas de olor* in instructions to cook meats and flavor broths. Each market in Mexico has its own stand of *yerbas*, displaying a huge variety of herbs, some for cooking, and others for medicinal teas. *Yerbas de olor* are commonly sold tied with a string, ready to use.

VEGETABLES:

CHAYOTE SQUASH:

Chayote is a delicately flavored, pear-shaped, light green squash with an edible flat seed in the middle. It may be smooth or spiny on the outside. This vegetable is becoming quite popular and is available almost all year-round.

CUITLACOCHE:

A fungus that develops on a type of corn grown in Mexico. This fungus forms in the kernels turning them dark, almost black. It is now available canned, prepared with onion and chopped serrano chiles. Usually eaten with warm corn tortillas or quesadillas or in more sophisticated dishes like crepes.

JICAMA:

A crisp, sweet and juicy, white root vegetable, shaped somewhat like a large turnip and covered with a brown, easy-to-peel skin. They vary widely in size, and are usually eaten raw with lots of lime juice and sprinkled with piquín chile.

NOPALES (CACTUS PADS):

These are the pads or leaves of the prickly pear cactus. They should be handled very carefully, as the needles are painfully sharp and must be removed before cooking. Please see page 171 for more information.

TOMATILLOS:

Also called *tomate verde*, this is not a green, underripe tomato, but a different vegetable. It stays green, even when fully ripened. Tomatillos are usually about the size of a plum tomato and have a papery husk that should be removed before cooking. Most of the time, they are cooked in stews and sauces, and eaten raw in salsas.

ZUCCHINI BLOSSOMS:

These are the yellow flowers of the zucchini. The blossoms are sautéed and cooked with epazote or cilantro and serrano chiles. They are a marvelous stuffing for crepes and quesadillas, among other dishes. Available fresh, in season, or canned in Hispanic markets.

Other Ingredients:

Achiote:

Also known as *annatto*, this comes from a small tropical tree that grows in southern Mexico and Central America. The pulp enclosing the seeds is yellow-orange and adds color and a very distinct flavor to any meat dish. Achiote is sold as a hard square that is usually mashed with bitter orange juice and prepared with cinnamon, cumin, cloves, oregano, and vinegar. It is also used for dyeing cloth.

Chorizo:

Chorizo is a spicy pork sausage seasoned with garlic, chile, cinnamon, cloves, oregano, cayenne pepper, vinegar, and salt. Spanish-style chorizo is usually milder than the Mexican-style chorizo.

Hominy:

Hominy is a type of corn mainly used in the popular *pozole*. It is called *cacahuazintle* and is considered to be of better quality than regular corn. Hominy is treated with lye to remove the skin and speed up the cooking process. When the base of the kernel is removed, it bursts open and looks like small flowers. White or yellow hominy is available now in cans. Either one can be used for *pozole*.

Masa:

This is the fresh corn dough used for making tortillas. You can only find fresh *masa* in *tortillerías* where tortillas are being made by the dozen and people stand in line to take them home, not only freshly made but hot and ready to eat.

Masa Harina:

Unbleached corn flour with a grainy texture. Outside of Mexico, *masa harina* is used to make tortillas and tamales. It is now widely available in major supermarkets and specialty stores. The most common brands are Maseca and Masa Harina; both are good and are used in the same proportions.

Plantains:

Mexico grows many varieties of bananas that differ in size, color and flavor. Plantain, or *plátano macho*, is a cooking banana, much larger than a normal banana, and is usually fried or baked. Plantains normally have their ends trimmed and are sliced lengthwise or in rounds.

Kitchen Implements

CAZUELA:

A loop-handled bowl or pot made out of clay. Before the era of aluminum, *cazuelas* were the pots that Mexicans used to cook everything. Now, these are only used for moles. Good restaurants that boast of serving very authentic dishes still use *cazuelas* for all their cooking. Some cooks claim that clay provides moles with an earthy flavor that cannot be achieved with any other kind of pot.

COMAL:

A *comal* is a round, flat pan without sides, very similar to a griddle. It has a small handle so it may be moved, if necessary, without burning your hands. It is quite a handy utensil to warm up tortillas, to make quesadillas and to roast chiles. The cast-iron ones are the best.

JARRO:

A pitcher made of clay, it is used to heat milk, *atole*, or chocolate. *Jarros* vary in size and color, and, because clay is known to keep heat longer, hot chocolate is traditionally made in a *jarro*.

MOLCAJETE:

A mortar and pestle made from volcanic stone. It is used for grinding ingredients into salsas. Before the blender came into being, salsas and guacamole were always made in a *molcajete*.

MOLINILLO:

Wooden utensil, about twelve inches long, round, with loose rings around the bottom part of the handle. Used for whipping hot chocolate. Readily available in markets in Mexico, with different, carved designs that make *molinillos* also a decorative piece in the kitchen. The more rings, the better the chocolate!

SALSERA:

A small bowl, usually ceramic, pewter, or clay, used to serve salsas.

BIBLIOGRAPHY

Calderón de la Barca, Marquesa. *La Vida en México*. Mexico: Libro Mex Editores, 1958.

Carreño King, Tania. *La Cocina Mexicana Através de los Siglos, VII El Pan de Cada Día*. Mexico: Editorial Clío, Libros y Videos, S.A. de C.V., 1997.

Carrillo, Ana María. *La Cocina Mexicana Através de los Siglos, La Cocina del Tomate, Frijol y Calabaza*. Mexico: Editorial Clío, Libros y Videos, S.A. de C.V., 1998.

De Benítez, Ana M. *Cocina Prehispánica*. Mexico: Ediciones Euroamericanas, 1974.

De Sahagún, Fray Bernardino. *Historia General de las Cosas de la Nueva España*. Mexico: Editorial Porrúa, 1985.

Díaz del Castillo, Bernal. *Verdadera Historia de la Conquista de la Nueva España*. Mexico: Ediciones Mexicanas, 1950.

Escalante, Jesús Flores. *Brevísima Historia de La Comida Mexicana*. Mexico: Asociación Mexicana de Estudios Fonográficos, 1994.

Jalisco Tequilana. *Historia del Tequila*. Revista de la Cámara Regional de la Industria Tequilera.

INDEX

achiote
  Baked Chicken in Achiote Sauce (*Pollo al Horno en Achiote*), 67
  Tacos Filled with Shredded Pork in Achiote Sauce (*Tacos de Cochinita Pibil*), 142–143

almonds
  Chicken Picadillo Filling (*Picadillo de Pollo*), 103
  Los Guajolotes Chicken in Mole Poblano (*Pollo en Mole Poblano Los Guajolotes*), 60–61
  Old-Fashioned Almond Cream (*Dulce Antiguo*), 231
  Pork Picadillo Empanadas (*Empanadas de Picadillo de Puerco*), 84
  Stuffed Poblano Chiles in Walnut Sauce (*Chiles en Nogada*), 116–117
  Sweet Tamales (*Tamales de Dulce*), 110
  Zacatecas-Style Roasting Hen (*Gallina Rellena Estilo Zacatecas*), 70–71

ancho chiles
  Ancho Chile Mole for Enmoladas (*Mole de Chile Ancho para Enmoladas*), 121
  Bread Soup with Garlic and Ancho Chile (*Sopa de Migas con Chile Ancho*), 37
  Fish Fillets in Adobo (*Filetes de Pescado en Adobo*), 92
  Leg of Pork in Ancho Chile Sauce (*Pierna de Puerco Enchilada*), 79
  Los Guajolotes Chicken in Mole Poblano (*Pollo en Mole Poblano Los Guajolotes*), 60–61
  Red Posole with Chicken (*Pozole Rojo*), 68–69
  Red Salsa with Fried Ancho Chile (*Salsa Roja con Chile Ancho Frito*), 155
  Spaghetti with Ancho Chile and Basil (*Spaghetti al Chile Ancho*), 51
  Spare Ribs in Adobo Sauce (*Costillas de Puerco Adobadas*), 83

ancho chiles (*continued*)
  Stuffed Ancho Chiles (*Chiles Anchos Rellenos*), 118
  Veracruz-Style Baked Tamal (*Tamal de Cazuela Estilo Veracruz*), 108–109

anise seeds
  Los Guajolotes Chicken in Mole Poblano (*Pollo en Mole Poblano Los Guajolotes*), 60–61

antojitos, 119–143

appetizers, 19–26
  Avocado Mousse (*Botana de Aguacate*), 17
  Baked Oysters on Toast (*Tostada de Ostiones al Horno*), 24
  Bologna Appetizer (*Entremés de Mortadela*), 21
  Garlic and Avocado Dip (*Dip de Ajo y Aguacate*), 18
  Hard-Boiled Eggs with Avocado (*Entremés de Huevos Duros con Aguacate*), 20
  Jicama and Avocado Appetizer (*Entremés de Jícama con Aguacate*), 19
  Oysters with Chipotle Adobo (*Ostiones Capeados con Chipotle*), 25
  Pollock Appetizer (*Cangrejo Frío*), 22
  Prawn Ceviche (*Ceviche de Camarón*), 23

apples
  Baked Chicken with Fruit and Vegetables (*Tapado de Pollo*), 72
  White Wine Sangria (*Sangria de Vino Blanco*), 214
  Zacatecas-Style Roasting Hen (*Gallina Rellena Estilo Zacatecas*), 70–71

Aunt Geor's Beef Tartare (*Carne Tártara de Tía Geor*), 78

avocados
  Avocado Mousse (*Botana de Aguacate*), 17
  Bajio-Style Shredded Beef (*Salpicón Estilo Bajío*), 77
  Fish with Avocado and Tomato Sauce (*Pescado con Salsa de Aguacate y Jitomate*), 94

avocados *(continued)*

Fusilli with Avocado Cream and Ricotta (*Tornillos con Crema de Aguacate y Queso Fresco*), 52

Garlic and Avocado Dip (*Dip de Ajo y Aguacate*), 18

Green Salsa with Avocado (*Salsa Verde con Aguacate*), 157

Guacamole, 149

Hard-Boiled Eggs with Avocado (*Entremés de Huevos Duros con Aguacate*), 20

Jicama and Avocado Appetizer (*Entremés de Jícama con Aguacate*), 19

Mesón del Angel Rice (*Arroz Estilo Mesón del Angel*), 46

Pickled Fish (*Pescado en Escabeche*), 95

Pollock Appetizer (*Cangrejo Frío*), 22

Pork Loin with Chipotle Chiles (*Tinga Estilo "Pitita"*), 82

Prawn Ceviche (*Ceviche de Camarón*), 23

Sardine, Tomato, and Feta Cheese Salad (*Ensalada de Sardinas*), 178

Shredded Beef Flautas with Avocado Sauce (*Flautas con Salsa de Aguacate*), 138

Aztec Casserole (*Budín Azteca*), 65

Baby Potatoes with Poblano Chiles (*Papitas Criollas con Rajas*), 173

bacon

Baked Oysters on Toast (*Tostada de Ostiones al Horno*), 25

Beans with Bacon and Beer (*Frijoles Borrachos*), 163

Oatmeal Soup (*Sopa de Avena*), 40

Bajio-Style Shredded Beef (*Salpicón Estilo Bajío*), 77

Baked Chayote Squash (*Chayotes al Horno*), 174

Baked Chicken in Achiote Sauce (*Pollo al Horno en Achiote*), 67

Baked Chicken with Fruit and Vegetables (*Tapado de Pollo*), 72

Baked Eggs on Refried Beans (*Huevos al Horno con Frijoles Refritos*), 169

Baked Oysters on Toast (*Tostada de Ostiones al Horno*), 25

Baked Prawns with Cheese and Jalapeños (*Camarones al Queso*), 97

Baked Scrambled Egg Taquitos (*Taquitos de Huevo al Horno*), 122

bananas

Baked Chicken with Fruit and Vegetables (*Tapado de Pollo*), 72

Basic Crepes (*Crepas Basicas*), 181

Basic Tamales (*Tamales*), 81–82

Basic Tomato Sauce (*Caldillo de Jitomate*), 29

basil

Red Snapper Fillets with Guacamole (*Filetes de Huachinango con Guacamole*), 96

Round Roast in Vinaigrette (*Cuete a la Vinagreta*), 75

Spaghetti with Ancho Chile and Basil (*Spaghetti al Chile Ancho*), 51

beans, 161–169

Baked Eggs on Refried Beans (*Huevos al Horno con Frijoles Refritos*), 169

Bean Sauce (*Salsa de Frijol*), 165

Beans in the Pot (*Frijoles de la Olla*), 164

Beans with Bacon and Beer (*Frijoles Borrachos*), 163

Pinto Beans with Roasted Red Peppers (*Frijoles con Chiles Morrones*), 167

Refried Beans with Totopos (*Frijoles Refritos con Totopos*), 168

Spanish-Style Beans (*Frijoles a la Española*), 166

beef, 73, 75–78

Aunt Geor's Beef Tartare (*Carne Tártara de Tía Geor*), 78

Bajio-Style Shredded Beef (*Salpicón Estilo Bajío*), 77

Breaded Beef Roulade (*Milanesas*), 76

Round Roast in Vinaigrette (*Cuete a la Vinagreta*), 75

Shredded Beef Flautas with Avocado Sauce (*Flautas con Salsa de Aguacate*), 138

Steak and Cheese Soft Tacos (*Tacos de Bistec con Queso*), 139 beer

   Beans with Bacon and Beer (*Frijoles Borrachos*), 163

   Drunken Salsa (*Salsa Borracha*), 153

   Lime-Spiked Beer (*Chelada*), 206

   Spicy Lime-Spiked Beer (*Michelada*), 207

Beet and Orange Juice Cooler (*Agua Fresca de Betabel y Jugo de Naranja*), 193

bell peppers

   Baked Prawns with Cheese and Jalapeños (*Camarones al Queso*), 97

   Chayote Squash and Eggplant Casserole (*Ensalada de Chayote y Berenjena*), 180

   Pickled Jalapeño Chiles (*Chiles en Vinagre*), 159

   Pinto Beans with Roasted Red Peppers (*Frijoles con Chiles Morrones*), 167

   Valencia-Style Paella (*Paella Valenciana*), 45

beverages, 191–214

   Beet and Orange Juice Cooler (*Agua Fresca de Betabel y Jugo de Naranja*), 193

   Cactus Juice (*Jugo de Nopales*), 194

   Cactus Pear Cooler (*Agua de Tuna*), 195

   Café au Lait (*Café con Leche*), 198

   Coffee from a Clay Pot (*Café de Olla*), 199

   Coffee with a Sting (*Café con Piquete*), 200

   Cucumber Cooler with Tequila (*Agua de Pepino con Piquete*), 196

   Easy Rice Cooler (*Horchata Fácil*), 181

   Flower of Azhar (*Flor de Azhar*), 213

   Fresh Fruit and Vegetable Juice (*Jugo de Frutas y Vegetales*), 197

   Hot Chocolate and Corn Drink (*Champurrado*), 203

   Hot Chocolate for Tamales and Churros (*Chocolate Caliente*), 204–205

   Lime-Spiked Beer (*Chelada*), 206

   Mexican Eggnog (*Rompope Casero*), 202

   Mexican Flag (*Bandera*), 213

   Mocambo (*Mocambo*), 212

   Prune and Rum Punch (*Ponche de Ciruela Pasa*), 209

   Spiced Tomato Juice Chaser (*Sangrita*), 210

   Spicy Lime-Spiked Beer (*Michelada*), 207

beverages *(continued)*

   Tequila Pop (*La Paloma*), 212

   Vampire (*Vampiro*), 208

   White Russian (*Ruso Blanco*), 208

   White Wine Sangria (*Sangria de Vino Blanco*), 214

black beans

   Baked Eggs on Refried Beans (*Huevos al Horno con Frijoles Refritos*), 169

   Bean Sauce (*Salsa de Frijol*), 165

   Beans in the Pot (*Frijoles de la Olla*), 164

   Northern-Style Taquitos (*Taquitos Norteños*), 125

   Refried Beans with Totopos (*Frijoles Refritos con Totopos*), 168

Bologna Appetizer (*Entremés de Mortadela*), 21

brandy

   Crepes Filled with Mango in Brandy Sauce (*Crepas de Mango en Almíbar con Brandy*), 227

bread crumbs

   Breaded Beef Roulade (*Milanesas*), 76

   Chicken Breasts in Orange Juice (*Pechugas de Pollo en Jugo de Naranja*), 57

   Chicken Breasts with Molcajete Salsa (*Pechugas en Salsa de Molcajete*), 58

   Breaded Beef Roulade (*Milanesas*), 76

   Oysters with Chipotle Adobo (*Ostiones Capeados con Chipotle*), 25

breads, 215–223

   Bread for the Day of Kings (*Rosca de Reyes*), 218–219

   Egg Yolk Buñuelos (*Buñuelos de Yema*), 220

   Fancy Churros (*Churros Elegantes*), 223

   Mexican Corn Bread (*Pan de Maiz*), 217

Bread Soup with Garlic and Ancho Chile (*Sopa de Migas con Chile Ancho*), 37

Buñuelos, Egg Yolk (*Buñuelos de Yema*), 220

burritas

   Flour Tortillas Filled with Ham and Cheese (*Burritas Norteñas*), 124

buttermilk

   Cream of Cauliflower Soup with Poblano Chile and Corn (*Sopa Crema de Coliflor con Chile Poblano y Elote*), 34

buttermilk *(continued)*
  Cream of Cucumber Soup (*Crema Fría de Pepino*), 35
  Crème Fraîche (*Crema Espesa*), 148

cabbage
  Nayarit-Style Prawn Tacos (*Tacos de Camarón Estilo Nayarit*), 134
cactus pads (*nopales*), 171
  Cactus Juice (*Jugo de Nopales*), 194
  Cactus Pad, Poblano Chile, and Chorizo Quesadillas (*Quesadillas de Nopales con Poblano y Chorizo*), 135
  Cactus Pads in Cheese and Mushroom Sauce (*Nopales en Salsa de Queso*), 179
  Cactus Pad Soup (*Sopa de Nopales*), 30
  Fresh Fruit and Vegetable Juice (*Jugo de Frutas y Vegetales*), 197
  Vegetable Casserole (*Cacerola de Verduras*), 188
  Warm Cactus Pad Salad (*Ensalada Caliente de Nopales*), 175
Cactus Pear Cooler (*Agua de Tuna*), 195
Café au Lait (*Café con Leche*), 198
candied fruit
  Bread for the Day of Kings (*Rosca de Reyes*), 218–219
  Stuffed Poblano Chiles in Walnut Sauce (*Chiles en Nogada*), 116–117
  Sweet Tamales (*Tamales de Dulce*), 110
capers
  Aunt Geor's Beef Tartare (*Carne Tártara de Tía Geor*), 78
  Christmas Cod (*Bacalao de Navidad*), 90–91
caramel
  Crepes with Cajeta and Coffee Liqueur (*Crepas de Cajeta con Licor de Café*), 226
  Meringue with Caramel and Coffee Liqueur (*Merengue Caramelizado*), 230
carrots
  Chicken in Cheese and Chipotle Chile Sauce (*Pollo en Salsa de Queso y Chipotle*), 59
  Chicken in Chorizo Sauce (*Pollo en Salsa de Chorizo*), 62
  Mole Casserole (*Budín de Mole*), 66

carrots *(continued)*
  Pickled Jalapeño Chiles (*Chiles en Vinagre*), 159
  Round Roast in Vinaigrette (*Cuete a la Vinagreta*), 75
  Sardine-Stuffed Poblano Chiles (*Chiles de Sardina en Frío*), 114
  Spicy Carrot Salad (*Ensalada Fría de Zanahoria con Picante*), 177
  Vegetable Casserole (*Cacerola de Verduras*), 188
  Vegetable-Filled Crepes (*Crepas de Verdura al Horno*), 184
Cascabel Chile Salsa (*Salsa de Chile Cascabel*), 150
casseroles
  Aztec Casserole (*Budín Azteca*), 65
  Chayote Squash and Eggplant Casserole (*Ensalada de Chayote y Berenjena*), 180
  Corn Tortilla and Pork Casserole (*Budín de Tortilla con Carne de Puerco*), 85
  Cuitlacoche and Zucchini Blossom Casserole (*Pastel de Cuitlacoche y Flor de Calabaza*), 186–187
  Mole Casserole (*Budín de Mole*), 66
  Spinach and Potato Casserole (*Budín de Espinaca*), 189
  Tortilla and Pasilla Chile Casserole (*Corona de Tortillas y Chile Pasilla*), 185
  Vegetable Casserole (*Cacerola de Verduras*), 188
  Xochitl Casserole (*Budín Xóchitl*), 64
  Zucchini Blossom, Poblano Chile, and Corn Casserole (*Budín de Flor de Calabaza y Elote*), 190
cauliflower
  Cream of Cauliflower Soup with Poblano Chile and Corn (*Sopa Crema de Coliflor con Chile Poblano y Elote*), 34
  Pickled Jalapeño Chiles (*Chiles en Vinagre*), 159
celery
  Chicken in Cheese and Chipotle Chile Sauce (*Pollo en Salsa de Queso y Chipotle*), 59

celery *(continued)*
   Chicken in Chorizo Sauce (*Pollo en Salsa de Chorizo*), 62
   Fresh Fruit and Vegetable Juice (*Jugo de Frutas y Vegetales*), 197
   Mole Casserole (*Budín de Mole*), 66
ceviche
   Prawn Ceviche (*Ceviche de Camarón*), 23
chayote squash
   Baked Chayote Squash (*Chayotes al Horno*), 174
   Chayote Squash and Eggplant Casserole (*Ensalada de Chayote y Berenjena*), 180
cheddar cheese
   Chicken in Cheese and Chipotle Chile Sauce (*Pollo en Salsa de Queso y Chipotle*), 59
cheese. *see* cheddar cheese; Chihuahua cheese; cream cheese; Edam cheese; farmer cheese; feta cheese; Manchego cheese; Monterey Jack cheese; mozzarella cheese; Oaxacan cheese; Parmesan cheese; queso fresco; ricotta cheese
Cheese Caramel Flan (*Queso Napolitano*), 222
chicken, 55–72
   Aztec Casserole (*Budín Azteca*), 65
   Baked Chicken in Achiote Sauce (*Pollo al Horno en Achiote*), 67
   Baked Chicken with Fruit and Vegetables (*Tapado de Pollo*), 72
   Chicken and Poblano Chile Tacos (*Tacos Poblanos*), 123
   Chicken Breasts in Orange Juice (*Pechugas de Pollo en Jugo de Naranja*), 57
   Chicken Breasts with Molcajete Salsa (*Pechugas en Salsa de Molcajete*), 58
   Chicken in Cheese and Chipotle Chile Sauce (*Pollo en Salsa de Queso y Chipotle*), 59
   Chicken in Chorizo Sauce (*Pollo en Salsa de Chorizo*), 62
   Los Guajolotes Chicken in Mole Poblano (*Pollo en Mole Poblano Los Guajolotes*), 60–61
   Chicken in Prune and Red Wine Sauce (*Pollo con Ciruelas y Vino Tinto*), 63

chicken *(continued)*
   Chicken Picadillo Filling (*Picadillo de Pollo*), 103
   Mole Casserole (*Budín de Mole*), 66
   Mole Poblano Chicken Filling (*Relleno de Pollo con Mole*), 105
   Mole Poblano Enchiladas (*Enchiladas de Mole Poblano*), 132
   Red Chile Chicken Filling (*Chile Rojo para Relleno*), 106
   Red Posole with Chicken (*Pozole Rojo*), 68–69
   Swiss Enchiladas (*Enchiladas Suizas*), 140–141
   Tomatillo Chicken Filling (*Chile Verde para Relleno*), 104
   Valencia-Style Paella (*Paella Valenciana*), 45
   Veracruz-Style Baked Tamal (*Tamal de Cazuela Estilo Veracruz*), 108–109
   Xochitl Casserole (*Budín Xóchitl*), 64
   Zacatecas-Style Roasting Hen (*Gallina Rellena Estilo Zacatecas*), 70–71
Chihuahua cheese
   Baked Chayote Squash (*Chayotes al Horno*), 174
   Corn Tortilla and Pork Casserole (*Budín de Tortilla con Carne de Puerco*), 85
   Refried Beans with Totopos (*Frijoles Refritos con Totopos*), 168
chiles. *see* ancho chiles; cascabel chiles; chiles de Árbol; chipotle chiles; guajillo chiles; jalapeño chiles; mulato chiles; New Mexico chiles; pasilla chiles; pickled chiles; poblano chiles; serrano chiles
Chile Sauce, 111
chiles de Árbol
   Chile de Árbol and Guajillo Salsa (*Salsa de Chile de Árbol y Guajillo*), 151
   Tomato Salsa with Chile de Árbol (*Salsa Roja de Chile de Árbol*), 158
chile rellenos
   Poblano Chiles Stuffed with Tamales (*Chiles Rellenos de Tamales*), 115
   Pork-Stuffed Poblano Chiles (*Chiles Rellenos de Picadillo de Puerco*), 113

chile rellenos *(continued)*

Sardine-Stuffed Poblano Chiles (*Chiles de Sardina en Frío*), 114

Stuffed Ancho Chiles (*Chiles Anchos Rellenos*), 118

Stuffed Poblano Chiles in Walnut Sauce (*Chiles en Nogada*), 116–117

chipotle adobo

Oysters with Chipotle Adobo (*Ostiones Capeados con Chipotle*), 25

Cactus Pad Soup (*Sopa de Nopales*), 30

Chicken in Cheese and Chipotle Chile Sauce (*Pollo en Salsa de Queso y Chipotle*), 59

Pork Loin with Chipotle Chiles (*Tinga Estilo "Pitita"*), 62

chipotle chiles

Baked Scrambled Egg Taquitos (*Taquitos de Huevo al Horno*), 122

Cactus Pad Soup (*Sopa de Nopales*), 30

Chicken and Poblano Chile Tacos (*Tacos Poblanos*), 123

Chicken in Cheese and Chipotle Chile Sauce (*Pollo en Salsa de Queso y Chipotle*), 59

Los Guajolotes Chicken in Mole Poblano (*Pollo en Mole Poblano Los Guajolotes*), 60–61

Corn Tortilla Dry Soup (*Sopa Seca de Tortilla*), 33

Pork Loin with Chipotle Chiles (*Tinga Estilo "Pitita"*), 82

Veracruz-Style Baked Tamal (*Tamal de Cazuela Estilo Veracruz*), 108–109

chocolate. *see* Mexican chocolate

chorizo sausage

Cactus Pad, Poblano Chile, and Chorizo Quesadillas (*Quesadillas de Nopales con Poblano y Chorizo*), 135

Chicken in Chorizo Sauce (*Pollo en Salsa de Chorizo*), 62

Rice with Chorizo Tacos (*Arroz Blanco con Taquitos de Chorizo*), 49

Quesadillas with Potato and Chorizo (*Quesadillas de Papa con Chorizo*), 137

Spanish-Style Beans (*Frijoles a la Española*), 166

chorizo sausage *(continued)*

Tortilla and Pasilla Chile Casserole (*Corona de Tortillas y Chile Pasilla*), 185

Valencia-Style Paella (*Paella Valenciana*), 45

Christmas Cod (*Bacalao de Navidad*), 90–91

Churros, Fancy (*Churros Elegantes*), 221

cilantro

Baked Eggs on Refried Beans (*Huevos al Horno con Frijoles Refritos*), 169

Beans in the Pot (*Frijoles de la Olla*), 164

Beans with Bacon and Beer (*Frijoles Borrachos*), 163

Bologna Appetizer (*Entremés de Mortadela*), 21

Fusilli with Avocado Cream and Ricotta (*Tornillos con Crema de Aguacate y Queso Fresco*), 52

Green Herb Spaghetti (*Spaghetti Verde*), 50

Green Salsa (*Salsa Verde*), 156

Guacamole, 149

Jicama, Red Onion, and Orange Salad (*Ensalada de Jícama y Cebolla Morada*), 176

Mesón del Angel Rice (*Arroz Estilo Mesón del Angel*), 46

Mushroom Quesadillas (*Quesadillas de Hongos*), 136

Peneques in Tomatillo Sauce (*Peneques en Salsa Verde*), 133

Pico de Gallo (*Pico de Gallo*), 154

Prawn Ceviche (*Ceviche de Camarón*), 23

Spiced Tomato Juice Chaser (*Sangrita*), 210

Warm Cactus Pad Salad (*Ensalada Caliente de Nopales*), 175

Xochitl Casserole (*Budín Xóchitl*), 64

cinnamon

Coffee from a Clay Pot (*Café de Olla*), 199

Easy Rice Cooler (*Horchata Fácil*), 201

Los Guajolotes Chicken in Mole Poblano (*Pollo en Mole Poblano Los Guajolotes*), 60–61

Pickled Fish (*Pescado en Escabeche*), 95

Prune and Rum Punch (*Ponche de Ciruela Pasa*), 209

cinnamon (*continued*)

Tacos Filled with Shredded Pork in Achiote Sauce (*Tacos de Cochinita Pibil*), 142–143

White Wine Sangria (*Sangria de Vino Blanco*), 214

Zacatecas-Style Roasting Hen (*Gallina Rellena Estilo Zacatecas*), 70–71

clams

Seafood Soup (*Sopa de Mariscos*), 41

Valencia-Style Paella (*Paella Valenciana*), 45

cloves

Chicken Breasts with Molcajete Salsa (*Pechugas en Salsa de Molcajete*), 58

Coffee from a Clay Pot (*Café de Olla*), 199

cod

Christmas Cod (*Bacalao de Navidad*), 90–91

coffee

Café au Lait (*Café con Leche*), 198

Coffee from a Clay Pot (*Café de Olla*), 199

Coffee Liqueur Mousse (*Mousse de Licor de Café*), 225

Coffee with a Sting (*Café con Piquete*), 200

coffee liqueur

Coffee Liqueur Mousse (*Mousse de Licor de Café*), 225

Coffee with a Sting (*Café con Piquete*), 200

Crepes with Cajeta and Coffee Liqueur (*Crepas de Cajeta con Licor de Café*), 226

Meringue with Caramel and Coffee Liqueur (*Merengue Caramelizado*), 230

Vampire (*Vampiro*), 208

condensed milk

Bread for the Day of Kings (*Rosca de Reyes*), 218–219

Cheese Caramel Flan (*Queso Napolitano*), 222

Guanajuato-Style Corn Flan (*Flan de Elote Estilo Guanajuato*), 224

Old-Fashioned Almond Cream (*Dulce Antiguo*), 231

coriander

Los Guajolotes Chicken in Mole Poblano (*Pollo en Mole Poblano Los Guajolotes*), 60–61

corn. *see also* hominy corn

Cactus Pad Soup (*Sopa de Nopales*), 30

Corn Soup (*Sopa de Elote*), 31

Corn Tortilla and Pork Casserole (*Budín de Tortilla con Carne de Puerco*), 85

Cream of Cauliflower Soup with Poblano Chile and Corn (*Sopa Crema de Coliflor con Chile Poblano y Elote*), 34

Cream of Corn Soup (*Sopa Crema de Elote*), 32

Cuitlacoche and Zucchini Blossom Casserole (*Pastel de Cuitlacoche y Flor de Calabaza*), 186–187

Guanajuato-Style Corn Flan (*Flan de Elote Estilo Guanajuato*), 224

Mesón del Angel Rice (*Arroz Estilo Mesón del Angel*), 46

Mole Casserole (*Budín de Mole*), 68

Pork with Green Mole Sauce (*Caldillo de Cerdo en Mole Verde*), 81

Veracruz-Style Baked Tamal (*Tamal de Cazuela Estilo Veracruz*), 108–109

Zucchini Blossom, Poblano Chile, and Corn Casserole (*Budín de Flor de Calabaza y Elote*), 190

Zucchini Blossom Lasagna (*Lasagna de Flor de Calabaza*), 53

Zucchini Blossom Soup (*Sopa de Flor de Calabaza*), 39

Corn Bread, Mexican (*Pan de Maiz*), 217

cornflakes

Cactus Pads in Cheese and Mushroom Sauce (*Nopales en Salsa de Queso*), 179

corn flour. *see also* Masa Harina; Maseca corn flour

Mexican Corn Bread (*Pan de Maiz*), 217

corn husks

Basic Tamales (*Tamales*), 101–102

Poblano Chiles Stuffed with Tamales (*Chiles Rellenos de Tamales*), 115

Sweet Tamales (*Tamales de Dulce*), 110

Zucchini Blossom and Poblano Chile Tamales (*Tamales de Flor de Calabaza*), 107

corn tortillas, 17
   Ancho Chile Mole for Enmoladas (*Mole de Chile Ancho para Enmoladas*), 121
   Aztec Casserole (*Budín Azteca*), 65
   Baked Scrambled Egg Taquitos (*Taquitos de Huevo al Horno*), 122
   Cactus Pad, Poblano Chile, and Chorizo Quesadillas (*Quesadillas de Nopales con Poblano y Chorizo*), 135
   Chicken and Poblano Chile Tacos (*Tacos Poblanos*), 123
   Rice with Chorizo Tacos (*Arroz Blanco con Taquitos de Chorizo*), 49
   Corn Tortilla and Pork Casserole (*Budín de Tortilla con Carne de Puerco*), 85
   Corn Tortilla Dry Soup (*Sopa Seca de Tortilla*), 33
   Cream of Corn Soup (*Sopa Crema de Elote*), 32
   Cuitlacoche and Zucchini Blossom Casserole (*Pastel de Cuitlacoche y Flor de Calabaza*), 186–187
   Fried Tortillas with Mole Poblano (*Enmoladas*), 128
   Guajillo Chile Enchiladas (*Enchiladas de Chile Guajillo*), 129
   Homemade Corn Tortillas (*Tortillas de Maiz Hechas en Casa*), 130
   Los Guajolotes Chicken in Mole Poblano (*Pollo en Mole Poblano Los Guajolotes*), 60–61
   Mole Casserole (*Budín de Mole*), 66
   Mole Poblano Enchiladas (*Enchiladas de Mole Poblano*), 132
   Mushroom Quesadillas (*Quesadillas de Hongos*), 136
   Nayarit-Style Prawn Tacos (*Tacos de Camarón Estilo Nayarit*), 134
   Peneques in Tomatillo Sauce (*Peneques en Salsa Verde*), 133
   Quesadillas with Potato and Chorizo (*Quesadillas de Papa con Chorizo*), 137
   Quick Mole Enchiladas (*Enchiladas Rápidas de Mole*), 131

corn tortillas (*continued*)
   Red Posole with Chicken (*Pozole Rojo*), 68–69
   Refried Beans with Totopos (*Frijoles Refritos con Totopos*), 168
   Shredded Beef Flautas with Avocado Sauce (*Flautas con Salsa de Aguacate*), 138
   Steak and Cheese Soft Tacos (*Tacos de Bistec con Queso*), 139
   Swiss Enchiladas (*Enchiladas Suizas*), 140–141
   Tacos Filled with Shredded Pork in Achiote Sauce (*Tacos de Cochinita Pibil*), 142–143
   Tortilla and Pasilla Chile Casserole (*Corona de Tortillas y Chile Pasilla*), 185
   Xochitl Casserole (*Budín Xóchitl*), 64
   Zacatecas-Style Enjitomatadas (*Enjitomatadas Estilo Zacatecas*), 126–127
   Zucchini Blossom, Poblano Chile, and Corn Casserole (*Budín de Flor de Calabaza y Elote*), 190
cream. *see also* whipping cream
   Corn Soup (*Sopa de Elote*), 31
   Cream of Cucumber Soup with White Wine (*Sopa de Pepino*), 36
   Mango Mousse with White Wine (*Mousse de Mango con Vino Blanco*), 229
cream cheese
   Avocado Mousse (*Botana de Aguacate*), 17
   Cactus Pads in Cheese and Mushroom Sauce (*Nopales en Salsa de Queso*), 179
   Cheese Caramel Flan (*Queso Napolitano*), 222
   Crepes Filled with Poblano and Pine Nuts (*Crepas de Rajas con Piñones*), 183
   Stuffed Poblano Chiles in Walnut Sauce (*Chiles en Nogada*), 116–117
   Whipped Orange and Cream Cheese Gelatin (*Gelatina Batida de Naranja con Queso Crema*), 232
Cream of Cauliflower Soup with Poblano Chile and Corn (*Sopa Crema de Coliflor con Chile Poblano y Elote*), 34
Cream of Corn Soup (*Sopa Crema de Elote*), 32

Cream of Cucumber Soup (*Crema Fría de Pepino*), 35

Cream of Cucumber Soup with White Wine (*Sopa de Pepino*), 36

Creamy Rice with Poblano Chile Strips (*Arroz Blanco con Rajas de Poblano*), 48

Crème Fraîche (*Crema Espesa*), 148

   Ancho Chile Mole for Enmoladas (*Mole de Chile Ancho para Enmoladas*), 121

   Chicken in Cheese and Chipotle Chile Sauce (*Pollo en Salsa de Queso y Chipotle*), 59

   Cuitlacoche and Zucchini Blossom Casserole (*Pastel de Cuitlacoche y Flor de Calabaza*), 186–187

   Fried Tortillas with Mole Poblano (*Enmoladas*), 128

   Guajillo Chile Enchiladas (*Enchiladas de Chile Guajillo*), 129

   Mole Casserole (*Budín de Mole*), 66

   Mole Poblano Enchiladas (*Enchiladas de Mole Poblano*), 132

   Peneques in Tomatillo Sauce (*Peneques en Salsa Verde*), 133

   Quick Mole Enchiladas (*Enchiladas Rápidas de Mole*), 131

   Tortilla and Pasilla Chile Casserole (*Corona de Tortillas y Chile Pasilla*), 185

   Vegetable Casserole (*Cacerola de Verduras*), 188

   Vegetable-Filled Crepes (*Crepas de Verdura al Horno*), 184

   Zacatecas-Style Enjitomatadas (*Enjitomatadas Estilo Zacatecas*), 126–127

   Zucchini Blossom Lasagna (*Lasagna de Flor de Calabaza*), 53

crepes, 181–184

   Basic Crepes (*Crepas Basicas*), 181

   Crepes Filled with Cuitlacoche (*Crepas Rellenas de Cuitlacoche*), 182

   Crepes Filled with Mango in Brandy Sauce (*Crepas de Mango en Almíbar con Brandy*), 227

   Crepes Filled with Poblano and Pine Nuts (*Crepas de Rajas con Piñones*), 183

crepes *(continued)*

   Crepes with Cajeta and Coffee Liqueur (*Crepas de Cajeta con Licor de Café*), 226

   Vegetable-Filled Crepes (*Crepas de Verdura al Horno*), 184

cucumbers

   Cream of Cucumber Soup (*Crema Fría de Pepino*), 35

   Cream of Cucumber Soup with White Wine (*Sopa de Pepino*), 36

   Cucumber Cooler with Tequila (*Agua de Pepino con Piquete*), 196

cuitlacoche

   Crepes Filled with Cuitlacoche (*Crepas Rellenas de Cuitlacoche*), 182

   Cuitlacoche and Zucchini Blossom Casserole (*Pastel de Cuitlacoche y Flor de Calabaza*), 186–187

cumin

   Cascabel Chile Salsa (*Salsa de Chile Cascabel*), 150

   Pickled Fish (*Pescado en Escabeche*), 95

   Zacatecas-Style Roasting Hen (*Gallina Rellena Estilo Zacatecas*), 70–71

custards. *see* puddings and custards

dill

   Cream of Cucumber Soup (*Crema Fría de Pepino*), 35

dips. *see also* salsas

   Garlic and Avocado Dip (*Dip de Ajo y Aguacate*), 18

   Guacamole, 149

Drunken Salsa (*Salsa Borracha*), 153

Easy Rice Cooler (*Horchata Fácil*), 201

Edam cheese

   Spinach and Potato Casserole (*Budín de Espinaca*), 189

Eggnog, Mexican (*Rompope Casero*), 102

eggplant

   Chayote Squash and Eggplant Casserole (*Ensalada de Chayote y Berenjena*), 180

eggs
 Baked Eggs on Refried Beans (*Huevos al Horno con Frijoles Refritos*), 169
 Baked Scrambled Egg Taquitos (*Taquitos de Huevo al Horno*), 122
 Cheese Caramel Flan (*Queso Napolitano*), 222
 Egg Yolk Buñuelos (*Buñuelos de Yema*), 220
 Guanajuato-Style Corn Flan (*Flan de Elote Estilo Guanajuato*), 224
 Hard-Boiled Eggs with Avocado (*Entremes de Huevos Duros con Aguacate*), 20
 Homemade Mayonnaise (*Mayonesa Hecha en Casa*), 147
 Mexican Eggnog (*Rompope Casero*), 202
 Northern-Style Taquitos (*Taquitos Norteños*), 125
 Pecan Caramel Flan (*Flan de Nuez*), 223
Empanadas, Pork Picadillo (*Empanadas de Picadillo de Puerco*), 84
enchiladas
 Guajillo Chile Enchiladas (*Enchiladas de Chile Guajillo*), 129
 Mole Poblano Enchiladas (*Enchiladas de Mole Poblano*), 132
 Quick Mole Enchiladas (*Enchiladas Rápidas de Mole*), 131
 Swiss Enchiladas (*Enchiladas Suizas*), 140–141
Enjitomatadas, Zacatecas-Style (*Enjitomatadas Estilo Zacatecas*), 126–127
Enmoladas, Ancho Chile Mole for (*Mole de Chile Ancho para Enmoladas*), 121
epazote
 Beans in the Pot (*Frijoles de la Olla*), 164
 Cuitlacoche and Zucchini Blossom Casserole (*Pastel de Cuitlacoche y Flor de Calabaza*), 186–187
 Mushroom Soup with Epazote (*Sopa de Hongos con Epazote*), 38
 Zucchini Blossom and Poblano Chile Tamales (*Tamales de Flor de Calabaza*), 107
 Zucchini Blossom Lasagna (*Lasagna de Flor de Calabaza*), 53

evaporated milk
 Mango Pudding (*Dulce de Mango*), 228

Fancy Churros (*Churros Elegantes*), 221
farmer cheese
 Baked Scrambled Egg Taquitos (*Taquitos de Huevo al Horno*), 122
 Corn Tortilla and Pork Casserole (*Budín de Tortilla con Carne de Puerco*), 85
 Quick Mole Enchiladas (*Enchiladas Rápidas de Mole*), 131
 Swiss Enchiladas (*Enchiladas Suizas*), 140–141
feta cheese
 Ancho Chile Mole for Enmoladas (*Mole de Chile Ancho para Enmoladas*), 121
 Aztec Casserole (*Budín Azteca*), 65
 Baby Potatoes with Poblano Chiles (*Papitas Criollas con Rajas*), 171
 Cactus Pad, Poblano Chile, and Chorizo Quesadillas (*Quesadillas de Nopales con Poblano y Chorizo*), 135
 Corn Tortilla Dry Soup (*Sopa Seca de Tortilla*), 33
 Drunken Salsa (*Salsa Borracha*), 153
 Fried Tortillas with Mole Poblano (*Enmoladas*), 128
 Guajillo Chile Enchiladas (*Enchiladas de Chile Guajillo*), 129
 Mole Poblano Enchiladas (*Enchiladas de Mole Poblano*), 132
 Poblano Chiles Stuffed with Tamales (*Chiles Rellenos de Tamales*), 115
 Sardine, Tomato, and Feta Cheese Salad (*Ensalada de Sardinas*), 178
 Shredded Beef Flautas with Avocado Sauce (*Flautas con Salsa de Aguacate*), 138
 Spaghetti with Ancho Chile and Basil (*Spaghetti al Chile Ancho*), 51
 Stuffed Ancho Chiles (*Chiles Anchos Rellenos*), 118
 Tortilla and Pasilla Chile Casserole (*Corona de Tortillas y Chile Pasilla*), 185

feta cheese (continued)

Vegetable-Filled Crepes (*Crepas de Verdura al Horno*), 184

Warm Cactus Pad Salad (*Ensalada Caliente de Nopales*), 175

Xochitl Casserole (*Budín Xóchitl*), 64

Zacatecas-Style Enjitomatadas (*Enjitomatadas Estilo Zacatecas*), 126–127

Zucchini Blossom, Poblano Chile, and Corn Casserole (*Budín de Flor de Calabaza y Elote*), 190

Zucchini Blossom Lasagna (*Lasagna de Flor de Calabaza*), 53

fish. see specific types

Fish Fillets in Adobo (*Filetes de Pescado en Adobo*), 92

Fish with Avocado and Tomato Sauce (*Pescado con Salsa de Aguacate y Jitomate*), 94

flan

Cheese Caramel Flan (*Queso Napolitano*), 222

Guanajuato-Style Corn Flan (*Flan de Elote Estilo Guanajuato*), 224

Pecan Caramel Flan (*Flan de Nuez*), 223

Flautas, Shredded Beef, with Avocado Sauce (*Flautas con Salsa de Aguacate*), 138

flour tortillas, 17

Flour Tortillas Filled with Ham and Cheese (*Burritas Norteñas*), 124

Steak and Cheese Soft Tacos (*Tacos de Bistec con Queso*), 139

Flower of Azhar (*Flor de Azhar*), 213

Fresh Fruit and Vegetable Juice (*Jugo de Frutas y Vegetales*), 197

Fried Fish Fillets in Tomato Sauce (*Pescado Rebozado en Caldillo de Jitomate*), 93

Fried Tortillas with Mole Poblano (*Enmoladas*), 128

Fusilli with Avocado Cream and Ricotta (*Tornillos con Crema de Aguacate y Queso Fresco*), 52

garlic

Bread Soup with Garlic and Ancho Chile (*Sopa de Migas con Chile Ancho*), 37

Christmas Cod (*Bacalao de Navidad*), 90–91

Garlic and Avocado Dip (*Dip de Ajo y Aguacate*), 18

Leg of Pork in Ancho Chile Sauce (*Pierna de Puerco Enchilada*), 79

Los Guajolotes Chicken in Mole Poblano (*Pollo en Mole Poblano Los Guajolotes*), 60–61

Pickled Jalapeño Chiles (*Chiles en Vinagre*), 159

gelatin

Avocado Mousse (*Botana de Aguacate*), 17

Mango Mousse with White Wine (*Mousse de Mango con Vino Blanco*), 229

Whipped Orange and Cream Cheese Gelatin (*Gelatina Batida de Naranja con Queso Crema*), 232

ginger ale

White Wine Sangria (*Sangria de Vino Blanco*), 214

grapefruit beverage, sparkling

Tequila Pop (*La Paloma*), 212

White Russian (*Ruso Blanco*), 208

grapefruit juice

Baked Chicken in Achiote Sauce (*Pollo al Horno en Achiote*), 67

green beans

Round Roast in Vinaigrette (*Cuete a la Vinagreta*), 75

Vegetable Casserole (*Cacerola de Verduras*), 188

Green Herb Spaghetti (*Spaghetti Verde*), 50

Green Salsa (*Salsa Verde*), 156

Poblano Chiles Stuffed with Tamales (*Chiles Rellenos de Tamales*), 115

Green Salsa with Avocado (*Salsa Verde con Aguacate*), 157

Nayarit-Style Prawn Tacos (*Tacos de Camarón Estilo Nayarit*), 134

Guacamole, 149
  Rice with Chorizo Tacos (*Arroz Blanco con Taquitos de Chorizo*), 49
  Red Snapper Fillets with Guacamole (*Filetes de Huachinango con Guacamole*), 96
guajillo chiles
  Chile de Árbol and Guajillo Salsa (*Salsa de Chile de Árbol y Guajillo*), 151
  Guajillo Chile Enchiladas (*Enchiladas de Chile Guajillo*), 129
  Red Posole with Chicken (*Pozole Rojo*), 68–69
Guanajuato-Style Corn Flan (*Flan de Elote Estilo Guanajuato*), 224

halibut
  Pickled Fish (*Pescado en Escabeche*), 95
ham
  Flour Tortillas Filled with Ham and Cheese (*Burritas Norteñas*), 124
  Stuffed Poblano Chiles in Walnut Sauce (*Chiles en Nogada*), 116–117
Hard-Boiled Eggs with Avocado (*Entremés de Huevos Duros con Aguacate*), 20
Homemade Corn Tortillas (*Tortillas de Maiz Hechas en Casa*), 130
Homemade Mayonnaise (*Mayonesa Hecha en Casa*), 147
hominy corn
  Red Posole with Chicken (*Pozole Rojo*), 68–69
Hot Chocolate and Corn Drink (*Champurrado*), 203
Hot Chocolate for Tamales and Churros (*Chocolate Caliente*), 204–205

jalapeño chiles. *see also* pickled chiles
  Baked Prawns with Cheese and Jalapeños (*Camarones al Queso*), 97
  Pickled Jalapeño Chiles (*Chiles en Vinagre*), 159
  Pork Picadillo Empanadas (*Empanadas de Picadillo de Puerco*), 84

jam
  Sweet Tamales (*Tamales de Dulce*), 110
jicama
  Jicama, Red Onion, and Orange Salad (*Ensalada de Jícama y Cebolla Morada*), 176
  Jicama and Avocado Appetizer (*Entremés de Jícama con Aguacate*), 19

ketchup
  Jicama and Avocado Appetizer (*Entremés de Jícama con Aguacate*), 23

leeks
  Corn Soup (*Sopa de Elote*), 31
  Vegetable-Filled Crepes (*Crepas de Verdura al Horno*), 184
Leg of Pork in Ancho Chile Sauce (*Pierna de Puerco Enchilada*), 79
lettuce
  Bajio-Style Shredded Beef (*Salpicón Estilo Bajío*), 77
  Baked Chicken in Achiote Sauce (*Pollo al Horno en Achiote*), 67
  Fish Fillets in Adobo (*Filetes de Pescado en Adobo*), 88
  Leg of Pork in Ancho Chile Sauce (*Pierna de Puerco Enchilada*), 79
  Sardine-Stuffed Poblano Chiles (*Chiles de Sardina en Frío*), 114
limes / lime juice
  Aunt Geor's Beef Tartare (*Carne Tártara de Tía Geor*), 78
  Avocado Mousse (*Botana de Aguacate*), 17
  Baked Prawns with Cheese and Jalapeños (*Camarones al Queso*), 97
  Beet and Orange Juice Cooler (*Agua Fresca de Betabel y Jugo de Naranja*), 193
  Bologna Appetizer (*Entremés de Mortadela*), 21
  Cream of Cucumber Soup (*Crema Fría de Pepino*), 35
  Cucumber Cooler with Tequila (*Agua de Pepino con Piquete*), 196

limes/lime juice *(continued)*

Fish with Avocado and Tomato Sauce (*Pescado con Salsa de Aguacate y Jitomate*), 94

Fresh Fruit and Vegetable Juice (*Jugo de Frutas y Vegetales*), 197

Fried Fish Fillets in Tomato Sauce (*Pescado Rebozado en Caldillo de Jitomate*), 93

Garlic and Avocado Dip (*Dip de Ajo y Aguacate*), 18

Hard-Boiled Eggs with Avocado (*Entremés de Huevos Duros con Aguacate*), 20

Jicama, Red Onion, and Orange Salad (*Ensalada de Jícama y Cebolla Morada*), 176

Jicama and Avocado Appetizer (*Entremés de Jícama con Aguacate*), 19

Lime-Spiked Beer (*Chelada*), 206

Mango Mousse with White Wine (*Mousse de Mango con Vino Blanco*), 229

Mexican Flag (*Bandera*), 213

Mocambo (*Mocambo*), 212

Oysters with Chipotle Adobo (*Ostiones Capeados con Chipotle*), 25

Pico de Gallo (*Pico de Gallo*), 154

Pollock Appetizer (*Cangrejo Frío*), 22

Prawn Ceviche (*Ceviche de Camarón*), 23

Prune and Rum Punch (*Ponche de Ciruela Pasa*), 209

Red Snapper Fillets with Guacamole (*Filetes de Huachinango con Guacamole*), 96

Sea Bass with Pickled Chiles (*Robalo al Horno*), 89

Seafood Soup (*Sopa de Mariscos*), 41

Shredded Beef Flautas with Avocado Sauce (*Flautas con Salsa de Aguacate*), 138

Spiced Tomato Juice Chaser (*Sangrita*), 210

Spicy Carrot Salad (*Ensalada Fría de Zanahoria con Picante*), 177

Spicy Lime-Spiked Beer (*Michelada*), 207

Steak and Cheese Soft Tacos (*Tacos de Bistec con Queso*), 139

Tacos Filled with Shredded Pork in Achiote Sauce (*Tacos de Cochinita Pibil*), 142–143

limes/lime juice *(continued)*

Tequila Pop (*La Paloma*), 219

White Russian (*Ruso Blanco*), 208

White Wine Sangria (*Sangria de Vino Blanco*), 214

Manchego cheese

Baked Scrambled Egg Taquitos (*Taquitos de Huevo al Horno*), 122

Cactus Pad Soup (*Sopa de Nopales*), 30

Corn Soup (*Sopa de Elote*), 31

Cream of Corn Soup (*Sopa Crema de Elote*), 32

Creamy Rice with Poblano Chile Strips (*Arroz Blanco con Rajas de Poblano*), 48

Crepes Filled with Cuitlacoche (*Crepas Rellenas de Cuitlacoche*), 182

Peneques in Tomatillo Sauce (*Peneques en Salsa Verde*), 132

Poblano Chile Strips Filling (*Rajas de Poblano para Relleno*), 112

Steak and Cheese Soft Tacos (*Tacos de Bistec con Queso*), 139

Swiss Enchiladas (*Enchiladas Suizas*), 140–141

mangoes

Crepes Filled with Mango in Brandy Sauce (*Crepas de Mango en Almíbar con Brandy*), 227

Mango Mousse with White Wine (*Mousse de Mango con Vino Blanco*), 229

Mango Pudding (*Dulce de Mango*), 228

Masa Harina

Homemade Corn Tortillas (*Tortillas de Maiz Hechas en Casa*), 130

Hot Chocolate and Corn Drink (*Champurrado*), 203

Maseca corn flour

Basic Tamales (*Tamales*), 101–102

Homemade Corn Tortillas (*Tortillas de Maiz Hechas en Casa*), 130

Poblano Chiles Stuffed with Tamales (*Chiles Rellenos de Tamales*), 115

Sweet Tamales (*Tamales de Dulce*), 110

mayonnaise
  Avocado Mousse (*Botana de Aguacate*), 21
  Bologna Appetizer (*Entremés de Mortadela*), 24
  Homemade Mayonnaise (*Mayonesa Hecha en Casa*), 147
  Jicama and Avocado Appetizer (*Entremés de Jícama con Aguacate*), 23
Meringue with Caramel and Coffee Liqueur (*Merengue Caramelizado*), 230
Mesón del Angel Rice (*Arroz Estilo Mesón del Angel*), 46
Mexican chocolate
  Hot Chocolate and Corn Drink (*Champurrado*), 203
  Hot Chocolate for Tamales and Churros (*Chocolate Caliente*), 204–205
  Los Guajolotes Chicken in Mole Poblano (*Pollo en Mole Poblano Los Guajolotes*), 60–61
Mexican Corn Bread (*Pan de Maiz*), 217
Mexican cream. see Crème Fraîche (*Crema Espesa*)
Mexican Eggnog (*Rompope Casero*), 202
Mexican Flag (*Bandera*), 213
Mocambo (*Mocambo*), 212
mole sauce
  Ancho Chile Mole for Enmoladas (*Mole de Chile Ancho para Enmoladas*), 121
  Fried Tortillas with Mole Poblano (*Enmoladas*), 128
  Los Guajolotes Chicken in Mole Poblano (*Pollo en Mole Poblano Los Guajolotes*), 60–61
  Mole Casserole (*Budín de Mole*), 66
  Mole Poblano Chicken Filling (*Relleno de Pollo con Mole*), 105
  Mole Poblano Enchiladas (*Enchiladas de Mole Poblano*), 132
  Pork with Green Mole Sauce (*Caldillo de Cerdo en Mole Verde*), 81
  Quick Mole Enchiladas (*Enchiladas Rápidas de Mole*), 131
Monterey Jack cheese
  Baked Chayote Squash (*Chayotes al Horno*), 174

Monterey Jack cheese (*continued*)
  Cactus Pad Soup (*Sopa de Nopales*), 30
  Corn Soup (*Sopa de Elote*), 31
  Cream of Corn Soup (*Sopa Crema de Elote*), 32
  Creamy Rice with Poblano Chile Strips (*Arroz Blanco con Rajas de Poblano*), 48
  Crepes Filled with Cuitlacoche (*Crepas Rellenas de Cuitlacoche*), 182
  Cuitlacoche and Zucchini Blossom Casserole (*Pastel de Cuitlacoche y Flor de Calabaza*), 186–187
  Flour Tortillas Filled with Ham and Cheese (*Burritas Norteñas*), 124
  Peneques in Tomatillo Sauce (*Peneques en Salsa Verde*), 133
  Poblano Chile Strips Filling (*Rajas de Poblano para Relleno*), 112
  Refried Beans with Totopos (*Frijoles Refritos con Totopos*), 168
  Steak and Cheese Soft Tacos (*Tacos de Bistec con Queso*), 139
  Vegetable Casserole (*Cacerola de Verduras*), 188
mousse
  Avocado Mousse (*Botana de Aguacate*), 17
  Coffee Liqueur Mousse (*Mousse de Licor de Café*), 225
  Mango Mousse with White Wine (*Mousse de Mango con Vino Blanco*), 229
mozzarella cheese
  Baked Oysters on Toast (*Tostada de Ostiones al Horno*), 24
  Baked Prawns with Cheese and Jalapeños (*Camarones al Queso*), 97
  Chayote Squash and Eggplant Casserole (*Ensalada de Chayote y Berenjena*), 180
  Mole Casserole (*Budín de Mole*), 66
mulato chiles
  Los Guajolotes Chicken in Mole Poblano (*Pollo en Mole Poblano Los Guajolotes*), 60–61
  Spare Ribs in Adobo Sauce (*Costillas de Puerco Adobadas*), 83

mushrooms
    Cactus Pads in Cheese and Mushroom
      Sauce (*Nopales en Salsa de Queso*), 179
    Chayote Squash and Eggplant Casserole
      (*Ensalada de Chayote y Berenjena*), 180
    Mushroom Quesadillas (*Quesadillas de
      Hongos*), 136
    Mushroom Soup with Epazote (*Sopa de
      Hongos con Epazote*), 38
    Pickled Jalapeño Chiles (*Chiles en Vinagre*),
      159

Nayarit-Style Prawn Tacos (*Tacos de Camarón
    Estilo Nayarit*), 134
New Mexico chiles
    Chile de Árbol and Guajillo Salsa (*Salsa de
      Chile de Árbol y Guajillo*), 151
    Guajillo Chile Enchiladas (*Enchiladas de
      Chile Guajillo*), 125
    Northern-Style Taquitos (*Taquitos Norteños*),
      125

Oatmeal Soup (*Sopa de Avena*), 40
Oaxacan cheese
    Cuitlacoche and Zucchini Blossom
      Casserole (*Pastel de Cuitlacoche y Flor de
      Calabaza*), 186–187
    Mole Casserole (*Budín de Mole*), 66
Old-Fashioned Almond Cream (*Dulce
    Antiguo*), 231
olives
    Chicken Picadillo Filling (*Picadillo de Pollo*),
      103
    Christmas Cod (*Bacalao de Navidad*), 90–91
    Fish with Avocado and Tomato Sauce (*Pescado
      con Salsa de Aguacate y Jitomate*), 94
    Pork Picadillo Empanadas (*Empanadas de
      Picadillo de Puerco*), 84
    Rice Salad, Andalusian Style (*Ensalada de
      Arroz a la Andaluza*), 47
    Swiss Enchiladas (*Enchiladas Suizas*), 140–141
    Zacatecas-Style Roasting Hen (*Gallina
      Rellena Estilo Zacatecas*), 70–71

onions
    Jicama, Red Onion, and Orange Salad
      (*Ensalada de Jícama y Cebolla Morada*), 176
    Los Guajolotes Chicken in Mole Poblano
      (*Pollo en Mole Poblano Los Guajolotes*), 60–61
oranges/orange juice
    Baked Chicken in Achiote Sauce (*Pollo al
      Horno en Achiote*), 67
    Beet and Orange Juice Cooler (*Agua Fresca
      de Betabel y Jugo de Naranja*), 193
    Cactus Juice (*Jugo de Nopales*), 194
    Chicken Breasts in Orange Juice (*Pechugas
      de Pollo en Jugo de Naranja*), 57
    Crepes with Cajeta and Coffee Liqueur
      (*Crepas de Cajeta con Licor de Café*), 226
    Drunken Salsa (*Salsa Borracha*), 153
    Egg Yolk Buñuelos (*Buñuelos de Yema*), 220
    Fish Fillets in Adobo (*Filetes de Pescado en
      Adobo*), 92
    Flower of Azhar (*Flor de Azhar*), 213
    Fresh Fruit and Vegetable Juice (*Jugo de
      Frutas y Vegetales*), 197
    Jicama, Red Onion, and Orange Salad
      (*Ensalada de Jícama y Cebolla Morada*), 176
    Prune and Rum Punch (*Ponche de Ciruela
      Pasa*), 209
    Sea Bass with Pickled Chiles (*Robalo al
      Horno*), 89
    Spiced Tomato Juice Chaser (*Sangrita*), 210
    Tacos Filled with Shredded Pork in
      Achiote Sauce (*Tacos de Cochinita Pibil*),
      142–143
    Whipped Orange and Cream Cheese
      Gelatin (*Gelatina Batida de Naranja con
      Queso Crema*), 232
    White Wine Sangria (*Sangria de Vino
      Blanco*), 214
oysters
    Baked Oysters on Toast (*Tostada de Ostiones
      al Horno*), 24
    Oysters with Chipotle Adobo (*Ostiones
      Capeados con Chipotle*), 25
    Seafood Soup (*Sopa de Mariscos*), 41

Paella, Valencia-Style (*Paella Valenciana*), 45

paprika

   Spanish-Style Beans (*Frijoles a la Española*), 166

   Valencia-Style Paella (*Paella Valenciana*), 45

Parmesan cheese

   Bread Soup with Garlic and Ancho Chile (*Sopa de Migas con Chile Ancho*), 37

   Chicken Breasts in Orange Juice (*Pechugas de Pollo en Jugo de Naranja*), 57

   Green Herb Spaghetti (*Spaghetti Verde*), 50

parsley

   Chayote Squash and Eggplant Casserole (*Ensalada de Chayote y Berenjena*), 180

   Christmas Cod (*Bacalao de Navidad*), 90–91

   Fresh Fruit and Vegetable Juice (*Jugo de Frutas y Vegetales*), 197

   Green Herb Spaghetti (*Spaghetti Verde*), 50

   Oysters with Chipotle Adobo (*Ostiones Capeados con Chipotle*), 25

   Pollock Appetizer (*Cangrejo Frío*), 22

   Pork Picadillo Empanadas (*Empanadas de Picadillo de Puerco*), 84

   Prawn Ceviche (*Ceviche de Camarón*), 23

   Rice Salad, Andalusian Style (*Ensalada de Arroz a la Andaluza*), 47

   Seafood Soup (*Sopa de Mariscos*), 41

   Stuffed Poblano Chiles in Walnut Sauce (*Chiles en Nogada*), 116–117

   Valencia-Style Paella (*Paella Valenciana*), 45

pasilla chiles

   Drunken Salsa (*Salsa Borracha*), 153

   Los Guajolotes Chicken in Mole Poblano (*Pollo en Mole Poblano Los Guajolotes*), 60–61

   Pasilla Chile and Tomatillo Salsa (*Salsa de Pasilla con Tomate Verde*), 152

   Spare Ribs in Adobo Sauce (*Costillas de Puerco Adobadas*), 83

   Steak and Cheese Soft Tacos (*Tacos de Bistec con Queso*), 139

   Tortilla and Pasilla Chile Casserole (*Corona de Tortillas y Chile Pasilla*), 185

pasta, 43, 50–51

   Fusilli with Avocado Cream and Ricotta (*Tornillos con Crema de Aguacate y Queso Fresco*), 52

   Green Herb Spaghetti (*Spaghetti Verde*), 60

   Spaghetti with Ancho Chile and Basil (*Spaghetti al Chile Ancho*), 51

   Zucchini Blossom Lasagna (*Lasagna de Flor de Calabaza*), 53

peanuts

   Los Guajolotes Chicken in Mole Poblano (*Pollo en Mole Poblano Los Guajolotes*), 60–61

peas

   Baked Chicken with Fruit and Vegetables (*Tapado de Pollo*), 72

   Round Roast in Vinaigrette (*Cuete a la Vinagreta*), 75

   Sardine-Stuffed Poblano Chiles (*Chiles de Sardina en Frío*), 114

pecans

   Crepes with Cajeta and Coffee Liqueur (*Crepas de Cajeta con Licor de Café*), 226

   Pecan Caramel Flan (*Flan de Nuez*), 223

Peneques in Tomatillo Sauce (*Peneques en Salsa Verde*), 133

pickled chiles

   Bajio-Style Shredded Beef (*Salpicón Estilo Bajío*), 77

   Baked Eggs on Refried Beans (*Huevos al Horno con Frijoles Refritos*), 169

   Christmas Cod (*Bacalao de Navidad*), 90–91

   Fish with Avocado and Tomato Sauce (*Pescado con Salsa de Aguacate y Jitomate*), 94

   Fried Fish Fillets in Tomato Sauce (*Pescado Rebozado en Caldillo de Jitomate*), 93

   Pickled Fish (*Pescado en Escabeche*), 94

   Pickled Jalapeño Chiles (*Chiles en Vinagre*), 159

   Sea Bass with Pickled Chiles (*Robalo al Horno*), 89

Pickled Fish (*Pescado en Escabeche*), 95

Pico de Gallo (*Pico de Gallo*), 154

pimientos
    Christmas Cod (*Bacalao de Navidad*), 90–91
    Rice Salad, Andalusian Style (*Ensalada de Arroz a la Andaluza*), 47
    Round Roast in Vinaigrette (*Cuete a la Vinagreta*), 75
    Stuffed Poblano Chiles in Walnut Sauce (*Chiles en Nogada*), 116–117

pineapple
    Baked Chicken with Fruit and Vegetables (*Tapado de Pollo*), 72
    Fresh Fruit and Vegetable Juice (*Jugo de Frutas y Vegetales*), 197

pine nuts
    Crepes Filled with Poblano and Pine Nuts (*Crepas de Rajas con Piñones*), 183

pinto beans
    Baked Eggs on Refried Beans (*Huevos al Horno con Frijoles Refritos*), 169
    Bean Sauce (*Salsa de Frijol*), 165
    Beans in the Pot (*Frijoles de la Olla*), 164
    Pinto Beans with Roasted Red Peppers (*Frijoles con Chiles Morrones*), 167
    Refried Beans with Totopos (*Frijoles Refritos con Totopos*), 168

piquín chile
    Jicama, Red Onion, and Orange Salad (*Ensalada de Jícama y Cebolla Morada*), 176
    Spicy Carrot Salad (*Ensalada Fría de Zanahoria con Picante*), 177

plantains
    Rice with Chorizo Tacos (*Arroz Blanco con Taquitos de Chorizo*), 49
    Los Guajolotes Chicken in Mole Poblano (*Pollo en Mole Poblano Los Guajolotes*), 60–61
    Pork Loin with Chipotle Chiles (*Tinga Estilo "Pitita"*), 82

poblano chiles
    Baby Potatoes with Poblano Chiles (*Papitas Criollas con Rajas*), 173
    Cactus Pad, Poblano Chile, and Chorizo Quesadillas (*Quesadillas de Nopales con Poblano y Chorizo*), 135

poblano chiles (*continued*)
    Chicken and Poblano Chile Tacos (*Tacos Poblanos*), 123
    Chile Sauce, 111
    Corn Soup (*Sopa de Elote*), 31
    Corn Tortilla and Pork Casserole (*Budín de Tortilla con Carne de Puerco*), 85
    Cream of Cauliflower Soup with Poblano Chile and Corn (*Sopa Crema de Coliflor con Chile Poblano y Elote*), 34
    Creamy Rice with Poblano Chile Strips (*Arroz Blanco con Rajas de Poblano*), 48
    Crepes Filled with Poblano and Pine Nuts (*Crepas de Rajas con Piñones*), 183
    Cuitlacoche and Zucchini Blossom Casserole (*Pastel de Cuitlacoche y Flor de Calabaza*), 186–187
    Mesón del Angel Rice (*Arroz Estilo Mesón del Angel*), 46
    Mole Poblano Chicken Filling (*Relleno de Pollo con Mole*), 105
    Northern-Style Taquitos (*Taquitos Norteños*), 125
    peeling, 111
    Poblano Chiles Stuffed with Tamales (*Chiles Rellenos de Tamales*), 115
    Poblano Chile Strips Filling (*Rajas de Poblano para Relleno*), 112
    Pork-Stuffed Poblano Chiles (*Chiles Rellenos de Picadillo de Puerco*), 113
    Quick Mole Enchiladas (*Enchiladas Rápidas de Mole*), 131
    Rajas de Poblano, 111
    roasting, 111
    Sardine-Stuffed Poblano Chiles (*Chiles de Sardina en Frío*), 114
    seeding, 111
    Stuffed Poblano Chiles in Walnut Sauce (*Chiles en Nogada*), 116–117
    Vegetable Casserole (*Cacerola de Verduras*), 188
    Zucchini Blossom, Poblano Chile, and Corn Casserole (*Budín de Flor de Calabaza y Elote*), 190

poblano chiles *(continued)*

Zucchini Blossom and Poblano Chile Tamales *(Tamales de Flor de Calabaza)*, 107

Zucchini Blossom Lasagna *(Lasagna de Flor de Calabaza)*, 53

Zucchini Blossom Soup *(Sopa de Flor de Calabaza)*, 39

Pollock Appetizer *(Cangrejo Frío)*, 22

pomegranates

Stuffed Poblano Chiles in Walnut Sauce *(Chiles en Nogada)*, 116–117

pork, 73, 79–85. *see also* bacon; ham

Corn Tortilla and Pork Casserole *(Budín de Tortilla con Carne de Puerco)*, 85

Leg of Pork in Ancho Chile Sauce *(Pierna de Puerco Enchilada)*, 79

Pork Chops in Spicy Tomato Sauce *(Chuletas en Salsa de Jitomate)*, 80

Pork Loin with Chipotle Chiles *(Tinga Estilo "Pitita")*, 82

Pork Picadillo Empanadas *(Empanadas de Picadillo de Puerco)*, 84

Pork-Stuffed Poblano Chiles *(Chiles Rellenos de Picadillo de Puerco)*, 113

Pork with Green Mole Sauce *(Caldillo de Cerdo en Mole Verde)*, 81

Spare Ribs in Adobo Sauce *(Costillas de Puerco Adobadas)*, 83

Stuffed Poblano Chiles in Walnut Sauce *(Chiles en Nogada)*, 116–117

Tacos Filled with Shredded Pork in Achiote Sauce *(Tacos de Cochinita Pibil)*, 142–143

Valencia-Style Paella *(Paella Valenciana)*, 45

Zacatecas-Style Roasting Hen *(Gallina Rellena Estilo Zacatecas)*, 70–71

potatoes

Baby Potatoes with Poblano Chiles *(Papitas Criollas con Rajas)*, 173

Chicken in Cheese and Chipotle Chile Sauce *(Pollo en Salsa de Queso y Chipotle)*, 59

Chicken in Chorizo Sauce *(Pollo en Salsa de Chorizo)*, 62

potatoes *(continued)*

Christmas Cod *(Bacalao de Navidad)*, 90–91

Mole Poblano Chicken Filling *(Relleno de Pollo con Mole)*, 105

Pork Chops in Spicy Tomato Sauce *(Chuletas en Salsa de Jitomate)*, 80

Pork with Green Mole Sauce *(Caldillo de Cerdo en Mole Verde)*, 81

Quesadillas with Potato and Chorizo *(Quesadillas de Papa con Chorizo)*, 137

Spinach and Potato Casserole *(Budín de Espinaca)*, 189

Vegetable Casserole *(Cacerola de Verduras)*, 188

Vegetable-Filled Crepes *(Crepas de Verdura al Horno)*, 184

Prawn Ceviche *(Ceviche de Camarón)*, 23

prawns. *see* shrimp (prawns)

prunes

Chicken in Prune and Red Wine Sauce *(Pollo con Ciruelas y Vino Tinto)*, 63

Los Guajolotes Chicken in Mole Poblano *(Pollo en Mole Poblano Los Guajolotes)*, 60–61

Prune and Rum Punch *(Ponche de Ciruela Pasa)*, 209

puddings and custards

Cheese Caramel Flan *(Queso Napolitano)*, 222

Guanajuato-Style Corn Flan *(Flan de Elote Estilo Guanajuato)*, 224

Mango Pudding *(Dulce de Mango)*, 228

Old-Fashioned Almond Cream *(Dulce Antiguo)*, 231

Pecan Caramel Flan *(Flan de Nuez)*, 223

puff pastry

Pork Picadillo Empanadas *(Empanadas de Picadillo de Puerco)*, 84

quesadillas

Cactus Pad, Poblano Chile, and Chorizo Quesadillas *(Quesadillas de Nopales con Poblano y Chorizo)*, 135

Mushroom Quesadillas *(Quesadillas de Hongos)*, 136

quesadillas *(continued)*

Quesadillas with Potato and Chorizo (*Quesadillas de Papa con Chorizo*), 137

queso fresco

Ancho Chile Mole for Enmoladas (*Mole de Chile Ancho para Enmoladas*), 121

Aztec Casserole (*Budín Azteca*), 65

Baby Potatoes with Poblano Chiles (*Papitas Criollas con Rajas*), 171

Cactus Pad, Poblano Chile, and Chorizo Quesadillas (*Quesadillas de Nopales con Poblano y Chorizo*), 135

Corn Tortilla Dry Soup (*Sopa Seca de Tortilla*), 33

Drunken Salsa (*Salsa Borracha*), 153

Fried Tortillas with Mole Poblano (*Enmoladas*), 127

Fusilli with Avocado Cream and Ricotta (*Tornillos con Crema de Aguacate y Queso Fresco*), 53

Guajillo Chile Enchiladas (*Enchiladas de Chile Guajillo*), 129

Mole Poblano Enchiladas (*Enchiladas de Mole Poblano*), 132

Poblano Chiles Stuffed with Tamales (*Chiles Rellenos de Tamales*), 115

Sardine, Tomato, and Feta Cheese Salad (*Ensalada de Sardinas*), 178

Shredded Beef Flautas with Avocado Sauce (*Flautas con Salsa de Aguacate*), 138

Spaghetti with Ancho Chile and Basil (*Spaghetti al Chile Ancho*), 51

Stuffed Ancho Chiles (*Chiles Anchos Rellenos*), 118

Tortilla and Pasilla Chile Casserole (*Corona de Tortillas y Chile Pasilla*), 184

Vegetable-Filled Crepes (*Crepas de Verdura al Horno*), 184

Warm Cactus Pad Salad (*Ensalada Caliente de Nopales*), 175

Xochitl Casserole (*Budín Xóchitl*), 64

Zacatecas-Style Enjitomatadas (*Enjitomatadas Estilo Zacatecas*), 126–127

queso fresco *(continued)*

Zucchini Blossom, Poblano Chile, and Corn Casserole (*Budín de Flor de Calabaza y Elote*), 170

Zucchini Blossom Lasagna (*Lasagna de Flor de Calabaza*), 53

Quick Mole Enchiladas (*Enchiladas Rápidas de Mole*), 131

raisins

Chicken Picadillo Filling (*Picadillo de Pollo*), 103

Los Guajolotes Chicken in Mole Poblano (*Pollo en Mole Poblano Los Guajolotes*), 60–61

Pork Picadillo Empanadas (*Empanadas de Picadillo de Puerco*), 84

Stuffed Poblano Chiles in Walnut Sauce (*Chiles en Nogada*), 116–117

Sweet Tamales (*Tamales de Dulce*), 110

Zacatecas-Style Roasting Hen (*Gallina Rellena Estilo Zacatecas*), 70–71

Red Chile Chicken Filling (*Chile Rojo para Relleno*), 106

Red Posole with Chicken (*Pozole Rojo*), 68–69

Red Salsa with Fried Ancho Chile (*Salsa Roja con Chile Ancho Frito*), 155

red snapper

Fish Fillets in Adobo (*Filetes de Pescado en Adobo*), 92

Fish with Avocado and Tomato Sauce (*Pescado con Salsa de Aguacate y Jitomate*), 94

Fried Fish Fillets in Tomato Sauce (*Pescado Rebozado en Caldillo de Jitomate*), 93

Red Snapper Fillets with Guacamole (*Filetes de Huachinango con Guacamole*), 96

Seafood Soup (*Sopa de Mariscos*), 41

Refried Beans with Totopos (*Frijoles Refritos con Totopos*), 168

rice, 39, 41–45

Creamy Rice with Poblano Chile Strips (*Arroz Blanco con Rajas de Poblano*), 48

Easy Rice Cooler (*Horchata Fácil*), 201

rice *(continued)*

Mesón del Angel Rice (*Arroz Estilo Mesón del Angel*), 46

Rice Salad, Andalusian Style (*Ensalada de Arroz a la Andaluza*), 47

Rice with Chorizo Tacos (*Arroz Blanco con Taquitos de Chorizo*), 49

Valencia-Style Paella (*Paella Valenciana*), 45

ricotta cheese

Fusilli with Avocado Cream and Ricotta (*Tornillos con Crema de Aguacate y Queso Fresco*), 52

Round Roast in Vinaigrette (*Cuete a la Vinagreta*), 75

rum

Mango Pudding (*Dulce de Mango*), 228

Mexican Eggnog (*Rompope Casero*), 202

Prune and Rum Punch (*Ponche de Ciruela Pasa*), 209

saffron

Valencia-Style Paella (*Paella Valenciana*), 45

salads

Jicama, Red Onion, and Orange Salad (*Ensalada de Jícama y Cebolla Morada*), 176

Rice Salad, Andalusian Style (*Ensalada de Arroz a la Andaluza*), 47

Sardine, Tomato, and Feta Cheese Salad (*Ensalada de Sardinas*), 178

Spicy Carrot Salad (*Ensalada Fría de Zanahoria con Picante*), 177

Warm Cactus Pad Salad (*Ensalada Caliente de Nopales*), 175

salsas, 145, 150–158

Basic Tomato Sauce (*Caldillo de Jitomate*), 29

Bean Sauce (*Salsa de Frijol*), 165

Cascabel Chile Salsa (*Salsa de Chile Cascabel*), 150

Chicken Breasts with Molcajete Salsa (*Pechugas en Salsa de Molcajete*), 58

Chile de Árbol and Guajillo Salsa (*Salsa de Chile de Árbol y Guajillo*), 151

Chile Sauce, 111

Drunken Salsa (*Salsa Borracha*), 153

salsas *(continued)*

Green Salsa (*Salsa Verde*), 156

Green Salsa with Avocado (*Salsa Verde con Aguacate*), 157

Pasilla Chile and Tomatillo Salsa (*Salsa de Pasilla con Tomate Verde*), 152

Pico de Gallo (*Pico de Gallo*), 154

Red Salsa with Fried Ancho Chile (*Salsa Roja con Chile Ancho Frito*), 155

Tomato Salsa with Chile de Árbol (*Salsa Roja de Chile de Árbol*), 158

salt cod

Christmas Cod (*Bacalao de Navidad*), 90–91

sardines

Sardine, Tomato, and Feta Cheese Salad (*Ensalada de Sardinas*), 178

Sardine-Stuffed Poblano Chiles (*Chiles de Sardina en Frío*), 114

sausage. *see* chorizo sausage

Sea Bass with Pickled Chiles (*Robalo al Horno*), 89

seafood and fish, 83–93. *see also* specific types

Seafood Soup (*Sopa de Mariscos*), 41

serrano chiles. *see also* pickled chiles

Avocado Mousse (*Botana de Aguacate*), 17

Aztec Casserole (*Budín Azteca*), 65

Baked Oysters on Toast (*Tostada de Ostiones al Horno*), 24

Baked Scrambled Egg Taquitos (*Taquitos de Huevo al Horno*), 122

Beans with Bacon and Beer (*Frijoles Borrachos*), 163

Bologna Appetizer (*Entremés de Mortadela*), 21

Chicken in Chorizo Sauce (*Pollo en Salsa de Chorizo*), 62

Cuitlacoche and Zucchini Blossom Casserole (*Pastel de Cuitlacoche y Flor de Calabaza*), 186–187

Fusilli with Avocado Cream and Ricotta (*Tornillos con Crema de Aguacate y Queso Fresco*), 52

serrano chiles *(continued)*
    Garlic and Avocado Dip (*Dip de Ajo y Aguacate*), 18
    Green Salsa (*Salsa Verde*), 156
    Green Salsa with Avocado (*Salsa Verde con Aguacate*), 157
    Guacamole, 149
    Hard-Boiled Eggs with Avocado (*Entremés de Huevos Duros con Aguacate*), 20
    Jicama, Red Onion, and Orange Salad (*Ensalada de Jícama y Cebolla Morada*), 176
    Mushroom Quesadillas (*Quesadillas de Hongos*), 136
    Mushroom Soup with Epazote (*Sopa de Hongos con Epazote*), 38
    Peneques in Tomatillo Sauce (*Peneques en Salsa Verde*), 133
    Pickled Jalapeño Chiles (*Chiles en Vinagre*), 159
    Pico de Gallo (*Pico de Gallo*), 154
    Pollock Appetizer (*Cangrejo Frío*), 22
    Pork Chops in Spicy Tomato Sauce (*Chuletas en Salsa de Jitomate*), 80
    Prawn Ceviche (*Ceviche de Camarón*), 23
    Red Chile Chicken Filling (*Chile Rojo para Relleno*), 106
    Red Salsa with Fried Ancho Chile (*Salsa Roja con Chile Ancho Frito*), 155
    Seafood Soup (*Sopa de Mariscos*), 41
    Shredded Beef Flautas with Avocado Sauce (*Flautas con Salsa de Aguacate*), 138
    Spiced Tomato Juice Chaser (*Sangrita*), 210
    Spinach and Potato Casserole (*Budín de Espinaca*), 189
    Swiss Enchiladas (*Enchiladas Suizas*), 140–141
    Tacos Filled with Shredded Pork in Achiote Sauce (*Tacos de Cochinita Pibil*), 142–143
    Tomatillo Chicken Filling (*Chile Verde para Relleno*), 104
    Xochitl Casserole (*Budín Xóchitl*), 64
    Zacatecas-Style Enjitomatadas (*Enjitomatadas Estilo Zacatecas*), 126–127
    Zucchini Blossom Lasagna (*Lasagna de Flor de Calabaza*), 53

sesame seeds
    Los Guajolotes Chicken in Mole Poblano (*Pollo en Mole Poblano Los Guajolotes*), 60–61
sherry
    Egg Yolk Buñuelos (*Buñuelos de Yema*), 220
    Old-Fashioned Almond Cream (*Dulce Antiguo*), 231
    Zacatecas-Style Roasting Hen (*Gallina Rellena Estilo Zacatecas*), 70–71
Shredded Beef Flautas with Avocado Sauce (*Flautas con Salsa de Aguacate*), 138
shrimp (prawns)
    Baked Prawns with Cheese and Jalapeños (*Camarones al Queso*), 97
    Nayarit-Style Prawn Tacos (*Tacos de Camarón Estilo Nayarit*), 134
    Seafood Soup (*Sopa de Mariscos*), 41
    Valencia-Style Paella (*Paella Valenciana*), 45
soups, 27–41
    Bread Soup with Garlic and Ancho Chile (*Sopa de Migas con Chile Ancho*), 37
    Cactus Pad Soup (*Sopa de Nopales*), 30
    Corn Soup (*Sopa de Elote*), 31
    Corn Tortilla Dry Soup (*Sopa Seca de Tortilla*), 33
    Cream of Cauliflower Soup with Poblano Chile and Corn (*Sopa Crema de Coliflor con Chile Poblano y Elote*), 34
    Cream of Corn Soup (*Sopa Crema de Elote*), 32
    Cream of Cucumber Soup (*Crema Fría de Pepino*), 35
    Cream of Cucumber Soup with White Wine (*Sopa de Pepino*), 36
    liquid versus dry, 27
    Mushroom Soup with Epazote (*Sopa de Hongos con Epazote*), 38
    Oatmeal Soup (*Sopa de Avena*), 40
    Seafood Soup (*Sopa de Mariscos*), 37
    Zucchini Blossom Soup (*Sopa de Flor de Calabaza*), 39

sour cream

Aztec Casserole (*Budín Azteca*), 65

Baby Potatoes with Poblano Chiles (*Papitas Criollas con Rajas*), 173

Baked Chayote Squash (*Chayotes al Horno*), 174

Baked Scrambled Egg Taquitos (*Taquitos de Huevo al Horno*), 122

Cactus Pad, Poblano Chile, and Chorizo Quesadillas (*Quesadillas de Nopales con Poblano y Chorizo*), 135

Corn Tortilla and Pork Casserole (*Budín de Tortilla con Carne de Puerco*), 85

Creamy Rice with Poblano Chile Strips (*Arroz Blanco con Rajas de Poblano*), 48

Green Herb Spaghetti (*Spaghetti Verde*), 50

Mango Mousse with White Wine (*Mousse de Mango con Vino Blanco*), 229

Mushroom Quesadillas (*Quesadillas de Hongos*), 136

Poblano Chiles Stuffed with Tamales (*Chiles Rellenos de Tamales*), 115

Sardine-Stuffed Poblano Chiles (*Chiles de Sardina en Frío*), 114

Xochitl Casserole (*Budín Xóchitl*), 64

Zucchini Blossom, Poblano Chile, and Corn Casserole (*Budín de Flor de Calabaza y Elote*), 190

Spaghetti with Ancho Chile and Basil (*Spaghetti al Chile Ancho*), 51

Spanish-Style Beans (*Frijoles a la Española*), 166

Spare Ribs in Adobo Sauce (*Costillas de Puerco Adobadas*), 83

Spiced Tomato Juice Chaser (*Sangrita*), 210

Mexican Flag (*Bandera*), 213

White Russian (*Ruso Blanco*), 210

Spicy Carrot Salad (*Ensalada Fría de Zanahoria con Picante*), 177

Spicy Lime-Spiked Beer (*Michelada*), 207

Spinach and Potato Casserole (*Budín de Espinaca*), 189

Steak and Cheese Soft Tacos (*Tacos de Bistec con Queso*), 139

Stuffed Ancho Chiles (*Chiles Anchos Rellenos*), 118

Stuffed Poblano Chiles in Walnut Sauce (*Chiles en Nogada*), 116–117

Sweet Tamales (*Tamales de Dulce*), 110

Swiss Enchiladas (*Enchiladas Suizas*), 140–141

tacos

Chicken and Poblano Chile Tacos (*Tacos Poblanos*), 123

Nayarit-Style Prawn Tacos (*Tacos de Camarón Estilo Nayarit*), 134

Rice with Chorizo Tacos (*Arroz Blanco con Taquitos de Chorizo*), 49

Steak and Cheese Soft Tacos (*Tacos de Bistec con Queso*), 139

Tacos Filled with Shredded Pork in Achiote Sauce (*Tacos de Cochinita Pibil*), 142–143

tamales, 99–110

Basic Tamales (*Tamales*), 101–102

Chicken Picadillo Filling (*Picadillo de Pollo*), 103

Mole Poblano Chicken Filling (*Relleno de Pollo con Mole*), 105

Poblano Chiles Stuffed with Tamales (*Chiles Rellenos de Tamales*), 115

Poblano Chile Strips Filling (*Rajas de Poblano para Relleno*), 112

Red Chile Chicken Filling (*Chile Rojo para Relleno*), 106

Sweet Tamales (*Tamales de Dulce*), 110

Tomatillo Chicken Filling (*Chile Verde para Relleno*), 104

Veracruz-Style Baked Tamal (*Tamal de Cazuela Estilo Veracruz*), 108–109

Zucchini Blossom and Poblano Chile Tamales (*Tamales de Flor de Calabaza*), 107

taquitos

Baked Scrambled Egg Taquitos (*Taquitos de Huevo al Horno*), 122

Northern-Style Taquitos (*Taquitos Norteños*), 125

tequila, 211–213
    Coffee with a Sting (*Café con Piquete*), 200
    Cucumber Cooler with Tequila (*Agua de Pepino con Piquete*), 196
    Flower of Azhar (*Flor de Azhar*), 213
    Mexican Flag (*Bandera*), 213
    Mocambo (*Mocambo*), 212
    Tequila Pop (*La Paloma*), 212
tomatillos
    Chile de Árbol and Guajillo Salsa (*Salsa de Chile de Árbol y Guajillo*), 151
    Green Salsa (*Salsa Verde*), 156
    Green Salsa with Avocado (*Salsa Verde con Aguacate*), 157
    Los Guajolotes Chicken in Mole Poblano (*Pollo en Mole Poblano Los Guajolotes*), 60–61
    Pasilla Chile and Tomatillo Salsa (*Salsa de Pasilla con Tomate Verde*), 152
    Peneques in Tomatillo Sauce (*Peneques en Salsa Verde*), 133
    Pork with Green Mole Sauce (*Caldillo de Cerdo en Mole Verde*), 81
    Tomatillo Chicken Filling (*Chile Verde para Relleno*), 104
    Xochitl Casserole (*Budín Xóchitl*), 64
tomatoes
    Aztec Casserole (*Budín Azteca*), 65
    Baby Potatoes with Poblano Chiles (*Papitas Criollas con Rajas*), 173
    Bajio-Style Shredded Beef (*Salpicón Estilo Bajío*), 77
    Baked Chicken with Fruit and Vegetables (*Tapado de Pollo*), 72
    Baked Oysters on Toast (*Tostada de Ostiones al Horno*), 24
    Baked Scrambled Egg Taquitos (*Taquitos de Huevo al Horno*), 122
    Basic Tomato Sauce (*Caldillo de Jitomate*), 29
    Beans with Bacon and Beer (*Frijoles Borrachos*), 163
    Cascabel Chile Salsa (*Salsa de Chile Cascabel*), 150
    Chicken in Chorizo Sauce (*Pollo en Salsa de Chorizo*), 62

tomatoes (*continued*)
    Chicken in Prune and Red Wine Sauce (*Pollo con Ciruelas y Vino Tinto*), 63
    Chicken Picadillo Filling (*Picadillo de Pollo*), 103
    Chile de Árbol and Guajillo Salsa (*Salsa de Chile de Árbol y Guajillo*), 151
    Christmas Cod (*Bacalao de Navidad*), 90–91
    Corn Tortilla and Pork Casserole (*Budín de Tortilla con Carne de Puerco*), 85
    Corn Tortilla Dry Soup (*Sopa Seca de Tortilla*), 33
    Crepes Filled with Poblano and Pine Nuts (*Crepas de Rajas con Piñones*), 183
    Fish Fillets in Adobo (*Filetes de Pescado en Adobo*), 92
    Fish with Avocado and Tomato Sauce (*Pescado con Salsa de Aguacate y Jitomate*), 94
    Guacamole, 149
    Guajillo Chile Enchiladas (*Enchiladas de Chile Guajillo*), 129
    Los Guajolotes Chicken in Mole Poblano (*Pollo en Mole Poblano Los Guajolotes*), 60–61
    Oatmeal Soup (*Sopa de Avena*), 40
    Pico de Gallo (*Pico de Gallo*), 154
    Pinto Beans with Roasted Red Peppers (*Frijoles con Chiles Morrones*), 167
    Poblano Chile Strips Filling (*Rajas de Poblano para Relleno*), 112
    Pollock Appetizer (*Cangrejo Frío*), 22
    Pork Chops in Spicy Tomato Sauce (*Chuletas en Salsa de Jitomate*), 80
    Pork Picadillo Empanadas (*Empanadas de Picadillo de Puerco*), 84
    Pork-Stuffed Poblano Chiles (*Chiles Rellenos de Picadillo de Puerco*), 113
    Prawn Ceviche (*Ceviche de Camarón*), 23
    Red Chile Chicken Filling (*Chile Rojo para Relleno*), 106
    Red Posole with Chicken (*Pozole Rojo*), 68–69
    Red Salsa with Fried Ancho Chile (*Salsa Roja con Chile Ancho Frito*), 155

tomatoes *(continued)*

Sardine, Tomato, and Feta Cheese Salad
(*Ensalada de Sardinas*), 178

Sea Bass with Pickled Chiles (*Robalo al
Horno*), 89

Seafood Soup (*Sopa de Mariscos*), 41

Spanish-Style Beans (*Frijoles a la Española*),
166

Spinach and Potato Casserole (*Budín de
Espinaca*), 189

Stuffed Ancho Chiles (*Chiles Anchos
Rellenos*), 118

Stuffed Poblano Chiles in Walnut Sauce
(*Chiles en Nogada*), 116–117

Tomato Salsa with Chile de Árbol (*Salsa
Roja de Chile de Árbol*), 158

Tortilla and Pasilla Chile Casserole (*Corona
de Tortillas y Chile Pasilla*), 185

Valencia-Style Paella (*Paella Valenciana*), 45

Veracruz-Style Baked Tamal (*Tamal de
Cazuela Estilo Veracruz*), 108–109

Zacatecas-Style Enjitomatadas
(*Enjitomatadas Estilo Zacatecas*), 126–127

Zacatecas-Style Roasting Hen (*Gallina
Rellena Estilo Zacatecas*), 70–71

tomato juice

Spiced Tomato Juice Chaser (*Sangrita*), 210

tomato sauce

Aztec Casserole (*Budín Azteca*), 65

Baby Potatoes with Poblano Chiles (*Papitas
Criollas con Rajas*), 173

Baked Scrambled Egg Taquitos (*Taquitos de
Huevo al Horno*), 122

Basic Tomato Sauce (*Caldillo de Jitomate*), 29

Cactus Pad Soup (*Sopa de Nopales*), 30

Chicken in Chorizo Sauce (*Pollo en Salsa de
Chorizo*), 62

Chicken Picadillo Filling (*Picadillo de Pollo*),
103

Christmas Cod (*Bacalao de Navidad*), 90–91

Corn Tortilla and Pork Casserole (*Budín de
Tortilla con Carne de Puerco*), 85

tomato sauce *(continued)*

Cuitlacoche and Zucchini Blossom
Casserole (*Pastel de Cuitlacoche y Flor de
Calabaza*), 186–187

Fried Fish Fillets in Tomato Sauce (*Pescado
Rebozado en Caldillo de Jitomate*), 93

Oatmeal Soup (*Sopa de Avena*), 40

Poblano Chiles Stuffed with Tamales (*Chiles
Rellenos de Tamales*), 115

Pork Chops in Spicy Tomato Sauce
(*Chuletas en Salsa de Jitomate*), 80

Pork Picadillo Empanadas (*Empanadas de
Picadillo de Puerco*), 84

Pork-Stuffed Poblano Chiles (*Chiles Rellenos
de Picadillo de Puerco*), 113

Red Posole with Chicken (*Pozole Rojo*),
68–69

Red Salsa with Fried Ancho Chile (*Salsa
Roja con Chile Ancho Frito*), 155

Seafood Soup (*Sopa de Mariscos*), 41

Spinach and Potato Casserole (*Budín de
Espinaca*), 189

Stuffed Ancho Chiles (*Chiles Anchos
Rellenos*), 118

Stuffed Poblano Chiles in Walnut Sauce
(*Chiles en Nogada*), 116–117

Tomato Salsa with Chile de Árbol (*Salsa
Roja de Chile de Árbol*), 158

Tortilla and Pasilla Chile Casserole (*Corona
de Tortillas y Chile Pasilla*), 185

Zacatecas-Style Enjitomatadas
(*Enjitomatadas Estilo Zacatecas*), 126–127

Zacatecas-Style Roasting Hen (*Gallina
Rellena Estilo Zacatecas*), 70–71

tortillas. *see* corn tortillas; flour tortillas

turnips

Corn Soup (*Sopa de Elote*), 31

Valencia-Style Paella (*Paella Valenciana*), 45

Vampire (*Vampiro*), 208

Vegetable Casserole (*Cacerola de Verduras*), 188

Vegetable-Filled Crepes (*Crepas de Verdura al
Horno*), 184

Veracruz-Style Baked Tamal (*Tamal de Cazuela Estilo Veracruz*), 108–109
vermouth
Flower of Azhar (*Flor de Azhar*), 213
vinegar
Bajio-Style Shredded Beef (*Salpicón Estilo Bajío*), 77
Baked Chicken in Achiote Sauce (*Pollo al Horno en Achiote*), 67
Bologna Appetizer (*Entremés de Mortadela*), 21
Chicken in Chorizo Sauce (*Pollo en Salsa de Chorizo*), 62
Homemade Mayonnaise (*Mayonesa Hecha en Casa*), 147
Leg of Pork in Ancho Chile Sauce (*Pierna de Puerco Enchilada*), 79
Pickled Fish (*Pescado en Escabeche*), 95
Pickled Jalapeño Chiles (*Chiles en Vinagre*), 159
Rice Salad, Andalusian Style (*Ensalada de Arroz a la Andaluza*), 47
Round Roast in Vinaigrette (*Cuete a la Vinagreta*), 75
Sardine-Stuffed Poblano Chiles (*Chiles de Sardina en Frío*), 114
Spaghetti with Ancho Chile and Basil (*Spaghetti al Chile Ancho*), 51
Tacos Filled with Shredded Pork in Achiote Sauce (*Tacos de Cochinita Pibil*), 142–143
Zacatecas-Style Roasting Hen (*Gallina Rellena Estilo Zacatecas*), 70–71

walnuts
Stuffed Poblano Chiles in Walnut Sauce (*Chiles en Nogada*), 116–117
Warm Cactus Pad Salad (*Ensalada Caliente de Nopales*), 175
Whipped Orange and Cream Cheese Gelatin (*Gelatina Batida de Naranja con Queso Crema*), 232
whipping cream
Coffee Liqueur Mousse (*Mousse de Licor de Café*), 225

whipping cream (*continued*)
Crème Fraîche (*Crema Espesa*), 148
Crepes with Cajeta and Coffee Liqueur (*Crepas de Cajeta con Licor de Café*), 226
Pecan Caramel Flan (*Flan de Nuez*), 223
Swiss Enchiladas (*Enchiladas Suizas*), 140–141
White Russian (*Ruso Blanco*), 204
White Wine Sangria (*Sangria de Vino Blanco*), 214
wine
Chicken in Prune and Red Wine Sauce (*Pollo con Ciruelas y Vino Tinto*), 63
Cream of Cucumber Soup with White Wine (*Sopa de Pepino*), 36
Drunken Salsa (*Salsa Borracha*), 153
Mango Mousse with White Wine (*Mousse de Mango con Vino Blanco*), 229
Seafood Soup (*Sopa de Mariscos*), 41
White Wine Sangria (*Sangria de Vino Blanco*), 214
Zacatecas-Style Roasting Hen (*Gallina Rellena Estilo Zacatecas*), 70–71

Xochitl Casserole (*Budín Xóchitl*), 64

Zacatecas-Style Enjitomatadas (*Enjitomatadas Estilo Zacatecas*), 126–127
Zacatecas-Style Roasting Hen (*Gallina Rellena Estilo Zacatecas*), 70–71
zucchini
Baked Chicken with Fruit and Vegetables (*Tapado de Pollo*), 72
Vegetable Casserole (*Cacerola de Verduras*), 188
Vegetable-Filled Crepes (*Crepas de Verdura al Horno*), 184
Zucchini Blossom, Poblano Chile, and Corn Casserole (*Budín de Flor de Calabaza y Elote*), 190
Zucchini Blossom Lasagna (*Lasagna de Flor de Calabaza*), 53
Zucchini Blossom Soup (*Sopa de Flor de Calabaza*), 39

zucchini blossoms

Cuitlacoche and Zucchini Blossom
Casserole (*Pastel de Cuitlacoche y Flor de
Calabaza*), 186–187

Zucchini Blossom, Poblano Chile, and
Corn Casserole (*Budín de Flor de
Calabaza y Elote*), 190

Zucchini Blossom and Poblano Chile
Tamales (*Tamales de Flor de Calabaza*),
107

Zucchini Blossom Lasagna (*Lasagna de Flor
de Calabaza*), 53

Zucchini Blossom Soup (*Sopa de Flor de
Calabaza*), 39